"A collection of reflections on the practice of compassion in everyday life that provides a recipe for a deeper life and a better world. It is written with minds and hearts wide open."

—DANIEL GILBERT, Edgar Pierce Professor of Psychology, Harvard University, author of *Stumbling on Happiness*

"An Open-Hearted Life shows us how to live a more meaningful, connected and a compassionate life. Bringing Buddhist teachings in a partnership with the techniques and insights of contemporary psychotherapy, the authors offer valuable guidelines to living a life with a truly open heart."

—THUPTEN JINPA, PhD, principal English translator to the Dalai Lama and author of *Essential Mind Training*

"A uniquely creative useful guide to improving your life."

—PAUL EKMAN, PhD, coauthor (with the Dalai Lama) of *Emotional Awareness*

"This wonderful book is easy and enjoyable to read, consisting of deep insights into the meaning of compassion and straightforward practices designed to help cultivate an open heart."

—KRISTIN NEFF, PhD, Professor of Educational Psychology, University of Texas at Austin

An Open-Hearted Life

Transformative Methods for
Compassionate Living from
a Clinical Psychologist
and a Buddhist Nun

Russell Kolts
&
Thubten Chodron

SHAMBHALA
Boston
2015

SHAMBHALA PUBLICATIONS, INC.
Horticultural Hall
300 Massachusetts Avenue
Boston, Massachusetts 02115
www.shambhala.com

9 8 7 6 5 4 3 2 1

First Edition
Printed in the United States of America

∞ This edition is printed on acid-free paper that meets the
American National Standards Institute z39.48 Standard.
♻ This book is printed on 30% postconsumer recycled paper.
For more information please visit www.shambhala.com.

Distributed in the United States by Penguin Random House LLC
and in Canada by Random House of Canada Ltd

Designed by Lora Zorian

LIBRARY OF CONGRESS CATALOGING-IN-PUBLICATION DATA
Kolts, Russell L., author.
[Living with an open heart]
An open-hearted life: transformative methods
for compassionate living from a clinical
psychologist and a Buddhist nun /
Russell Kolts and Thubten Chodron.
pages cm
Previously published: London: Constable & Robinson Ltd.,
2013, under the title "Living with an open heart."
ISBN 978-1-61180-211-5 (paperback)
1. Spiritual life—Buddhism. 2. Psychotherapy—Religious aspects
—Buddhism. 3. Compassion—Religious aspects—Buddhism.
I. Thubten Chodron, 1950–, author. II. Title.
BQ5612.K65 2015
177'.7—dc23
2014024858

This book is dedicated to
His Holiness the 14th Dalai Lama of Tibet.

And to all sentient beings,
who wish only to be happy and to not suffer.

For as long as space endures,
And for as long as sentient beings remain,
Until then may I too abide
To dispel the misery of the world.[1]

Contents

PART THREE

Cultivating Compassion

Preface

Western psychology has focused on the scientific study of mind and, to a large extent, the individual. It has concentrated on mental health problems, aggression, assertiveness, self-esteem, how to compete better in the world, how to have better bodies and better sex. In fact, there is increasing evidence that over the last thirty years we have become more self-focused, grasping and narcissistic, increasingly preoccupied with our sense of self and our self-presentations, whether in the "real" world of work or dating, or via social media. We have, as the late Christopher Lasch noted, been turned into theatrical performers riddled with self-criticism and shame, fearful of rejection if our performance does not win the approval of others. Unfortunately, the consequence of our material wealth and "do more, have more, be more" attitudes is not always greater happiness, but increased risk of depression and anxiety, which are increasing in Western society, especially among younger cohorts.

So what happens when we turn this on its head, so that it is not so much self-enhancement that is the key to happiness but compassion, the wish to be open to the suffering of self and others with a commitment to try to engage with it, alleviate and prevent it? What happens when we see the suffering in ourselves and others not as something that has gone wrong, or an indication of personal failure or weakness, but rather as a normal process of living that requires us to develop insight and courage?

This was the journey of the Buddha twenty-five centuries ago. He was born a prince, and to protect him from the suffering of life his father built him high-walled golden palaces where all his desires could be satisfied—the best food, wine and ladies. So for the first thirty years or so he was able to simply live a life of the fulfilment of worldly pleasures. In a way, of course, this is what Western society today tells us we should be doing—to buy more, have more, do more, be more—to indulge ourselves in the pleasures of food, drink, holidays, cars and TV shows, and not to notice too much the suffering in our own hearts or in those around us.

However, Siddhartha (the Buddha-to-be) sensed something beyond the walls, beyond his life of pleasures, so with an attendant he went outside the palace. There he encountered four messengers: an old man in the process of decaying, a sick person in pain, and a decomposing corpse. He became aware that no matter how much one is distracted by the pleasures or the strivings of this life, ultimately suffering is always nearby. The fourth messenger was a holy man he saw wandering in the town. When he asked his attendant who he was, the attendant replied that he was a holy man seeking the causes of suffering and the cessation of suffering. Opening to the realities of suffering, the Buddha decided he also needed to discover the causes and cessation of suffering; to get to the bottom of things.

I've often wondered if I had been in that situation whether I would have taken the same road or if I would have said to myself: "Hey man, it is a Hell outside these gates. I'm staying here with my wine, women, song and fine clothes." This is what most of us do—we try to close out suffering and hope that the world won't treat us too badly. Yet in our hearts we know that this does not actually work. We see the world becoming more problematic: the planet gradually being destroyed for our grandchildren; banks and other economic institutions courting greed and immoral behavior, doing terrible damage to the social fabric of society; arms manufacturers making huge profits on the basis of conflicts that we don't know how to solve; and millions dying every year from starvation and preventable disease. In our own lives we know we are not invulnerable to the uncertainty of economic conditions, relational conflicts and break-ups, disappointments, sickness, ageing and the eventual death of ourselves and our loved ones.

So what happens if we take a completely different approach and stop trying to focus on how to have more, more and more, and turn around to look at the real nature of life? What happens if we actually take the Buddha's path? The first thought of course is: "You must be crazy! How can you want me to explore the existence of suffering when I want to be happy, for suffering just go away?!" But the reality is actually that when we engage with suffering we put our capacity for happiness on a much firmer footing. The importance of engaging with the unsatisfactory aspects of life is not some masochistic joke for us to wallow in misery, but a real journey to change and enhance our minds. The cultivation of compassion is at the heart of this journey.

Until recently we've had to rely on personal testimonies that compassion really does create the conditions for producing greater happiness; that it can bring greater harmony in our relationships, help us to become less self-critical and prone to feelings of shame, foster a more caring relationship with the world we live in and help us create peace, joyfulness and contentment within ourselves. Thankfully, partly with the encouragement of the Dalai Lama, Western sciences have begun to look at this. It turns out that cultivating compassion for oneself and others does amazing things to our brains and bodies. Cultivating compassion increases the workings of parts of the brain involved with positive emotion—it has positive effects on our cardiovascular system and our immune system. The cultivation of compassion does real physical good. In our minds, too, the cultivation of compassion creates deeper insights into the nature of our suffering, and rather than being self-critical and shame prone we become more self-accepting, wise and caring of ourselves. Cultivating compassion allows us to become more thoughtful and caring in our relationships, and those relationships are more likely to flourish if we don't constantly feel disappointed and critical.

We have the wisdom of over two-and-a-half thousand years of Buddhist practices and insights into the mind, and a new science that has explored the physiological and psychological benefits of compassion. There is no question whatsoever now that compassion can be and should be at the heart of all that we do—at the heart of our education and how we treat and teach our children, at the heart of our businesses, at the heart of our relationships with each other and very much at the heart of our relationships with ourselves.

In this remarkable and wonderful book, my friend Russell Kolts, a professor of psychology, and Buddhist nun Thubten Chodron have come together to explore how to bring the wisdom of compassion into our lives. The book is organized into six sections that unfold in easy-to-follow ways, beginning with understanding the real nature of compassion and disbanding myths about it. Compassion can sometimes be seen as weak or a bit fluffy. It is neither of those. Compassion starts by looking at suffering and for that reason courage is at its core. Sometimes people think compassion is a way of letting people off the hook, but again this is a wrong idea, as you will see. As we gain clarity into the genuine nature of compassion, we gain the capacity to look closely at experiences that we'd previously chosen to avoid or escape. We learn to use our human capacity of awareness to gain more insight into what our minds are up to. Rather than just feeling angry and speaking and acting on that, we have an opportunity to "mindfully" begin to notice what is going on in our minds. Armed with this capacity to bring our attention under personal control, we can now focus on who and what we need to cultivate compassion for. Bringing together the wisdom of traditional Buddhist insights and scientific understanding, Russell and Chodron outline a set of practices for helping to build compassion into our everyday lives. This is crucial because while some approaches suggest meditation each day, for many of us that's difficult. What is more important is to wake up to each moment and to try as best we can to be fully aware of the opportunity we have to bring compassion to whatever we are doing at that time. The exercises Russell and Chodron offer will help enormously with this endeavor.

Relationships of course are at the heart of much of our source of happiness. We are an evolved social species and our minds have been designed over many millions of years for social relationships. From the day we are born to the day we die the kindness of others has a huge impact on the quality of our lives. The quality of relationships children experience will influence their genetic expression and brain maturation. Children who grow up feeling loved and valued develop in different ways to those who grow up abused, criticized and stressed. Thus trying to create harmony with others can be a source of joy for them and for ourselves. But as with all journeys, problems arise and unforeseen obstacles get in the way. So in the latter section Russell and Chodron guide us through potential sources of difficulty on the way.

It is a delight and honor to be able to recommend this book to you. Even in times of suffering and doubt may the words in these pages help you find peace and joy. They have for me.

—PROFESSOR PAUL GILBERT, OBE,
author of *The Compassionate Mind*

THE DALAI LAMA

I always tell people that my religion is kindness, because kindness is "in our bones." Without kindness, none of us could survive. When we are born we are welcomed with kindness and compassion. Due to the kindness of others, we have food, shelter, clothing, and medicine—all that we need to stay alive. As children, under the care of others, we receive an education and learn good values that help us in life. Having enjoyed the benefits of others' kindness, it is only natural that we repay it.

However, sometimes our sense of self-interest prevents us from doing so. What's more, some people say we are genetically predisposed to seek our own benefit regardless of others. I don't believe we need be confined by such simple instincts. It's natural for us to pursue our own interests, but we have to do so wisely, not foolishly. And the wise course is to take others into consideration too.

Today, more and more scientists are finding that consciously cultivating compassion has a positive role in brain function and strengthens particular neural pathways. In other words, our marvellous human brains can be transformed in the process of nurturing our best qualities—such as generosity, compassion, love, tolerance, forgiveness, fortitude, patience, and wisdom. And the ancient methods based on reason that the Buddha taught for releasing disturbing emotions and cultivating positive emotions can provide a way to do this.

Our world is increasingly interdependent, but I wonder if we truly understand that our interdependent human community has to be compassionate; compassionate in our choice of goals, compassionate in our means of cooperation and our pursuit of these goals. Compassion affirms the principles of dignity and justice for all. From the Buddhist viewpoint all things originate in the mind. Real appreciation of humanity, compassion and love, are the key issues. If we develop a good heart, whether the field is science, commerce or politics, since the motivation is so very important, the result will be more beneficial. With a positive motivation that takes account of other people's interests as well as our own, our activities can help humanity; without such a motivation our actions are likely to be detrimental. This is why compassion is so very important for humankind.

I am especially pleased that this book, *An Open-Hearted Life,* has been written by a psychologist and a Buddhist nun working together. The respective traditions to which they belong are both rich in knowledge and wisdom, and have much to share with and learn from each other. Having been involved in a dialogue between modern science and Buddhist science for many years, I'm happy to see others taking part and enriching the conversation. The authors present the topic of compassion in language that is easy to understand and in ways that are appropriate for people to apply, whatever faith, or none, to which they belong. The short reflections at the end of each entry give readers simple, yet effective means to begin to cultivate the most beneficial of human qualities—compassion.

AUGUST 29, 2013

Introduction

An old Cherokee is teaching his grandson about life. "A fight is going on inside me," he said to the boy.

"It is a terrible fight and it is between two wolves. One is anger, envy, sorrow, regret, greed, arrogance, self-pity, guilt, resentment, inferiority, lies, false pride, superiority and ego."

He continued, "The other is joy, peace, love, hope, serenity, humility, kindness, benevolence, empathy, generosity, truth, compassion and faith.

"The same fight is going on inside you—and inside every other person, too."

The grandson thought about it for a minute and then asked his grandfather, "Which wolf will win?"

The old Cherokee simply replied, "The one you feed."

—NATIVE AMERICAN LEGEND[1]

THIS BOOK IS ABOUT LEARNING to feed the wolf of goodness.

Compassion is based in the desire for others to be free from suffering and the aspiration to help alleviate that suffering. There are many reasons to cultivate compassion. We may have observed suffering in the world and found ourselves moved by it. We may have found ourselves struggling with an on-going sense of dis-contentment and are searching for ways to imbue our lives with meaning. We may have noticed ourselves behaving in ways that aren't consistent with our values and want to change that. We may have found ourselves inspired by someone who embod-ies compassion, kindness, perseverance and thoughtfulness, and want to be more like him or her. We may wish to improve our relationships with others, reduce conflicts and increase our own warmth and kindness. In a world filled with difficulty, challenges and suffering, we may want to become part of the solution. To do this, we have to begin with ourselves.

When we cultivate compassion, we learn to stop being so self-centered, jealous and competitive and instead focus on the well-being of ourselves *and* all other beings. When we act from a compassionate perspective that desires all beings to have hap-piness and freedom from suffering, we are better prepared to take care of ourselves, others and the world.

Most people have busy lives and may think that there isn't the time or the space for practicing compassion. However, it's possible to bring compassion into our lives even when we are at our busiest. Cultivating compassion doesn't have to involve *adding* anything to our lives; it's about *changing* the way we understand and approach ourselves, other people and the ac-tivities we already do.

We've arranged this book as a series of relatively brief en-tries. Some entries introduce ideas about compassion, some present practices for developing compassion and related strengths, and some provide information about our emotions and ways for us to understand and work with them.

As you open your heart to compassion, your life will begin to change. The drive to trounce others will be replaced by the desire to benefit others; feelings of isolation will be replaced by feelings of connection with others. Learning to accept our emotions—even negative ones, such as jealousy and anger—we'll stop mentally beating ourselves up for having them and will be better able to address them. As we deepen our empathy, love and compassion for other people, we'll find that the need to judge and criticize others will fade, replaced by the desire to understand and help them. Compassion is a gateway to happiness, emotional stability and good relationships.

Our Approach

This book features two authors: one a clinical psychologist and the other a Buddhist nun. When I (Russell) considered the idea of a book featuring brief readings and practices for cultivating compassion, I wanted to draw from both Western psychology and Buddhism as both seek to understand and alleviate suffering. I fantasized about how great it would be to have a Buddhist teacher as a coauthor. Luckily, I knew the perfect person. As I had visited Sravasti Abbey and benefited greatly from her writings, teachings and example in my own efforts to cultivate compassion, I was thrilled when Venerable Thubten Chodron agreed to join me on this journey. My aim was to show how Buddhism and psychology can work together towards the same goal—helping us to live with open hearts, to cultivate kindness and compassion for ourselves and others even in the context of busy lives. Compassion is something we can bring into every moment of our lives, and as you'll see, both the ancient traditions of Buddhism and the more recent approaches of psychology have much to contribute to this effort.

While there is a good deal of overlap between our approaches, each field offers its own unique perspectives. We were excited to combine these traditions.

Both of us value compassion highly, try to cultivate it in our daily lives and strive to share with others our knowledge and experiences of compassion. Both of us have deep reverence for people—be they well-known or not—who provide living examples of compassion in action. We have both benefited greatly from Buddhist teachings on compassion and have utilized Western psychological approaches to compassion in our own lives and teaching.

We think there are also interesting differences in our approaches. Chodron, a nun in the Tibetan Buddhist tradition, approaches compassion chiefly from a spiritual perspective, having spent decades studying and practicing teachings of the Buddha and great Buddhist masters. These teachings describe step-by-step methods for eliminating anger and cultivating forgiveness as well as for developing unbiased love and compassion for all beings.

As a clinical psychologist and through his work as a therapist, researcher and university professor specializing in areas such as mood disorders, mindfulness, anger and Compassion Focused Therapy, Russell draws more heavily upon the scientific perspective of Western psychology. This is reflected in how he approaches compassion as well, bringing in an emphasis on the evolved brain's role in helping shape our emotional responses, as well as the practice of mindfulness as it is currently taught in Western psychology.

We have had many interesting discussions together about compassion, informed by our different backgrounds, educations and experiences. But above all, we share a unified commitment to the application of compassion, kindness and tolerance to the alleviation of suffering. We've enjoyed writing and exploring compassion together, and we hope that you, too, will enjoy the shared approach found in this book.

Mind and Brain

At various points, we will discuss the mind, the brain and the interaction between the two, so it's useful to start by defining what we mean by these. By "mind," we are referring to mental activity—the part of us that thinks, perceives, feels and experiences; this includes the conscious, cognitive, intelligent and emotive parts of us as human beings. Unlike the brain, the mind isn't made of matter.

Buddhists view the mind as being mere clarity and awareness. *Clarity* refers to the immaterial nature of the mind, as well as to the mind being like a mirror in that it is able to reflect whatever appears to it. *Awareness* indicates the mind's capacity to perceive, experience and engage with objects.

The fundamental nature of the mind is pure and untainted, although it is sometimes clouded by disturbing emotions such as clinging attachment, anger and confusion. An analogy may be helpful here: the mind resembles the clear sky, while its contents—thoughts, emotions and so on—are like clouds passing through it. The sky-like nature of the mind itself is pure; the cloud-like thoughts and emotions are not an inherent part of it. Disturbing emotions cloud the mind so that we cannot see things as they are. Fortunately, this can be reversed through the cultivation of wisdom, enabling us to see the sky-like pure nature of our minds.

In contrast, the brain is a physical organ shaped by evolution, composed of cells called neurons and operating through complex electrochemical processes. The interaction between the mind and the brain is complicated, and this is one area in which we have slightly different perspectives. Chodron views the relationship between the brain and the mind as correlational: that the brain often mirrors and reflects mental activities and emotions, but rarely directly causes them. Russell places a greater emphasis on the brain's role in shaping our experience of reality, viewing its physical activity as a part of the causal chain that gives rise to our mental experiences, even as it is shaped in turn by these mental experiences. When it comes to cultivating compassion, this difference is a minor one. While the perspectives we take in our entries may differ a bit, our goals for this book are the same—learning how we can use our minds and brains to our best advantage in cultivating compassion, in order to create better lives and a better world.

Format and Overview

Our goal in writing this book is to give you practical tools for transforming your mind, so that you can express your deepest values such as kindness, love, compassion and generosity throughout your day, however unglamorous your tasks and interactions may seem. You may even find that, when imbued with compassion, no task or interaction is mundane.

To accomplish our purpose, we have composed a series of brief entries giving you ideas and practices to carry into your day. These entries will help you become more aware of how to bring compassion into your daily life and to face obstacles that challenge our ability to be compassionate. Each entry is followed by a reflection that will help you think about and apply the points in that entry to your life.

The entries are organized into six major sections:

- Section I centers on defining compassion, clarifying what it is and what it isn't, and exploring the reasons why it is worth incorporating into our lives.
- Section II helps us prepare to cultivate compassion by increasing our awareness of others and learning how our emotions work.

- Section III focuses on how to cultivate compassion and presents a number of practices and strategies to help you incorporate compassion into your everyday life.
- Section IV explores the relationship between compassion and how we connect and communicate with others.
- Section V addresses the obstacles and challenges that we may come across while cultivating compassion.
- Section VI focuses on specific applications of compassion in our lives and society.

While the entries are laid out in sequential fashion and can be read in order, most of the entries can also be read on their own. You may enjoy flipping the book open and reading an entry at random, reflecting on the entry as you go about your day. Since cultivating compassion is an ongoing practice in our lives, you may want to read this book again and again, soaking up more wisdom each time.

Symbols

Given that we bring two different traditions to bear in our exploration of compassion, we thought that it would be useful for you to know whose voice is primary in the various entries. As a reminder of this, we've included symbols at the beginning of each entry to indicate who authored it. Russell is represented by Ψ, the Greek letter Psi, which is often used as a symbol for the field of psychology. Chodron's entries are indicated with a Dharma wheel, ❀, a common symbol in Buddhism. The Buddha is said to have "turned the wheel of the Dharma," that is, he gave teachings describing the way to fully actualize our human potential. On those entries in which both authors contributed significantly, the symbol of a lotus is used, ✿. The lotus is a beautiful flower that grows out of the mud but is not tainted by it. So, too, people who have developed their compassion to its fullest extent can live in the world with its suffering and confusion but not be adversely influenced by it. In Buddhist art, the Buddha is often depicted sitting or standing upon a lotus. For your convenience, we've also indicated below who wrote which entries:

- Russell: 1, 2, 6, 8–10, 12, 13, 15, 16, 19, 20, 31–4, 36, 40, 48, 53–5, 60, 61, 64, 66, 69.
- Chodron: 3-5, 7, 11, 14, 17, 18, 21–30, 35, 37–9, 41, 46, 47, 49, 50–2, 56–9, 62, 63, 65, 67, 68.
- Both: 42–45.

Acknowledgments

Both authors would like to express our sincere gratitude and respect to His Holiness the Dalai Lama for his enlightening example of compassion in action. We are grateful to Fritha Saunders and all at Constable & Robinson and Shambhala who made this book possible.

Russell

I would like to express my gratitude to all who have committed themselves to cultivating and teaching compassion, both ancient masters and contemporary teachers and scholars. I wish to convey deep thanks to Professor Paul Gilbert and the rest of the Compassion Focused Therapy community, to my ever-supportive colleagues and students at Eastern Washington University and elsewhere, and to my family—in particular, my wife Lisa, son Dylan and my parents John and Mary Kolts. I'm also fortunate to have a number of friends who continually offer me support and compassion, and I would particularly like to thank Randy Hartsock, Chris Schwarz, and Shane Smith, whose influence in my life directly contributed to the writing of this book.

Chodron

I would like to express my appreciation to the Buddha and to the eighth-century Indian sage Shantideva who so eloquently gave instructions on the method for cultivating compassion, as well as to all of my teachers. I also appreciate the patience and support of the community at Sravasti Abbey.

An Open-Hearted Life

1 : Setting Our Motivation

Ψ THIS BOOK IS ABOUT LEARNING to weave compassion into our everyday lives, no matter how busy or hectic those lives may be. When starting out on an important journey, it's worth it to do some preparation—and this particular journey is one that *matters*. So let's begin preparing for our journey together by considering motivation, which is a crucial component of compassion.

Have you ever considered why you do the things you do? We have many different motivations, linked to a wide range of goals—we may want to form and maintain relationships; acquire money, status or possessions; pursue meaning and happiness in life. At other times, we may not be aware of our motivations at all—going through the day checking off items on a "to do" list, disconnected from the awareness of *why* we're doing these things. However, it's possible for us to *choose* and *consciously cultivate* a motivation in our minds, just as we cultivate seeds in a garden. Specifically, we can resolve to do whatever it is we're doing for beneficial reasons. There are considerable advantages to doing this: the motivation behind an action—the *reason* we're doing it—deeply influences the manner in which we do the action, how we feel while we're doing it, as well as the outcome of the activity. Over time, pausing to consciously cultivate a compassionate motivation before we act transforms our mental state, assisting us to make wise decisions and enhancing our lives.

We all have various responsibilities in our jobs and homes. Imagine that one of yours is to cook dinner for your family or roommates. When you get home from a busy and tiring day, it might be easy to approach preparing the meal as just another item to be checked off of your "to do" list. You might even resent having to do it, thinking, "This is something I *have* to do," even if it's a task you've agreed to do and may often enjoy.

Suppose you were to approach cooking dinner a bit differently. What if you shifted gears after you got home by taking a few quiet minutes for yourself, or simply taking a minute to breathe in a relaxed way and release the tension in your muscles? What if you then generated *the motivation to prepare a nutritious meal to feed and nurture these people you care about, to make their lives better*? Imagine yourself preparing this meal with purpose—a purpose that is a reflection of the values that you hold most dear, such as kindness, love, compassion and generosity. Picture those you care about being happy and well nourished by the food that you've lovingly prepared for them.

Including compassion in our motivation can transform even the most mundane tasks. We can wash dishes so others may eat without becoming ill. As parents and teachers, we can guide and occasionally discipline children with the motivation to help them develop qualities that will serve them well as they grow in life. We can interact with customers with the intention of helping them find what they need and will enjoy. Buddhist teachers encourage us to examine our motives before we act, making sure they are not selfish or unkind, and that our ultimate goal is to benefit others and free them from suffering. Imagine acting with the motivation to free all beings— including yourself—from suffering. Try not to get caught up in thinking, "That's silly, there's no way I could possibly do that." Simply imagine how you would feel, think and behave if you *had* such a motive.

REFLECTION

Working with Motivation

As we begin our conversation about compassion, consider reading this book—contemplating the ideas, trying out the practices—with the intention to cultivate positive qualities so you can contribute to the happiness of everyone with whom you come into contact, including yourself. Imagine acting with the sincere motivation to make the world around you a kinder, happier place and to reduce the suffering of those you interact with. Try taking a moment to set your motivation each morning before getting out of bed: "Today I will do my best to show kindness and compassion to those with whom I interact." "Today I will try to be less judgmental." "Today, I will provide a model of patience and perseverance for my children, so they will learn these qualities." Experiment with setting your motivation in this way each morning and see how this impacts your day.

PART ONE

Compassion

What It Is, What It Isn't and Why It's Worth Cultivating

2 : What Is Compassion and Why Do We Need It?

Ψ DEFINITIONS OF COMPASSION, whether drawn from the dictionary or the Dalai Lama, generally involve two components: *sensitivity* to suffering and the *motivation* to help alleviate it. The first involves openness to being moved in the face of pain and suffering—we allow ourselves to bear witness to the difficulties that we and others face, and to be touched by this suffering. This experience of being moved by suffering gives rise to the second component: the motivation to help make things better.

His Holiness the Dalai Lama frequently says, "If you want others to be happy, practice compassion. If you want to be happy, practice compassion." Why do His Holiness and so many others feel that this particular virtue is worth cultivating?

Life can be difficult, and we're all in it together. Even if we are born into an advantaged position with parents who love us and care for us, an abundance of food, comfortable shelter and access to education and medical care, each of us will still have to deal with great difficulty in our lives. All of us face aging, sickness and death. We will all lose people we love. Sometimes we will do our best and not succeed. Most of us will have our hearts broken, if not once, then several times. We will sometimes feel other painful emotions: fear, sadness, anger or anxiety. This is the pain that comes with being human. It's the price of admission. Added to this is the fact that many of us are born into situations that are far more difficult than others—abusive or neglectful home environments, extreme poverty and cultural contexts that systematically advantage some people while disadvantaging others. Life is challenging, and the playing field is anything but level.

In the face of all this pain and hardship, compassion is the only response that makes sense. Sure, we could do lots of other things. We could become upset, look for people to blame, and get mad at them. We could simply close our eyes to the things we don't like, pushing away painful feelings or numbing them with drugs or alcohol. We could look the other way when confronted with the suffering of others or even blame them for their struggles. The trouble is that the challenges in life—whether they are feelings inside of us we'd rather not have, conflicts with other people or problems in the world—don't go away when we ignore them. In fact, they generally get bigger.

While it isn't easy to bring ourselves face-to-face with pain and difficulty, there is a huge benefit to doing so. Once we've stopped denying, avoiding or ignoring our problems, we can work to make things better. Viewing the world with compassion allows us to relinquish the need to judge and shame ourselves or other people for having entirely human feelings. Instead, we can learn to balance our emotions so we will be at our best. Our confidence grows as we learn that we *can* face, tolerate and work to improve difficult emotions and situations. This confidence helps us relate to life on its own terms, without being crippled by fear and worry. It allows us to shift from an anxious vigilance that is continually keeping watch for potential mistakes or difficulties to a more open, balanced experience that helps us respond to challenges while savoring the good things in life and being grateful for them.

I (Russell) developed a Compassion Focused Therapy

group at a state prison. This program is designed to help the men there learn compassionate ways of working with their anger. Many of them enter the group sceptically, thinking that compassion means being weak and vulnerable: "just being nice all the time." But their view of compassion changes dramatically over the course of group therapy as they discover that compassion requires *courage*—the courage to bring ourselves face-to-face with the difficulties of life and the powerful emotions that sometimes arise within us. It requires courage and commitment to *stay*, to tolerate the distress and discomfort we feel when encountering these difficulties as we learn to work with them. Compassion is anything but weakness.

There are more benefits to compassion. Recognizing we're all in this together, we stop finger-pointing or sticking our heads in the sand and begin to support one another. All our lives are filled with challenges, and we all sometimes struggle with powerful emotions. We're better able to face these challenges when we encourage one another and kindly hold ourselves accountable when we're the ones causing the problems. When we feel safe, accepted and valued, we are able to face problems in life and take responsibility for them. This is a gift we can give to others and to ourselves; it's a gift that benefits the giver as much as the recipient.

REFLECTION

Three Students and Three Teachers

Imagine three children attempting to learn a difficult new task such as playing an instrument or solving an algebra problem. All three struggle with the task. One child has a teacher who ignores her, oblivious to her struggles. Another has an impatient teacher who constantly points out what he is doing wrong and criticizes his mistakes. The third has a compassionate teacher, who gently coaches her, letting her know that this is difficult in the beginning, encouraging her to keep at it and pointing out her progress. Which child will make the best progress? Which teacher would you prefer to have?[1]

3 : Compassion, Interdependence and Universal Responsibility

We must all learn to live together as brothers or we will perish together as fools. This is the great challenge of the hour. This is true of individuals. It is true of nations. No individual can live alone. No nation can live alone.

—MARTIN LUTHER KING JR.

As MARTIN LUTHER KING JR. pointed out, none of us can live alone; we are all dependent on each other. What do we need to learn in order to live together as brothers and sisters? The answer is compassion. Feeling compassion means being concerned about the suffering of others and wishing them to be free from suffering and its causes. Compassion is closely related to love, which is the wish for living beings to have happiness and its causes.

Having compassion makes sense. If we don't care for others, all of us will suffer—either because our needs are not being met or because we will be surrounded by unhappy people—a situation that will make our own lives miserable. For these reasons, His Holiness the Dalai Lama counsels, "If you want to be selfish, be wisely selfish and take care of others."

Compassion applies to all areas of our lives—on a personal

level, compassion for ourselves, for friends and family, for our colleagues and our boss, and even for the people who sometimes disturb us; on a community level, compassion of one group for other groups; on an international level, compassion of one nation for the citizens of other nations. Compassion is the opposite of and the antidote to our usual self-centeredness that urges us to get the best and most for ourselves in order to ensure our own happiness. Self-centeredness results in difficulties for those around us, and their problems disturb not only their tranquillity but ours as well.

Many years ago some of the people in the city where I (Chodron) lived did not want to pay increased property taxes in order to support schools and afterschool activities for children and teens. They figured that since their children were already grown, there was no reason for them to pay for the education of other people's children. However, they *were* willing for their taxes to be used to build more prisons to protect them from criminals. What they didn't see was that these things were related.

When children don't receive a good education, and afterschool activities such as sports and art are cut, they can easily get involved with drugs. Using drugs requires money, so some turn to theft. The stores that they shoplift from and the houses that they burgle often belong to the people who voted against increased property tax. When children do not have the facilities and education that they need and are not cared for by their families, schools and society in general, everyone is affected. We are all interconnected.

Although we may win arguments when we care only for ourselves or for those who are on our side, when we humiliate people and ignore their misery, it will almost always come back to haunt us. Conflicts and wars throughout world history attest to this fact. Therefore, if we want to be happy ourselves, it is essential to care for the welfare of others. Rather than categorizing some people as "enemies" whose needs are not important, we can instead care for their well-being. When we respect them as human beings and help them to meet their basic needs—such as their need for food, clothing, shelter and medicine, and their need to be respected, to give and receive care and affection, and to contribute to the welfare of a group—there will be no reason for them to be antagonistic towards us; we will have done everything that we could to ensure their happiness and end their suffering. An enemy will become a friend. History shows many instances of this, some even in our lifetime. For example, Britain and the U.S. saw Germany and Japan as enemies in the 1940s, and now these countries are allies and work well together.

Human beings are more dependent on each other now than in any other time in human existence. Unlike centuries ago, very few people grow their own food, make their own clothes or construct their own homes. Many of us do not know how to do these activities and we depend on others who do, as well as on those who make the roads we drive on, who invent the technology we use and who teach us everything we know, to name a few. Once we recognize that we are inextricably interconnected, we see that caring for each other is more crucial than ever before.

At a gathering with inner city children who live in violent communities and are at risk for turning to violence themselves, the Dalai Lama said, "Violence is old-fashioned. War is old-fashioned. We have exceptional human brains, something no other species has, so we have to use our intelligence to help each other. Then all of us will benefit and live together peacefully." Compassion is the way to do this.

REFLECTION

Bringing Compassion into the World

Consider a situation in the world or in your own life that might be improved by compassion. Imagine how this situation could be different if the people involved in it felt, thought and acted with compassion, wishing others not to suffer.

4 : Genuine Compassion

COMPASSION IS A QUALITY of mind that can be deliberately cultivated. Unlike mental states that are caused by distorted perceptions and misconceptions, such as anger and greed, compassion is developed with a more rational state of mind that does not exaggerate either the positive or negative aspects of a person, object, idea or situation. Moreover, compassion influences our other thoughts and emotions. Anger, jealousy and contempt can be eliminated through compassion, while mind-states such as love can be purposefully cultivated and deepened.

Compassion is not like a well that will one day run dry. Rather, the more we open our hearts with compassion, the more compassion increases. It is not the case that if we have compassion for one group, there won't be enough to share with another group. Compassion spreads; the more there is, the more there will be.

Compassion is an internal attitude that may manifest in our behavior. However, compassion is not the behavior itself, for one behavior can be done with different motivations. For example, we may take care of a sick relative because we have genuine affection for him. Conversely, we may care for him because we want to inherit his estate. The action is the same, but the motivations differ. The first motivation is prompted by genuine compassion, the second by self-concern.

Acting with compassion entails being creative and knowing that one behavior is not suitable for all occasions. In some circumstances, we may be compassionate by sharing our possessions; while in others, we may show it by saying, "no." In this way, compassion must be combined with good judgment to be effective.

REFLECTION

Compassionate Intention

As you go through the day, try to be creative in bringing a compassionate intention to the situations you face. For example, when washing dishes, consider that you are doing so that others may eat without contracting disease. When interacting with others, do so with the intention to make their day a bit brighter. Pick a few situations you regularly encounter during the day, and experiment with how you could bring a compassionate intention to the situation and see how it affects your experience of the situation.

5 : Abandoning Misconceptions and Making Peace with Our Fears

WHEN WE HEAR THE WORD "COMPASSION," a variety of images may come to mind: a mother tenderly caring for her child, Mother Teresa's loving care for the dying, feeling sympathy for another's misery. But other less benevolent images may also arise: being overwhelmed by others' suffering, being taken advantage of and going along with actions that we don't agree with.

Understanding the true meaning of compassion is not easy. It requires contemplation, making peace with our fears and dispelling misconceptions. In doing this, our hearts will open to ourselves and others in a way we may never have thought possible.

One misconception is that compassion means pitying or feeling sorry for someone. Imagine that Ben stands back and with a superior attitude looks at a homeless person and thinks, "How terrible! Poor you! I feel sorry for you," with the unspoken subtext, "It's a shame that you aren't as intelligent as I am and did stupid things so that you ended up on the streets." This is not compassion, but condescension combined with pity.

Acting with compassion towards others means seeing them as equal to us. We are all human beings who want happiness and do not want suffering. The eighth century Buddhist sage, Shantideva, illustrates this with the analogy of our hand pulling a thorn out of our foot. The hand doesn't think, "I, the great and glorious hand, am bequeathing compassion on you, the stupid foot, that didn't watch where you were going even though I told you to look out for thorns. So now you're in this mess, and you're so fortunate to have me around because I'm going to rescue you yet again. Foot, I really wish you would get it together and take care of yourself. It's very troublesome for me to help you, but I'll do it anyway. So don't forget what I'm doing for you because now you owe me a good turn."

Whew, that's a lot for the hand to dump on the foot which is already suffering from the thorn. Neither the hand nor the foot is happy with the situation.

In a situation of genuine compassion, the hand and foot realize that they are part of the same organism. There's no power imbalance, no condescending ego trips, no infliction of guilt or obligation. Rather, the hand reaches down and pulls the thorn out of the foot without thinking twice about it. It's the hand's natural instinct and they both benefit. Likewise, when we extend help to others, we need to be mindful to do it with genuine compassion.

Respect for others is an essential ingredient for compassion, and real compassion fosters respect. For most people, being treated with respect is more important than being physically comfortable. Those of us who are usually treated with respect may take it for granted and not understand how important it actually is to us. However, people who are deprived of respect—the poor, ill, physically challenged, incarcerated and oppressed—know the pain of disrespect only too well.

During a class that I (Chodron) was teaching on compassion, I asked my students to try to do at least one action motivated by genuine compassion each day. The next week one of the students recounted that he had been in the downtown area where a woman was sitting on the sidewalk, with her hands out begging. His compassion aroused, he wanted to help. He didn't have much money with him but pulled out a dollar and, looking her in the eyes, he smiled and handed it to her with both hands, saying, "I wish I could give you more but this is what I have with me."

The woman looked up and met his gaze with tears in her eyes, "That's the first time someone treated me with respect since I've been here," she said, "That means more to me than the money."

REFLECTION

Compassion and Respect

Try to recall a time that you've been treated with pity, a time when you thought that someone was looking down on you or not respecting you. If you can't remember such a time, imagine what it might be like. Explore how that feels.

Now bring to mind a time when someone showed you compassion—perhaps respectfully offering help when you needed it, doing something kind to brighten your day or simply holding your hand as you grieved. Once again, allow yourself to notice the emotions that arise.

Now notice the differences in how pity and respectful compassion affect your mental state. Our attitudes towards other people can have a huge impact on the way they think and feel. Consider how you want to affect others. What do you want to inspire in them?

6 : Courageous Compassion

Ψ WHEN HEARING THE WORD "COMPASSION," some people think it means giving in to what other people want. Others think compassion means trying to create a world in which everything is perfect, with everyone joining hands and humming inspirational songs. In this imaginary world, no one ever struggles or cries, all conflict is smoothed over, there is no pain or difficulty and we all live happily ever after.

Some imagine compassion means being above it all, serenely transcending all worldly troubles and moving through life unscathed and unaffected by difficulties. We may fantasize about drifting through life with sublime smiles on our faces, magically interacting with others in ways that instantly and effortlessly free them from their struggles and inspire them to completely turn their lives around. We may imagine how wonderful the world would be if everyone saw things from our viewpoint, if all those poor people could just understand what *we* understand.

Here's a news flash: That's not compassion. It's self-indulgence, smacking of what Chögyam Trungpa called "idiot compassion." Compassion is not airy-fairy. It is not pretentious. It does not mean just being comfortable and sweet all of the time, and it isn't an excuse to consider ourselves better than others.

Imagine being a plumber and someone calls because his toilet isn't working properly. He reports a terrible smell coming from underneath the house, likely indicating a broken sewage pipe that needs replacing. Showing up in our clean, white uniforms, we chat with him about the problem and offer well-meant advice, "These things often sort themselves out. Be careful not to flush the wrong things down the toilet. Have a nice cup of tea and a biscuit—you'll feel better shortly." This is all well and good, but it isn't going to solve the problem. We need to open up the crawlspace under the house, crawl in to diagnose the problem, lug our tools in through the muck and replace the broken pipe. It's going to be uncomfortable. The smell will be nasty. Those white uniforms will definitely get soiled. But that's what is necessary if we want to help.

Similarly, compassion requires a willingness to bring ourselves into contact with pain and suffering—our own and that of those we want to help. Compassion requires us to stay when things get tough, to tolerate the difficult emotions that arise when we come into contact with suffering and those who experience it. Compassion is courageous.

It isn't easy to be around people who are suffering. Our brains play a role in this: they have cells called "mirror neurons" that enable us to feel a bit of what those we come into contact with are feeling. This is why we cringe when we see others in pain—on a psychological level, we feel some of their hurt. Witnessing suffering can bring up powerful emotions in us, emotions we must learn to tolerate and work with if we are going to help. The feelings that arise when we see others (or even ourselves) suffering can be painful, but this isn't a bad thing. It's a crucial part of compassion, one we're "wired" to feel.

We can try a brief exercise. Take a few breaths and notice the feelings and thoughts you're experiencing. Now say to yourself: "hungry child." Notice any feelings that arise when you say those words and allow them to sink in. You may find yourself feeling touched or sad, feelings I experienced when writing them. That's no accident. We're born with the capacity to share each other's pain and are equipped with the tools of compassion to respond to it.

We need courage and patience to face this pain. It isn't easy, because we have powerful instincts that motivate us to recoil from things that cause us discomfort. But if we allow ourselves to constantly pull away from the suffering that we see around us or feel within us, we won't be able to understand it well enough to help. We have to be willing to put ourselves into the shoes of those who are suffering, to see the world through their eyes. We have to be able to *stay* and to *listen*. This means *stopping* our habitual tendency to escape the situation, assign judgmental labels, or give thoughtless advice so we can move on. Rather, we need to look deeply at the suffering in order to understand its nature, its causes and its remedies. Then, when we act in compassion, we can do so wisely and confidently.

REFLECTION

Getting to Know Ourselves

Consider some situations that make you uncomfortable, that you tend to avoid. For example, how do you feel and react when you are with others who are in physical pain, or who are feeling sadness, grief, fear, anger or hopelessness? Notice the experiences you are comfortable sharing with them and which ones prompt you to pull back.

7 : Confusion about Compassion

 WHILE EVERYONE ADMIRES compassion, there is a lot of confusion about it. In addition to learning what compassion is, it's good to also know what it isn't.

Having compassion does not mean we become people-pleasers. The motivation of a people-pleaser is self-protection. It is not genuine care for another person, but wanting other people to think well of us or be nice to us. Such a motivation centers on protecting our ego, not on benefiting someone else.

Compassion does not involve interfering in other people's lives and fixing their problems. Becoming Ms. or Mr. Fix-It brings the focus back to us. We think, "I can't stand to see another person suffer. I've *got* to do something about it." With this thought, we risk getting more involved than the other person wants. We become so energized by the thought, "I'm going to solve her problem," that we may inadvertently make the other person feel powerless and helpless. No one wants other people to control their life out of a mistaken sense of compassion. Sometimes the most compassionate thing to do is to teach others how to help solve their own problems and then to step back and give them the opportunity to do so. When they succeed, their self-confidence will increase. If they don't, hopefully they will learn from their mistakes. If they ask us for tips on how to deal with the situation, we can do that while at the same time respecting their autonomy.

Compassion does not entail becoming a doormat that others trample on or allowing others to take advantage of us. Compassion does not involve misdirected forgiveness such as in the case of domestic violence: "It's okay, dear. You beat me last night and the night before. I have compassion for you and forgive you. You can beat me again if you wish." That is not compassion; that is foolishness that helps neither others nor us. When our children or we are in danger, we should leave the situation immediately and not return until the other person has received the help he needs so that the violence has ceased and the situation is safe. Although we maintain compassion for others who are overwhelmed by disturbing emotions, we do not allow them to harm us. This is not only for our own safety, but also for their benefit since they will face many problems due to their violent behavior.

In fact, compassion may entail acting in a way that the other person does not like at all. With genuine compassion, we may even have to jeopardize a relationship with someone we care about in order to benefit that person. A man once told me that as a teenager he acted out and got in a lot of trouble with the law. Each time, his mother would go to court and get him out, and then he'd steal, drink or sell drugs yet again. But one time his mother looked at the judge and said, "My son is out of control. You keep him," and left the court. He was stunned and sat in jail for a while. At first he was quite upset, but it made him reflect on his behavior and stop taking his mother's kindness for granted. As a result, he began to settle down.

Compassion also gives us the confidence to say "no" when faced with someone's manipulative behavior. Giving into their scheming or pleas helps neither them nor us in the long run. Although the other person may be angry, we do not doubt our decision when we know that what we are doing is a good choice done with a compassionate motivation.

Compassion is a gift that we give freely to others. Expecting something in return, even a thank-you, can lead to disappointment. Even if someone thanks us, it is the person who gives thanks, not the one who receives it, who benefits the most. The person who gives thanks experiences happiness because she is showing her appreciation for—and her willingness to return—kindness. When someone doesn't thank us, that doesn't have to diminish our joy or our compassion. In other words, our pleasure comes from the act of giving, not from someone showing appreciation for what we have done. We feel content because we acted in accordance with our own values.

We may encounter many different situations during the course of our lives when feelings of compassion arise naturally within us. Moved by the suffering that we've observed, we may find ourselves motivated to act to make things better. In these situations, it's important to honestly assess what we are capable of doing—and what we aren't. Then we can act effectively, contributing what we're able to, without inappropriately trying to shoulder burdens that we're incapable of handling or which aren't ours to carry. For example, if we observe a co-worker struggling at a task that he's been given, we may be tempted to just do it for him, even if we know that it's his responsibility and we're already busy with our own work. But it may be better to simply offer a kind, sympathetic ear and perhaps some words of encouragement. If we push ourselves out of guilt or out of a sense of obligation to do more, we will become resentful, which will take the joy out of giving. Guilt and compassion don't go together. Compassion given freely is best for others and us.

Sometimes our feelings of compassion are greater than what we—or anyone else—are capable of doing in response. For example, after the 2010 earthquake in Haiti, we may have felt a strong compassion for those left homeless or injured.

However, as one individual we are incapable of remedying the entire tragedy. Instead, we must do what we are capable of doing, for example making a donation to a charity organization. To maintain a compassionate state even when we are unable to extend practical help, we can also do the "taking and giving" meditation, which will be described in entry 30.

REFLECTION

Removing Confusion about Compassion

Recall a time when you had a mistaken notion of compassion; for example, you thought that being compassionate meant pleasing other people or helping someone out of a sense of obligation or guilt. How could you have changed your attitude into one of actual compassion? Imagine doing that. Then, imagine yourself acting with genuine compassion.

8 : A Different Kind of Strength

Ψ WHILE CULTIVATING COMPASSION may be challenging and uncomfortable at times, *it's worth it.* Compassion enables us to live our values, help other people, address problems in our communities and to make a better world. Approaching challenges with compassion enables us to transform our minds, have a positive effect on the situations and people with whom we come into contact, and to support others and ourselves when we're faced with things we can't change.

The more we practice compassion, the easier it gets. We discover *we can do it.* We find we can bear all the scary thoughts we've built up in our minds and the feelings we thought were completely unbearable. As we courageously face the things that scare us over and over again, they stop being so scary.

Psychologists call this *habituation.* It means that when we're repeatedly exposed to things that scare us and nothing terrible happens, our fear gradually decreases over time. As Shantideva wrote in *The Way of the Bodhisattva*:[1] "There is nothing whatsoever that is not made easier through acquaintance."

When we sit together with those who are feeling grief-stricken, terrified or furious and have a compassionate attitude towards them, we begin to understand that we can be in the presence of others' strong emotions without having to react to them, fix the situation or escape. When we spend time with people whose background, manners, beliefs or lifestyles may initially put us off, we begin to understand that they are valuable people who have hopes and dreams just like us, who only want to be happy and not suffer just like us.

When I (Russell) first started running Compassion Focused Therapy anger management groups in prison, I was a bit intimidated. Some of the men were in prison because of rape, murder and other violent offences, and I was there to work with the really angry ones! However, I soon discovered that these men were just like me in so many ways, and when given an opportunity and shown compassion they not only claimed responsibility for their crimes, but also actively took responsibility for changing their lives and committed to replacing their anger with compassion.

After running these groups for more than three years I can honestly say I've never worked with a more committed, hard-working group of people. While it took a few sessions for these men to connect with the idea of seeing themselves as "compassionate," they almost immediately began putting the compassionate understandings and practices I was teaching them to work. Instead of rushing to judge and condemn themselves and others, they began to seek understanding. Instead of reacting to small irritants (and large ones) with fury and violence, they began to slow down, take a moment to soothe themselves and try to take a broader perspective. Instead of indifference, they began extending kindness to others in the prison—even going so far as to enthusiastically teach their "cellies" (cellmates) and other men on their units what they were learning. Perhaps the most frequent comment I've heard from these men is how often other people, from corrections officers to family members, have asked them, "What happened? You're different—what are you doing?" Their answer? "Compassion."

When we compassionately allow ourselves to experience the full range of our emotions, including those that may seem overwhelming or off-putting, we begin to understand we *can* experience them without being overwhelmed. Becoming intimately familiar with our own fear, anger, grief, craving and/or disgust, we learn it is possible to move into and out of these feelings without becoming forever trapped in them. We can learn to direct warmth and compassion towards ourselves when we're struggling with our difficult emotions, just as we do to others. In this way, we gradually discover ways to feel safe as we allow ourselves to feel whatever emotions are there for us to feel. We learn to express empathy and develop compassionate skills we can draw upon as we go through life.

When all of this comes together—habituation, understanding and new skills—we have a new kind of strength. We begin to experience a confidence and fearlessness that is truly powerful. It's the strength to face life head-on, exactly as it comes.

Our fear is replaced with a confidence that "Whatever happens, I can find a way to work with it." By recognizing what connects us, the concept of "enemies" becomes ridiculous. No longer threatened by perspectives that are different from our own, we become wiser, and the need to constantly assert our own viewpoints gives way to the eagerness to listen to and learn from others.

Recognizing that the urgency we feel when a strong emotion arises is simply a property of the emotion itself, we can see when a situation calls for a more balanced, nuanced approach. Consider an argument with a partner or family member in which you've become angry and are absolutely certain your perspective is correct. The anger or frustration arises, and you feel an intense urge to continue the conversation—to keep trying to hammer your point home—even when the other person's body language is clearly telling you *nothing is getting through right now.* In such situations, we can recognize that the urgency we feel to continue the conversation has little to do with what would *be helpful,* and everything to do with the way anger plays out in our minds. Understanding this, we can instead choose to slow things down. It's remarkable how being able to slow down and listen to others helps make them much more motivated to slow down and listen to *us.* We also learn we can *accept* our emotions without having to act on them, recoil from them or shame ourselves for having them. Instead, we can relate to them warmly, as old friends we value but who sometimes can mislead us: "Anger, I recognize you. While I understand that you're just trying to protect me, your methods aren't very well suited to the situation at hand. Let me help you."

Think of the people you may consider as models of compassion: His Holiness the Dalai Lama, Jesus Christ, Mahatma Gandhi, Nelson Mandela, Mother Teresa. They all exhibit *fearlessness* in the face of situations that would make many of us cower. They keep going when many would turn aside. It's not that they were never afraid. It's that they weren't *afraid of being afraid.* They accepted their fear and kept going anyway. That's the courage of compassion.

REFLECTION

We All Want to be Happy and Free from Suffering

At the heart of compassion is the realization *we all want to be happy and free from suffering.* We are all united by this simple truth. Consider your deepest desires: aren't all of the activities you do each day centered on the wish to be happy and not to suffer?

This is true for everyone else, too. That person in front of you in the queue talking loudly on her mobile phone wants to be happy and not suffer. The politician on the television viciously attacking his opponent wants to be happy and not suffer. The man begging for change on the side of the road wants to be happy and not suffer. When we can look beneath the external appearance of everyone's actions, we'll see a heartfelt wish to be happy and not suffer.

As you go through your day and encounter different people, remind yourself that like you, one of their deepest, innermost wishes is to be happy and not suffer. When you're at a red light, on the train, walking down the street or waiting in a queue, look at the people around you and reflect, "This person, like me, wants to be happy and avoid suffering." Let this knowledge enter your heart.

Then take it a step further and extend a kind wish to them, "*May you be happy and free from suffering.*" Similarly, we can extend this kind wish to ourselves. Repeatedly extending compassionate wishes can transform our minds: as we gradually build compassionate habits, they replace our habits to judge, criticize and shame that keep us caught up in anger, anxiety and negativity.

PART TWO

The Building Blocks
of Compassion

9 : Mindful Awareness

Ψ A COMMON OBSTACLE to compassion occurs when our minds are swept away by troublesome emotions or thoughts. It's relatively easy to experience kindness and compassion when everything is going well. The trouble comes when anger, fear, jealousy, anxiety, critical thoughts and so on leap into our minds. If we're not paying attention, we can lose ourselves in such thoughts and emotions, and our compassion quickly fades away.

Over the last few decades, Western mental health professionals have used mindfulness approaches adapted from traditional Buddhist practices to help their patients work with difficult thoughts and emotions. A quickly growing body of research shows that the regular practice of mindfulness meditation can even lead to growth in areas of the brain linked with emotion regulation, sense of self-identity, compassion and empathy.[1] There are many excellent books and resources on mindfulness if you are interested in learning more; what follows is a brief introduction on how increasing our mindfulness can aid us in developing our compassionate potential.

What exactly is mindfulness? In the psychological community, we generally define mindfulness as purposeful, non-judgmental awareness of what is happening inside of us and around us in the present moment. With mindful awareness, we neither cling to nor reject our experiences; we simply notice and accept them as they are. For example, we can discuss a sensitive issue with a family member and notice our voice is growing louder with an edge to it. We then become aware that this is because we feel threatened and are getting defensive and angry. This mindful awareness gives us the ability to make wise choices—for example, to slow down and to think before we speak. If we fail to notice troublesome thoughts and emotions and to recognize them as temporary *mental experiences*, it can be easy to be swept away by them.

We can consider a couple of examples. I (Russell) have done a lot of therapy work both with parents who are struggling to parent their challenging children and with adults who have had terrible childhood relationships with their own parents. Imagine a situation in which a child does something that really pushes our buttons—say, my son gets excited and accidentally bumps into my favorite acoustic guitar, sending it careening off of its stand on to the brick fireplace and putting a deep gouge into its side. In the heat of the moment, anger rapidly rising within us, it might be easy to thoughtlessly say things that can cause our loved one great pain, things that we would *never* say when we are at our best: "Why can't you look where you're going? Are you stupid? I can't have anything nice without you destroying it! Get out of my sight!" These comments can cause long-lasting harm; particularly if they are repeated time and time again over the course of many years.

Mindful awareness can help us notice when we are overcome by powerful emotions, so we steer ourselves towards a better course of action: "Wow . . . I am *really* angry right now. Anything I say to him while I'm feeling this way is likely to be hurtful, so I'd better keep quiet for the time being." Having taken a step back from the powerful emotion, a host of other possibilities open up, like slowing down my breathing, reminding myself it was an accident, it was only a guitar, and if I'm really *that* concerned about keeping it unblemished, I'd be better off keeping it in its case rather than on a tippy stand in a high-traffic area near a brick fireplace! Once I've calmed myself, I might even become aware of this as a valuable teaching experience—a chance to demonstrate to my son how to handle stressful situations in a calm, balanced manner, rather than flying off the handle—the way I'd want him to handle such situations as an adult. Over time, such interactions can help him develop the ability to deal with frustrating situations in helpful ways himself.

Since we're on the topic of parenting, it's worth noting that mindfulness can also be applied to other emotions like fear and anxiety. One of the tricks of good parenting is being able to tolerate some discomfort or fear when our children start to venture out on their own. This occurs throughout their development—from when they begin to walk, run and play independently on playgrounds (jumping around, inevitably falling) to when they begin dating, applying for jobs and eventually leave home. In each case, good parenting requires us to balance giving our children the support they need *and* the freedom to learn to manage challenging life situations on their own. If we're unable to observe and accept feelings of fear, or our desires to have control, we can easily become overprotective and controlling in the effort to make sure our children never come into contact with harm, while inadvertently crippling them in the process.

If we're overwhelmed by these emotions, we may engage in perhaps an even less helpful strategy—ignoring or turning away from our children entirely, because we can't handle the discomfort that comes from watching them struggle. Mindful awareness allows us to observe, accept and take responsibility for our own emotions, so we can work with them, rather than having these emotions dictate our actions: "Of course it's hard to watch my daughter go through this (and "this" could be anything from falling off playground equipment to going through a painful breakup), but this is how she's going to learn to manage such situations on her own. What would help me manage my own emotions so I can be here for her when she needs me but still allow her to develop as an individual?"

To return to the subject of troublesome thoughts and emotions, we often take our thoughts to be the absolute truth, experiencing them as "the way it is," and, unsurprisingly, have powerful reactions to them. Our emotions are very powerful—but they often aren't terribly *clever*, they're not very good at distinguishing between what is happening to us in the outside world and the thoughts and images we produce in our own minds.

For example, imagine that halfway through Joe's public talk (and twenty minutes before the bank closes), Gina, a woman sitting in the front row, recalls she forgot to deposit a check into her bank account needed to cover a number of debits that will be due over the weekend. Frowning and grumbling to herself because she forgot to take care of this, she quickly stands up and leaves the room. Imagine Joe notices this and interprets her behavior in a self-critical way: "She thinks I'm incompetent and that my talk is nonsense." He'll likely experience the same emotions as if she had said those things to him directly: shame, anxiety, embarrassment and perhaps hostility towards Gina. But we know, in fact, the situation had nothing to do with Joe—he completely misinterpreted Gina's actions. We tend to be very sensitive to perceived threats, which can lead to problems such as mistakenly interpreting events in the worst possible way, and having powerful emotional responses to mental events—thoughts, imagery, fantasies—that have little to do with what's actually going on.

Now try to imagine Joe responding differently. Imagine he is aware of the thought, "Gina thinks I'm incompetent and my talk is nonsense" and recognizes it as simply a thought. He pauses to reflect, "I wonder if there is another explanation for her behavior? She seemed to be engaged and interested during the rest of my talk. Perhaps something else is going on of which I'm unaware." Imagine how different Joe's emotional response would be when he is aware of what is happening in his mind.

With mindfulness, we train ourselves to recognize and accept our mental experiences *as* temporary mental experiences, without judging or clinging to them. Relating to our thoughts and emotions as temporary experiences rather than identifying them as *who we are* or as *the way things are* gives us some space to work with them. It's the difference between getting completely caught up in anger and instead observing, "I am *really* angry right now. I wonder what would help me work with this feeling?"

The acronym RAIN can be useful in helping us to remember the psychological process involved in mindfulness:

R   Recognize what is going on inside of us.
A   Accept and allow our experience to be what it is.
I   Investigate our experience, looking closely at what
     is happening within us.
N   Nonidentification, which means observing our
     experience without becoming one with it.[2]

Mindfulness allows us to have an accepting, nonjudgmental awareness of our thoughts and emotions, without necessarily buying into them. This changes how we think and talk about our emotions, for example recognizing that "I am feeling anger" rather than "I *am* angry." The first statement recognizes anger as an experience within the larger body of our awareness, a temporary mental state. The second reflects identification; we feel fused with the emotion and can't see a way to work with it.

Mindfulness helps us develop compassion, because the more aware we are of our shifting thoughts and emotional states, the better prepared we'll be to work with the difficult ones and to cultivate the mental experiences that we *want* to have (like compassion!). We can also choose to bring compassion into our mindful awareness. In this way, we practice mindfulness and self-compassion in tandem, thinking, "I'm feeling anxious (angry, jealous, sad) right now. How can I help myself work with this suffering?"

A common method of training in mindfulness begins with mindfully observing the breath. To do this, we sit upright and gently settle our attention on the breath. When our attention wanders as thoughts or distractions come to mind, we notice and accept them, and gently bring our attention back to the breath. There's no need to get frustrated when we find ourselves carried away by our thoughts. It's natural that distractions arise and we'll gradually get better at not getting carried away by them. In fact, these distractions help us get better at learning to notice movement in the mind—noticing when thoughts and emotions arise in our minds—which will help us work with these experiences. Over time, we'll notice these thoughts more quickly, accept them, release them and bring our mindful awareness back to the breath. The purpose of returning our attention to the breath is not to suppress or ignore our thoughts or emotions; it is to help us learn to notice them, and to give us some mental space so we don't automatically get caught up in unproductive thoughts that make us miserable. There are many good books and resources available to help us learn mindfulness (a number of recommendations are provided in the "Further Reading" section at the end of this book), and guided audio-meditations of mindful-breathing exercises can be found at www.compassionatemind.net.

REFLECTION

Mindful Checking In

The following exercise will help you become aware of what you are experiencing at a given moment and learn to notice, distinguish and accept various thoughts and emotions that arise in your mind. Try to pause a few times each day to notice your experience, and observe the effects that doing so has on your life.

- Start by bringing attention to your breath and noticing the feeling of your breath entering and leaving your body. Do this for thirty seconds or so.
- Shift your attention to your external bodily sensations—notice the sounds and sights coming in through your senses. Notice other bodily sensations—temperature, the pressure of your body making contact with the floor or chair, etc.
- Then shift your attention to your internal bodily sensations—heart rate, breathing, tension, hunger or fullness, aches and pains you may be feeling, temperature.
- Be aware of your mental experiences—notice what you are thinking, e.g., "This is odd." "What is it *now?*" "I don't feel like this is going to work."
- Now notice your emotions—Interest? Irritation? Anticipation? Boredom? Anxiety? Notice how the content of your thoughts can impact how you feel.
- Now bring awareness to your motivation (what you

want to do) and mental imagery (pictures or fantasy playing out in your mind).

Bring awareness to these experiences, noticing and accepting your thoughts, emotions, motivations and mental images as *temporary* mental events. As we do this process of "checking-in," we will become better at recognizing these mental and bodily experiences for what they are—temporary experiences—rather than being carried away by them. We'll also learn to notice how one mental experience can lead to the next, like a line of dominoes falling one at a time.

10 : Compassionate Understanding of Emotions

Ψ Do you ever look around at the world and wonder how it is we humans do such crazy, stupid things? Perhaps you occasionally look back at your own life and see decisions you've made that now make you cringe—almost as if you can't believe that was you. We may try to explain these things we do by attaching labels, "He's short-sighted." "I've got no self-control." "People are idiots!" However, to develop compassion, we need a nonjudgmental approach, imbued with acceptance and kindness.

Understanding how our emotions work is a big help. Bring to mind an emotion you've had recently, perhaps a challenging one such as anger or anxiety. Looking closely, you'll find this emotion can impact your mind in a number of different ways. Emotions "organize" our minds by affecting many aspects of our mental experience:

- *Bodily experience*: emotions play out in terms of feelings in the body. Some emotions arouse our bodies, while others relax them.
- *Attention*: emotions shape how narrowly or broadly our attention is focused, as well as what we pay attention to.
- *Thinking and reasoning*: emotions shape how flexibly we're able to think and also what we tend to think about.

43

- *Imagery*: often, emotions involve mental imagery, like little movies or pictures that we play in our minds.
- *Motivation*: emotions help to shape what we find ourselves wanting to do and why we want to do it.
- *Behavior*: emotions shape our behavior; we behave very differently depending upon what emotions we're feeling.

Now recall a positive emotion such as affection or joy. Reflect on how this emotion affects these factors in very different ways.

Considering all of these factors together, we can see how our emotions—particularly "negative" ones—can be difficult to manage and how we can get caught up in them so easily. They can interact with one another to produce a sort of emotional inertia, organizing our minds in ways that can be difficult to quickly change. For example, when we're angry, we are prone to feeling stimulation and tension in our bodies, our attention narrowly focused on the object of our anger. We tend to be absolutely certain of our own perspective and to obsess about the situation, repeatedly playing it over in our minds like a movie. We'll likely be motivated to attack—perhaps to criticize the other person or say something nasty about them behind their back. That's a lot going on for just one emotion! With so many responses to just one feeling, perhaps we *can* begin to understand how we end up doing such silly, counterproductive things when we're in the grips of different emotions.

Here's an example. One of my (Russell's) clients, Jim, decided to quit smoking, and had been doing quite well at it. Jim described the feeling of resisting the urge to smoke as somewhat similar to resisting the powerful urge to act on an emotion—not really painful, but very uncomfortable, like having an intense itch he was trying not to scratch. Once, Jim recounted having been at the bar having a pint with some of his friends, when one of them pulled out a cigarette and began to light up. The craving organized Jim's mind quite quickly in the way we've described—attention focused, motivation set, heart rate picking up and so on. But what stuck out most in his memory was how it affected his thinking and reasoning: "As my friend held out the pack to offer me one, thoughts leapt into my mind: 'I've done great—two weeks with no smoking. It's just one cigarette. It won't matter. I can just have this one and then go right back to not smoking.'" At the time, Jim found this line of reasoning quite convincing, and had a smoke. What happened next was fascinating: "From the first puff, my reasoning completely flipped on its head. The stream of thoughts that now came was entirely different: 'Well, I've screwed it up now! I'd been doing so well, but now I've blown it. Might as well go buy a pack!'" We see how powerfully that emotion—in this case, the craving—influenced Jim's thinking and, through it, his behavior.

Now that we know a bit about how we—and everyone else—can get hijacked by our emotions and end up doing things that aren't good for anyone, what do we do about it? Having awareness of how it all works is a good start. When we're mindfully aware of what is happening in our minds and bodies—what we're feeling, thinking, motivated to do and so on—it gives us some space to evaluate and rethink our intentions, to observe and take steps to manage the emotions that we're experiencing, and to plan how to proceed: "Wow, I'm working really hard to convince myself to have this cigarette. Is this really what I want to do, or is it just part of the craving I need to learn to resist if I'm going to quit smoking?"

Having a compassionate understanding of how emotions organize our minds can help us to decide how to act. To take this compassionate understanding even further, we need to grasp that there's no reason to blame ourselves for how this works—we didn't choose for this process to play out so powerfully. It's just how our brains (at the physical level) and minds (at the level of our awareness) work. But once we're aware of it, we can take responsibility for the process.

That's where compassion comes in. Just as emotions such as anger and experiences such as addictive craving can organize the mind in powerful ways, so can compassion and kindness. The good news is that compassion organizes our minds in really *helpful* ways, focusing our attention on suffering and what might be helpful in addressing it. Bringing compassion into our minds, we use our thinking ability to our advantage. We can imagine ourselves behaving in different ways to figure out what would be most helpful; we can use our reasoning to ask questions: "How does it make sense that he might feel this way?" "What would help her to feel safe?" "What would be helpful to do in this situation?" We can work with all of these mental activities to bring about a compassionate state of mind:

- Focus our *attention* on things that are helpful and which help us to feel more compassionate.
- Work with our *motivation*, committing ourselves to becoming more compassionate.
- Use mental *imagery* to imagine how we would think, feel and act as deeply compassionate beings, and to practice compassionate actions in our minds.
- Use our *thinking and reasoning* to develop our motivation, empathy and other compassionate qualities.
- Practice engaging in compassionate *behavior*.
- Work with the ways that our emotions reveal themselves in our bodies (for example, the arousal and

tension that tend to accompany anger), slowing our bodies down so that we can shift out of irritation and into more compassionate states of mind.

Having a compassionate understanding of how emotions play out in our minds gives us a roadmap for managing our thoughts. We can sit back and let our emotions run the show, or we can choose to think, pay attention, imagine and behave in ways that help us to develop the mental qualities that we *want* to have.

REFLECTION

How Compassion Affects the Mind

Take a moment to connect with compassion. Slow down your breathing a bit, and try to recall a time in which you were touched by suffering, perhaps of someone you cared about, and were motivated to help them. Feel this experience of wanting them to be free from suffering. Notice what was happening in your mind. What were you feeling? What were you paying attention to? What were you thinking about and what were you telling yourself? What were you imagining? What sensations did you feel in your body (tension, activation, etc.)? What were you motivated to do? What actions did you take? Notice how compassion affects your mind.

11 : The Power of Optimism

AN OPTIMISTIC ATTITUDE is crucial in order to maintain our compassion and live a happy life in general, and there are many reasons to be optimistic. When we experience discomfort, unpleasantness, suffering or pain, there is always a cause or condition that has created these feelings: having no food causes us to become hungry; being sick causes us to experience pain and discomfort. But these causes and conditions are not permanent. They abate and often disappear, causing our suffering to stop. To use the example of illness, we may be miserable due to having bacterial pneumonia. But when antibiotics destroy the cause of our illness—the bacteria—our feelings of misery from illness also end. Even when alleviating the immediate cause or condition of our suffering is beyond our control—for example, when there has been the death of a pet or loved one—we know that the pain we feel will lessen over time.

Some years ago, an American reporter interviewed the Dalai Lama. She asked, "You seem like such a happy person, yet you became a refugee decades ago and have not been able to return to Tibet. There has been genocide and environmental devastation in Tibet and your people have suffered tremendously, both those who remained in Tibet and those who followed you into exile in India. Why aren't you angry at the illegal occupation of your country by the Communist Chinese?"

The Dalai Lama gave one of his infectious smiles and responded, "If I were angry, I would be miserable. I wouldn't be able to sleep or eat properly and my health would suffer. That would be of no use to anyone. So I look at all that is good, rejoice in it and keep my mind happy."

From the Dalai Lama's answer, we can see that even in terrible circumstances it is possible to be optimistic and joyful. Reflecting on the benefits of compassion for others and ourselves gives us hope and confidence. We can use this positive attitude to transform our minds and increase our good qualities by developing compassion.

Genuine compassion does not mean ignoring ourselves. In fact, it is important to have compassion for ourselves: we are living beings who experience suffering like everyone else. When we are aware of our desire to be compassionate, we can pay attention to ourselves in ways that allow us to acknowledge our own suffering and deal with it. This is quite different from being self-centered, where we interpret every situation from the limited view of how it relates to *me*, as if our happiness were more important than anyone else's and our suffering hurt more than others' suffering. Even in dire circumstances, it is possible to be optimistic and joyful when we reflect on the benefits of compassion for others and ourselves.

It is not the case that to be truly compassionate towards others we have to suffer. Some people believe that if they feel the least bit of joy, it means that they are selfish: "There is so much pain and suffering in the world. If I don't constantly feel weighed down by it, I am not truly compassionate." However, this way of thinking is wrong. There is nothing wrong with being happy—that's what we all want! It is possible to be joyful without being selfish. In fact, compassion stops us from being self-centered by focusing on the happiness of others as well as ourselves and brings us more joy as a result. That joy in turn makes it easier to cultivate compassion.

REFLECTION

Compassionate Self-Understanding

Consider your response when you see or learn of another person's suffering. Do you feel guilty because you are happy while they are suffering? Think about whether this makes you more or less able to be helpful to them. If we require ourselves to suffer in order to be compassionate, our compassion will soon drain us, and that doesn't help anyone. See if it is possible for you to feel some positive emotions—such as being pleased that you are able to be moved by suffering and are able to feel empathy and compassion—when you are faced with a situation that involves real suffering. It can be inspiring to see our guilt replaced by concern for others.

12 : Three Types of Emotion

Ψ IN WORKING TO DEVELOP compassion, we need to
focus our efforts in two ways. First, we need to develop ourselves as compassionate beings, by cultivating and strengthening our motivation and ability to feel, think,
act and relate compassionately. Second, we need to learn to
work with the obstacles that prevent us from feeling compassion and can keep us from acting on our best intentions.

Earlier, we discussed how different emotions organize the
mind in very powerful ways. This is no accident. From the
perspective of evolutionary psychology, the reason we have
all of these emotions is that they helped our ancestors survive
and pass their genes along to us.[1] From this perspective, we
can consider human emotions as falling into three different
categories: those that evolved to help us detect and respond
to perceived threats, those that evolved to help us pursue goals
and acquire the things we need to survive and reproduce, and
those that evolved to help us feel safe, connected with others, content and at peace. In Compassion-Focused Therapy,
we refer to these as the threat system, the drive system and the
safeness system respectively.

The trouble comes when these systems of emotion become
imbalanced. For example, this can happen when our minds
become obsessively focused on real or imagined threats or the
pursuit of things we want, and we become blind to the needs

of others (and sometimes to our own needs as well). This is one of the major obstacles to compassion. The threat and drive systems are powerful, and when they're running the show the voice of our better nature can be drowned out by feelings of anger, hostility, anxiety, materialistic desire, lust, or cold and selfish ambition.

Although all of these responses are related to the desire to achieve happiness and avoid suffering, they can cause problems. We're not at our best when we're caught up in threat and drive responses. We may be very good at spotting these problems in others—finding ourselves getting irritated with people who are behaving in ways that seem hostile, hesitant or greedy—and struggle to feel warmth and compassion for them. Shortly afterwards, we may notice we're even criticizing ourselves for feeling or acting in similar ways! It's easy to fall into these patterns, and equally easy to judge, blame or shame other people and ourselves for doing so: "He's just an idiot." "I'm a weak person." We may feel justified in these judgments; they may seem to fit very well. But looking more closely, we can see these harsh judgments as yet another example of our threat response taking control of our minds, attacking others (or ourselves) when they aren't behaving the way we think they should. It's understandable, but it isn't *helpful*.

So part of my (Russell's) answer to the question, "What is compassion?" involves the awareness that much of our suffering is related to powerful emotions that can arise without our conscious awareness—emotions we may inadvertently fuel with our thoughts and behavior, making things worse rather than better. Instead of criticizing ourselves and other people for having and expressing these emotions, having compassion involves accepting that we all sometimes have them, and committing ourselves to dealing with them when they come up. Rather than judging, being compassionate means trying to understand. It means asking, "What would be helpful as I work to manage this feeling?" Likewise, it involves recognizing that it's silly to blame ourselves for having these normal human emotions, while also acknowledging that if we're going to have the lives that we want, we need to take hold of the reins and steer our minds in the direction we want them to go.

This awareness can be transformative. It enables us to understand the challenging behaviors of others (and ourselves) not as "something wrong with them/me," but as the products of emotional responses that have become imbalanced. Understanding that emotions such as anger and anxiety are produced when we feel threatened (whether the threat is real or something we dreamed up in our minds), we can experience compassion for those who are caught up in these emotions. When we see someone behaving in a hostile manner, instead of thinking, "What an idiot!" we can shift out of judgment mode into the understanding that comes with compassion: "His threat system is activated right now. I know what that feels like! What could I do that might help him feel safe, or at least not feel even more threatened?"

Compassionately seeking to *understand* rather than judging and labeling, we often find solutions to problems that seemed unsolvable before. We start to see people as valuable beings who are struggling, rather than as idiots who are creating problems for us. We can do this for ourselves, as well. We can stop beating ourselves up for having normal human emotions, even as we commit to working with these emotions more helpfully. As we begin to let go of the critical judgments that keep us and other people feeling threatened, compassion becomes easier and easier.

Towards the beginning of one of my (Russell's) prison groups, Officer Sanders, an officer at the facility, politely poked her head into the group and asked Richard, a group member, to step out with her. Richard asked why, and she told him that he was in the wrong group—that he was scheduled to attend an alternate, mandatory group held at the same time. (In the prison, there are certain groups that the men are required to take. Ours is not one of them.) At this point, Richard attempted to explain that he had addressed this situation with another member of staff and that arrangements had been made for him to attend our group instead. Officer Sanders said she was not aware of any such arrangement and that she needed him to come with her immediately. The interaction continued in a back-and-forth manner, in front of the group, for a few more moments. As it continued, both Richard and Officer Sanders began to grow more tense and irritated. After a bit, they both wisely concluded this was a conversation better handled in private and went to sort the situation out.

In difficult situations like the one described above, it's easy to feel threatened. Thinking, "I'm right and you're wrong," we focus on defending ourselves from attack. In such challenging situations, we tend to stop listening and may raise our voices, talk over the other person or speak more quickly. The problem is that these behaviors are ineffective ways to get our point across because they activate the *other person's* threat system. Not feeling heard or understood, she may start doing the very same things, such as not listening or talking loudly herself—which then keeps the cycle going by fueling our threat response in turn. It's like our threat systems start bouncing off of each other, and the situation can rapidly escalate into a heated argument. When this happens in a public context—in front of other people—the negative emotions we feel are magnified, as we're aware of being observed by other people and can feel embarrassed.

Once we're aware of this process, we see that a change of strategy can make all the difference. Rather than continuing to pummel the other person's threat system, we can slow down our breathing for a bit to calm our own threat response and then alter our behavior to help the other person feel safe. For example, rather than continuing to restate our own perspective, we could say, "I'm sorry, I've been caught up in making my own point and haven't been listening very well. Could you explain again where you are coming from so I can make sure that I understand?" Imagine being in the middle of a heated argument and having someone say this to you. Can you see how a statement like this, which communicates respect and a lack of threat, could take the steam out of an angry interaction?

When we're feeling threatened or we are single-mindedly in pursuit of a goal, our attention and thinking are rigid and narrow. Completely focused on ourselves, it can be almost impossible to see the other person's point of view. If we mindfully recognize our threat or drive systems are running the show and we're caught up in the motivation to defend ourselves or push through our own agendas, we can slow things down and shift to a more open and inclusive perspective in which everyone feels safe and heard. Doing this, we often find common ground. We may even discover we didn't really disagree at all!

In the case of Richard and Officer Sanders, it was a simple breakdown in the channels of communication, which happens often in complicated settings like prisons or workplaces. Richard had indeed gone through the proper channels and had been given permission to finish our group before beginning the next. Officer Sanders had not been notified of this and was attempting to do her job, making sure the prison population was where they were supposed to be. Both felt threatened by having the conversation in front of others, Richard because he was embarrassed and frustrated, and Officer Sanders because she was being publicly challenged rather than obeyed in a prison setting where everyone's safety depends on her authority being followed. Luckily, both of them recognized this and sensibly moved the conversation to a more private location where each felt safe, and things were resolved almost immediately.

REFLECTION

Compassion and Emotions

Think of a time when you were behaving aggressively or when you completely shut down and refused to communicate with another person. What emotions did you feel at that time? Now think of a time when you were behaving kindly and compassionately. How did you feel then? You'll find that as you move from feeling threatened to feeling safe in a situation, your ability to experience and act with compassion increases.

13 : Working with Unwanted Thoughts and Emotions

Ψ

A MAJOR OBSTACLE to self-compassion is the tendency to blame ourselves for our own thoughts and emotions. Noticing that we're having thoughts that run contrary to our values, we may blame and shame ourselves: "I'm a terrible person!" "What a hypocrite I am!" This can also happen when we find ourselves feeling emotions we'd prefer not to have, or emotions we've been taught we shouldn't feel. We notice jealous thoughts and criticize ourselves: "I'm so selfish and greedy." We observe fear and anger and quickly label ourselves: "I'm so weak!" "I'm out of control!"

We may think this self-condemnation helps us—that somehow, if we attack ourselves enough for thinking and feeling things that we don't like, we'll change and become the person that we want to be. We may be afraid that if we aren't hard on ourselves, these undesirable thoughts and emotions will wreak havoc in our minds, causing us to lose control, or giving ourselves permission to misbehave. However, the problem with attacking and shaming ourselves is that it fuels our sense of being threatened and keeps us stuck in feeling angry, anxious and defensive. This mental state isn't a fertile ground for cultivating compassion or other positive qualities. Shaming ourselves reinforces qualities in ourselves that we are ultimately trying to change, such as being judgmental of others.

Finding the best way to work with difficult or unwanted thoughts or emotions requires skill. We need to *stop blaming ourselves* for thoughts and emotions that arise in us as a result of our previous conditioning and experiences, and at the same time step up to *take responsibility* for working with those unhelpful thoughts and emotions and for cultivating more helpful ones. Refraining from blaming and attacking ourselves doesn't mean we're being self-indulgent or irresponsible. We accept that these troublesome thoughts and emotions exist in our minds and know that it's our job to resolve them. At the same time, aspiring to cultivate our minds in ways that fit with our values doesn't mean attacking ourselves when we fall short of our goals. Rather than continually fueling our own threat responses by criticizing ourselves, we want to stimulate our drive and safeness responses, *creating a sense and space of safety* from which we can work with scary or challenging thoughts, feelings and situations and *inspiring ourselves* to act in more compassionate ways.

Consider a recent example from one of my (Russell's) therapy groups. Jeremy, who had a history of physical and verbal aggression, had been working to reduce his angry behavior, and to cultivate more kind, understanding ways of relating to others. One day, an acquaintance harshly criticized Jeremy about his past in a way that he experienced as very hurtful. Although Jeremy handled the situation adeptly, telling the other person that he wasn't willing to discuss his past with someone he didn't know well, he became embarrassed and angry. Observing his anger, he became very self-critical: "There I go again! I'm not making any progress. This is hopeless!" Crestfallen, Jeremy told the group about his "failure." But instead of condemning Jeremy (as he was condemning himself), the other members urged Jeremy to stop being so self-critical and to take a second look at the situation. With their help, he was able to see that he had actually done a good job at handling an uncomfortable experience, avoiding both aggression and harsh speech. Further, they helped him to recognize this as a situation that would be hard for anyone—it *hurts* to have your past thrown back in your face when you're doing your best to improve—and rather than beating himself up for getting upset, he could consider what might help him feel safe in the face of such harsh criticism. This coaching worked, and after practicing over a few more similar situations (we can usually find challenging situations to practice on!), Jeremy learned to notice and redirect his criticism of himself before it got the better of him.

At various times, we'll have *all kinds* of thoughts—kind thoughts and cruel thoughts, sad thoughts and happy thoughts, supportive thoughts and judgmental thoughts, nurturing thoughts and wildly spicy sexual thoughts. That goes with the territory when you have a human mind. Some of these thoughts will surprise us, particularly if they are very different from how we like to see ourselves. If we see ourselves as "a kind person," we may find ourselves dismayed when a cruel thought leaps to mind about that person who just cut us off in traffic. We can find ourselves trying to drive these thoughts out of our minds or ignoring them in the attempt to avoid the discomfort they cause us.

It turns out that these strategies—suppressing or ignoring troublesome thoughts and feelings—don't work very well. Research shows that trying to *avoid* thinking of something actually makes us *more* likely to think of it![1] It also keeps us from dealing with the situation. If we are able to accept our unwanted thoughts and emotions for what they are, we can approach them without fear, anger or revulsion, and work to replace them with compassionate thoughts. It's similar to being at a dinner and being given a plate of food we don't like, for example, cabbage. We can try to pretend the cabbage isn't there, but that doesn't get rid of it and it doesn't get us something we *can* eat either. Accepting an uncomfortable emotion doesn't mean we decide to like it; it means we acknowledge its presence and consider our options. In the case of cabbage, we could eat it anyway, leave it and eat the other food on the plate, or politely ask for something else. Similarly, accepting what we are thinking or feeling doesn't mean we endorse these experiences and want to continue having them. Rather, acceptance creates a place of safety from which we can work with our internal experiences.

Working with our experiences means that instead of ignoring, denying or simply trying to push unwanted thoughts out of our minds, we try a different strategy: noticing unwanted thoughts as mental events, we accept the presence of these thoughts without following or engaging them, and gently redirect our minds to more helpful thoughts or experiences. This approach invigorates our efforts by helping us reconnect with the motivation to improve the world and ourselves by practicing compassion. For example, if we notice ourselves delighting in the misfortune of someone we don't like, instead of beating ourselves up, we can respond differently:

- Accept and acknowledge the thought or emotion: "I notice I'm enjoying how much she is struggling."
- Empathize with ourselves and redirect ourselves towards our goal: "It makes sense that I'd feel and think this way, given how my relationship with her has gone in the past. But I want to be a compassionate person, not someone who delights in others' misfortune."

- Feel good that we noticed this habit and now have the opportunity to work with it: "I want to change this kind of habit and work to cultivate compassion in my life. Good thing I caught myself thinking this way."
- Bring up a compassionate motivation: "This is an opportunity to see the benefit of having compassion for people who push my buttons and to generate that compassion. Deep down, I *do* want her—and everyone else—to be happy and to not suffer."
- Gently shift our minds to a thought that reflects our commitment to compassion: "May she have peace and support as she copes with this challenge."

Though it is easier to attack ourselves than to practice this more lengthy compassionate approach, the compassionate approach is much more likely to create positive changes in our minds without creating *more* unhelpful thoughts and emotions. For example, Jenna, a student, would sometimes observe herself having very critical or cruel thoughts about one of her classmates and was appalled: "She just seemed so smug, and I thought, 'She's so awful. I hate her. I hope that she *fails* this test.' I couldn't believe that I wished that for her! I feel like such a terrible person."

As she examined her feelings, Jenna became aware that the negative thoughts she had about her classmate were prompted by feelings of threat—for example, the classmate had achieved a higher score than Jenna on several previous exams. Jenna's feelings were then *magnified* when she attacked herself for having negative thoughts ("I felt like I not only wasn't as smart as she is, but that I was a bad person as well!"). Once Jenna was able to notice her negative thoughts and evaluate them, she found herself able to practice compassion both towards herself and her classmate: "I was feeling threatened, but that wasn't her fault. She's just trying to do the best that she can, just like me. Attacking her doesn't make me feel better about my test scores, but maybe there are other things that would help me feel more confident. Ultimately, I really want *both of us* to succeed."

Instead of wishing ill for her classmate, Jenna was able to notice the real issue—her own fears of not doing well. Furthermore, she found that cultivating compassion for both herself and her classmate ("We're both just trying to succeed in a really demanding program.") helped them develop a relationship that improved their performances—they began studying together—which also provided social support that helped reduce Jenna's stress.

Similarly, it's not helpful to attack ourselves for having human emotions such as fear, anger or lust. These emotions will sometimes arise in us, and it's our responsibility to find ways to work with them. As we discussed above, shaming ourselves for having these emotions simply creates *more* challenging emotions for us to cope with, creating a cycle that can easily end in avoidance, denial and more suffering for ourselves.

Here, too, we start by *accepting* our emotions and then generating other thoughts and emotions, such as compassion for others and ourselves that can help alleviate these difficult experiences. Jeremy, whom you read about earlier in this section, gives us a good example of this. After his group-mates helped him to recognize that he was needlessly attacking himself, he continued having occasional experiences of irritation and anger, and was sometimes tempted to criticize himself for it. Instead, he learned to coach himself through these episodes: "I'm getting angry again, and I'm feeling a bit frustrated with myself. But look at how quickly I noticed the anger—I was able to step out of the situation and calm myself down before things got out of control, and then come back and resolve the situation without getting aggressive. I never would have done that before. Even the fact that I grow frustrated with myself for becoming angry shows how committed I am to becoming a compassionate person. Being compassionate doesn't mean I'll *never* grow irritated or angry. It means taking responsibility and working with these difficult feelings when they come up. That's what I'm doing."

As Jeremy got better at noticing his anger and began to view himself and others with compassion ("It's hard to work with anger when you've struggled with it all your life, and I'm making real progress."), he found the anger and irritation arose less often than before. He also observed that when he wasn't fueling his threat system with self-critical thoughts, his anger dissipated much more quickly, replaced with a sense of safeness and confidence in his ability to handle his emotions when they came up.

As we work over time to replace troublesome thoughts and emotions with more compassionate ones, we will establish new, compassionate mental habits. Gradually, the frequency and strength of our disturbing thoughts and emotions will start to decrease, while the compassionate thoughts and emotions we've cultivated will naturally increase. We'll notice that troubling thoughts and emotions seem to come less often, and that other thoughts and feelings—those that reflect the sort of people who we want to be—will arise of their own accord. We'll observe our tendency to make quick judgments about others being replaced by the ability to slow down, look closely and understand a difficult situation. Anxiety and anger will come less frequently as we notice ourselves feeling safer, more confident and more fearlessly able to engage with all that life has to offer.

REFLECTION

Working with Unwanted Thoughts and Emotions

Think of an unwanted mental experience, such as cruel thoughts you may have had about someone, angry or fearful thoughts you have experienced, or other feelings to which you usually respond with self-blame. Imagine working with them by going through the process described above. Begin by accepting and acknowledging the unwanted thoughts or emotions. Empathize with your own experience and then release the thoughts or emotions, not by pushing them away but by redirecting your mind towards your motivation to cultivate compassion. Feel grateful that by noticing this experience you now have an opportunity to change it. Generate a compassionate thought or image in your mind, wishing the other person and yourself well, envisioning them—and you—having peace, happiness and all the conditions enabling you to be at your best.

14 : Becoming Friends
with Ourselves

As LIVING BEINGS, our deepest wish is to be happy, peaceful and free from suffering. When we operate on the premise that the causes of happiness and suffering lie *outside of* ourselves—in other people, possessions, positions or places—we often quarrel with others, disparage them, try to ruin their reputation, steal from them or even physically harm them. Holding the view that happiness comes from outside drags us into a tug of war with the external world, as we try to get what we like and think will make us happy and try to avoid what we dislike and believe will cause us pain. However, we will never succeed in changing other people or the environment into what we want them to be. Even if we could manage to get everything just the way we want it, in the next moment things would change. We would end up living in a state of constant frustration and anxiety, feeling that our emotions and our lives are beyond our control.

In this process we fail to look inside ourselves and to realize that it is how we are thinking, interpreting and viewing situations that determines whether we are happy or miserable. With a little reflection, this fact becomes evident. Remember a day when you were in a bad mood even though nothing special happened to provoke it. It is likely that you found many of the people you encountered that day to be rude and disagreeable. Meanwhile on the days when you are in a good mood, even if you get some unexpected criticism, you're able to listen and take it in. This demonstrates that our moods influence how we interpret the situations we encounter and thus how we experience them.

Nowhere in our present education system are we taught to observe how our internal moods and ideas influence whether we experience delight or unhappiness. Instead, we buy into the idea that happiness comes from outside of ourselves, for example, from material possessions or other people. When we think like this, it is easy to become self-centered, viewing other people as if their only purpose is to bring us happiness, and if they do not do a very good job of it, we feel that we're entitled to complain. When our happiness is dependent on the actions of others, which are out of our control, we will never be happy.

For this reason, setting aside some time each day for spiritual practice is important. This is a quiet time that we can use to "get in touch" with ourselves, to become our own friend. We check in with ourselves, "What is of real importance in my life? How do I feel? What are the ethical principles that guide my life?" If our minds are filled with many confusing thoughts or emotions, we can use this time to meditate or do spiritual reading in order to rebalance ourselves. In this way, we learn to live with integrity, in a way that corresponds to our ethical principles and not just chase after external things in order to convince others and ourselves that we "have a life." We need to treat ourselves with respect, not self-indulgence, so that we can cultivate our good qualities and counteract our faults.

It is often said that to feel love and compassion for others we must first feel love and compassion for ourselves. A lack of love and compassion for ourselves leads to harsh criticism of ourselves, which, in turn, carries over to how we feel about and speak to others. Furthermore, a judgmental attitude towards ourselves will make us miserable and inhibit us from cultivating and experiencing love and compassion. Therefore it is important to become friends with ourselves, have a caring attitude and be kind when talking to ourselves.

To do this, first we need to question our thoughts. When we find ourselves thinking, "I'm worthless," we can ask ourselves, "Is that true?" It doesn't take long to realize that it isn't. We do contribute to others' lives and each of us has talents. Thinking that we are worthless or incapable is wrong and not very helpful.

Strange as it may initially sound, not everything that we think is true! Thoughts are merely thoughts; they are not necessarily an accurate description of reality. When we are feeling very down or very excited, our thoughts are usually skewed, exaggerating either the negative or the positive aspects of whatever we are thinking about. We can tell that our self-deprecating thoughts are unrealistic because they all center on ourselves: "I am the worst lawyer/parent/student/teacher in the world." This is a little bit self-inflating, don't you think? We are not so important that we can make everything go wrong! Focusing only on ourselves is an imbalanced way to look at the world; there are always other people and conditions to be considered. Knowing this, we don't have to buy into our self-deprecating thoughts, thinking that they are true. They are simply thoughts drifting through the mind. They come and they go. They do not describe an objective reality.

Once we begin to doubt the negative thoughts that we have about ourselves, which have been created by adopting a self-centered perspective on our lives, we can turn our attention to our good qualities. Some people find this hard to do because they are accustomed to denigrating themselves or worry about becoming arrogant if they think anything good about themselves. However, acknowledging our talents and good qualities involves seeing what is there. It is not about exaggerating; we *do* have those qualities and abilities.

Arrogance is different: it inflates these qualities and is a proud attitude that arises from a lack of self-confidence. In our desperate attempt to feel good about ourselves, we exaggerate our good qualities, thinking that if we can convince others we are wonderful then we must *be* wonderful. In contrast, recognizing our talents and abilities does not involve exaggeration. We're simply being factual—we have this knowledge or those abilities—and we can use them in the service of others.

Whereas self-centeredness is inflated preoccupation with ourselves, having healthy self-esteem involves acknowledging our abilities and appreciating what we have to offer the world. With healthy self-confidence we appreciate and respect ourselves just as we would appreciate and respect any other living being. We are neither worthless nor more important than others. With a balanced attitude, we are able to extend kindness and compassion to ourselves and to others.

Becoming friends with ourselves requires being kind to ourselves. Having an attitude of kindness towards ourselves is not self-indulgence; it is simply treating ourselves with the same respect and consideration that we would treat any other person. There is nothing selfish about this. When we say, "I want to be kind and compassionate to all living beings," the word "all" includes ourselves. "All" doesn't mean everyone except me! We are as deserving of our own kindness as everyone else, so we practice being patient with ourselves, encouraging ourselves and celebrating our own successes.

An example of this may be helpful. When we compare ourselves to one of our friends, we may regard her as more athletic or more financially successful than we are. If we are self-deprecating, we immediately think: "She's so much better than I am. I'm not very good. I've tried to do my best but I'm just not cut out for this. I'm such a loser." There is no need to compare ourselves to another person. Each of us is unique with our own talents and gifts. Our friend has skills in one area and we have skills in another. Instead of feeling downhearted, we can respect each other's qualities and recognize that each of us offers something different to the collective group. Personally, I (Chodron) am glad other people are better at certain things than I am; otherwise this planet would be in big trouble! I know nothing about electricity, plumbing, cars and many other things. On the other hand, I have certain talents: I can write an essay that makes sense and I'm okay speaking in public. Seeing this, I can rejoice in others' talents and also in my own.

Doing this entails practice, and practice means repetition. It may take time to learn how to stop criticizing ourselves. First we need to notice that self-critical internal dialogue is going on. Then we can ask ourselves, "Is this true?" "Am I actually bad at my job or do I just lack confidence in my ability?" "Am I really the worst parent in the world, or am I doing the best I can?" When we challenge our self-criticism in this way, we'll find that many of our thoughts are exaggerated. When we recognize our self-criticism for what it is, we can then press the mental "stop" button on this internal dialogue and replace it with a kinder, more tolerant and encouraging internal dialogue. In this way, we become friends with ourselves, enjoying our own company and respecting ourselves.

REFLECTION

Noticing Our Self-Talk

Try to notice the different ways you talk to yourself. Is your internal voice harsh and critical, or kind, validating and encouraging? When you observe that your self-talk is serving no purpose other than to keep you locked into negative emotions, come back to observing your breath and let your mind settle. Then shift your thoughts to an internal voice that is more reality-based, helpful and encouraging. Recognize that you have good qualities and talents. Rejoice in them and aspire to use those qualities and talents to benefit all living beings.

15 : "Follow Your Line"

Ψ LIVING IN THE INLAND PACIFIC NORTHWEST of the United States, there are lots of fun opportunities for outdoor recreation. I (Russell) enjoy several of these, including skiing, hiking and going on the occasional backpacking trip. One of my favorites, though, is mountain biking. There's just something amazing about riding a bicycle through a narrow path in the middle of a lush pine forest or making my way down a steep, rocky hill, dropping off the back of my seat to keep the bike from pitching over on itself. It's one of the reasons I love living in Spokane.

When I first started mountain biking, though, I used to crash. *A lot.* When you're riding backwoods trails, there are lots of obstacles—rocks, stumps, tree roots and the occasional fallen tree. Working your way through these is part of the fun. However, for the novice mountain biker, it can be really intimidating, and can seem like you're drawn straight towards the obstacles that you are trying to avoid—again and again and again. It can get really frustrating (and occasionally painful!).

Mountain biking was like this for me, until my good friend Michael gave me a really amazing (and refreshingly brief) piece of advice. He said, "*Follow your line.*" The idea was simple but brilliant: notice the obstacles you wish to avoid, but don't stare at them—because the bike will follow your gaze. We can't help it—we just tend to ride in the direction we're looking. Instead, the key is to pick a safe "line" through the obstacles, picking out the path we wish to ride, and keeping our eyes focused on that line. My trouble riding occurred because I was constantly "staring at stumps"... and rocks, and roots ... rather than at the way I wanted to go. Once I started following my line, my biking experience changed almost overnight, and I found myself effortlessly threading my way through rough terrain that would have given me fits (or at least skinned knees) beforehand.

Life is a lot like mountain biking. When obstacles come up—challenging situations, difficult emotions—it won't work to just ignore them, because they'll trip us up. But we also don't want to constantly stare right at them either. Continually thinking about and focusing our attention on our difficulties, failings and problems keeps us mentally pointed right at them, and doesn't help us to find solutions or to feel better. Instead, we want to notice, accept and be aware of our challenges, but then to really focus our attention on the path we wish to follow. Rather than beating ourselves up for our previous failings, we need to think about how we want to improve ourselves and make efforts to do so. Rather than continually worrying about the overwhelming task before us, we can ask ourselves, "What would be helpful in getting started on this project?" Rather than obsessing over the argument you had with your partner this morning and fueling the negative emotions you felt then, you can focus on how you might approach things in order to have a better interaction next time and repair the relationship. We mindfully acknowledge the obstacles, and then pick our line forward and follow it.

We can apply this approach to the development of compassion. As we've mentioned, when we're beginning to cultivate compassion, we'll likely act in ways that aren't at all reflective of the changes we're trying to effect in our minds, for example, speaking harshly to someone when we are working on feeling compassion for everyone. Instead of beating ourselves up when we don't measure up to our hopes or standards, we can notice the obstacles in our way—for example, becoming more aware of things that push our buttons or situations that trigger less-than-compassionate thoughts and behaviors in us—and consider how we might do better in the future. We can also begin to pay more attention to our thoughts when we are struggling, to notice when we're "staring at stumps," and gently redirect ourselves to once again follow our lines.

REFLECTION

"Following Your Line"

Consider a situation or challenge that has been an obstacle for you—perhaps a challenge over which you've spent a lot of time thinking and stewing, or a conflict or grudge you've held on to and continue to have negative feelings about. Consider how you have been focused on this obstacle and see if you can redirect your attention to the positive efforts you could make to address it or, if this is impossible, to accept it and let it go in a positive way. In choosing your "line" in this way, you can draw upon the many compassionate approaches described in this book. When you find your mind being drawn back to the difficulty or obstacle in unproductive ways (ruminating in ways that just keep negative emotions going, for example), try to gently bring your attention back to your line—the path of compassion.

16 : A Healthy Diet for the Mind

Ψ IN A LOT OF WAYS, cultivating compassion is like engaging in a "mental fitness" program for the mind. We may have noticed our bodies getting older, putting on weight, aching in places that we hadn't noticed before and getting out of breath walking up just a few flights of stairs. We can get like this mentally, too—mentally obese with worries and cravings, with flighty minds that get worked up over lots of little details, unable to handle even minor situations that don't go our way.

Seeing this, we decide it's time to get in shape. Most "get-in-shape" regimens involve two major components: diet and exercise. In this way, we manage what goes into the body and how we use it. If you're going to lose weight, get in shape and have a healthy body, you need to eat healthily. This can be hard if you're used to fast-food meals and your house is stocked with unhealthy food. These can be hard to give up, as they're specifically designed to trigger cravings in us. They stimulate us and we like them.

But even in the face of these cravings, there are things we can do to make it easier to eat healthily. First, we use what psychologists call "stimulus control." A stimulus is anything in our environment that can prompt us, making different behaviors more or less likely. For example, the presence of different types of food affects what we will tend to eat. If the behavior we're looking to change involves eating more healthily, a good way to start is to clean out the house—get rid of all the junk food and replace it with healthy food. We gather up most of the chips and cookies, the boxes of preservative-laden products with ingredient labels you need a chemistry degree to understand, and throw them out. We then buy some fresh fruit and vegetables and healthier snacks—you know, stuff that our grandmothers might actually recognize as food. When we reach for that apple or a handful of nuts, we might sometimes find ourselves wishing they were french fries instead, but it will be a lot easier to eat healthily if apples are what's available. So we plan ahead, buying food when we're not hungry, so that when hunger hits, the food that's available is good for us. Likewise, if we want to quit smoking, the first thing we can do is to discard all the cigarettes in the house, and perhaps avoid being around friends who are smoking.

We can do the same things with our minds. Computer folk have a phrase: "garbage in, garbage out." This means computers can't tell the difference between good information and bad information; they just run the numbers. So if the information we put into the computer is nonsensical, the results the computer churns out will be equally meaningless. Our emotions are like this as well: they just work with what we give them, and they're not always good at telling the wheat from the chaff. For example, if we continually watch television programs featuring commentators who are working really hard to make us angry, we are likely to feel hostile and angry a lot of the time.

There's a lot of garbage out there. Invasive tabloid newspapers spread titillating and malicious gossip about public figures, deifying them one day and attacking them the next. We're constantly bombarded with images of impossibly thin models held up as the ideal of feminine attractiveness. These images can easily impact one's self-image if we fall into the trap of comparing ourselves to them. This is particularly true in a digital age in which anyone who's good with imaging software can trim an inch off the thigh, or add a size or two to the bust-line. We might not even recognize a model from the cover of a magazine if we met her on the street. Similarly, the internet is filled with pornographic material that can warp our ideas about what constitutes "normal" sexual behavior and condition our arousal patterns so that the delightful reality of everyday sex is no longer enough for us. Television and video games can be filled with gratuitous violence as well as gender and racial stereotypes, desensitizing us to things which would otherwise leave us horrified and outraged.

But we have a choice—*we don't have to accept it*. Just as our physical bodies "are what we eat," the content of our minds are shaped by what we pay attention to, and by what is available in the environments we inhabit. We can prepare to fill our minds with nutritious substances by first choosing to avoid media that glorifies and desensitizes us to violence, pornography and other objectified depictions of sexuality, and material that depicts people in stereotyped or exploitive ways.

If we look, we find there is a world of healthy mental "food" out there for us to feast on—for every "junk food" film out there, there is an inspiring story of kindness, a documentary of someone who has overcome adversity we can't even dream of, a movie that provokes us to mentally explore the world in new ways. I (Russell) have found the healthiest way to use the internet is to do so *purposefully,* seeking specific things, be it news, information about things that I'm interested in or ways to connect with like-minded people. I've found if I just "surf," I'll often find myself in rather polluted waters, having wasted a good bit of time in getting there.

Best of all, we can go out and actually connect with each other and with nature. Text messages are great for efficient communication, but they can't capture the warmth of real human interaction between people who like and respect one another, and the internet can't capture the feeling of sitting beneath a tree at the edge of a beautiful body of water.

Nourishing our minds with healthy experiences doesn't mean we can't have fun. I'm not talking about swearing off action movies and rock-and-roll music, or rebuking ourselves every time we appreciate attractive people or images. That would be no fun at all! We don't need to be terrified that our fragile minds are constantly being poisoned by the messages with which we're surrounded. Rather, it's about bringing *intentionality* to what we put in our minds. This means we *choose* what our minds are exposed to, knowing that the things we attend to become a part of us. They change us and shape our experience of the world, other people and ourselves. Remember the phrase "garbage in, garbage out": rather than consuming whatever is put in front of us, we can consider the potential effects of how we attend to things. We can expose ourselves to things that will help shape the compassionate mental states we want to create in ourselves.

REFLECTION

How We Feed Our Minds

Think about the diet you've been feeding your mind. What things have you watched, listened to and thought about that have helped you become more like the person you want to be? Have you exposed yourself to things that have served little purpose but to create distress or to reinforce unhealthy or unwanted habits, thoughts or emotions? Think about how you could fill your mind with more nutritious substances.

17 : Being Responsible
for Our Emotions

SOMEONE ONCE COMMENTED to me (Chodron), "I want to appear responsible, but I don't want to be responsible." Many of us have that attitude. Nevertheless, we are responsible for our emotions. That doesn't mean it's our fault if we experience disturbing emotions such as anger and fear but it does mean we have to work with them when they come up. Whether disturbing emotions arise due to ignorance, misconceptions, and our interpretations of previous experiences (the Buddhist perspective) or from the interaction of our current experience, previous learning history and the tendencies of our "animal brains," we do not need to blame ourselves for having them. Instead, we need to deal with the present situation: our disturbing emotions are present, and now we have the choice of how to respond to them. Do we fuel them by dwelling on them or do we subdue them by applying an antidote? The choice is ours.

My hesitancy to emphasize the role of our "animal brains" or genes in accounting for our destructive emotions is because it is all too easy for us to then shrug our shoulders and say, "What can I do? I was born that way." For example, an alcoholic could easily excuse his drinking and have a defeatist attitude when someone suggests that he goes to AA by saying, "Alcoholism runs in my family. That's the way I am. I can't go beyond what my biology and brain chemistry dictate." While it's true that we didn't choose our genes or our brains, we give up our own power when we think that they control us. Regardless of the genes an alcoholic inherited, he is the one who chooses whether to drink or not.

It is similar when we think, "I had a horrible childhood that emotionally damaged me." Yes, it may be true that we experienced dreadful circumstances as a child, but to then continually identify ourselves as emotionally damaged can keep us stuck in a negative self-image that guarantees that we will continue to suffer. It is more helpful to think, "I experienced certain conditioning factors. Some are genetic, others biological, others derive from experiences that I had in the past. These things affected me, but their effects are not impossible to change."

Why? From the Buddhist perspective, as soon as we say the word "conditioning"—be it conditioning by our brains, our genes or our previous experiences—we are talking about causality; in other words, cause and effect. If things are caused, it means that they can be changed (or ended). That is their very nature. They cannot remain the same even if we want them to. For example, the sperm and egg of our parents cause our bodies to form. From the moment that we are conceived our body changes: it grows, ages and eventually dies. Everything that arises due to causes changes, including our disturbing emotions and unhelpful emotional habits.

Who can change these disturbing emotions and unbeneficial emotional habits? We can. In fact, no one else can alleviate our disturbing emotions, even though others may influence us in positive ways and help us to do so. For example, while a friend or a therapist may give us good advice on how to manage our anger, we are the ones who must put the advice into practice and change ourselves. Just as we can't ask someone to sleep for us so that we'll feel rested, we can't ask or pay for someone else to transform our minds. That is our responsibility, and it is a wonderful responsibility at that. It means we can slowly recondition ourselves to become calmer, wiser and more compassionate.

We had little control over our experiences when we were young children; adults told us things or treated us in certain ways and we generally followed along. Since adults are not perfect, as children we would inevitably have been exposed to their cravings, frustration, grief and other emotions. As children, we didn't have the ability to challenge adults, so we generally accepted whatever they told us. If an adult was in a bad mood and hollered that we were stupid, we believed them. If they threatened to hit us, we thought that they would.

In this way, as children we received a lot of conditioning and some of it may have been harmful. Being young, we didn't have the ability to evaluate adults' behavior objectively and so the effects of it remained with us even as we grew into adulthood. One nice thing about being an adult is that we have the ability to assess the conditioning we received in the past. We can look back at our experiences and the things we heard and ask ourselves, "Is this something true and beneficial that I want to keep in my life, or is it something untrue and harmful that I would be better off letting go of?" If we decide we would be better off letting go of those thoughts and emotions, we can then go about freeing ourselves from whatever we learned that was harmful. For example, we can learn to cultivate more reasonable and beneficial emotional responses, such as compassion, and in that way change our habitual emotional responses to certain situations.

For example, adults who were shouting may have terrified us when we were young and conditioned us to withdraw in order to feel safe. That emotional and behavioral habit may have followed us into adulthood, but now it doesn't serve us very well. By training our minds in compassion, we can change that previous conditioning so that now when we hear shouting voices we will feel compassion, both for those who are shouting and for ourselves for our past experiences. In doing so, we'll be able to better respond to a negative situation and decide on a helpful response.

This means taking responsibility for our emotions. Instead of seeing our anger, anxiety and fear as huge walls we can never get beyond, we see they are only conditioned responses that can be changed. The more we learn how to cultivate compassion and wisdom, the more we'll be able to reflect on them and in that way change our habitual emotional responses and actions.

REFLECTION

Identifying and Taking Responsibility for Emotional Habits

During the process of growing up, most of us will have picked up emotional habits that may not help us in the present. See if you can identify things that you do or ways that you react that get in the way of your happiness. Try to understand where you learned these habits or responses. Taking responsibility for these habits and responses, try to commit to figuring out ways to replace these tricky reactions with strategies that work better and to learn to cope with the emotions that accompany them. Keep this goal in mind as you progress throughout the book.

18 : Beyond Blame

WHILE ANGER AND THE TENDENCY TO BLAME may arise in our mind, they are contrary to the qualities all of us admire such as love, compassion, tolerance and forgiveness. From our own experience, we know that when anger and blame arise in our minds, there is no space for love and compassion at that moment. Therefore to cultivate the qualities that bring peace in ourselves, in our relationships, and in society, we will want to seek ways to subdue their opposites.

We often say, "That person made me so mad!" as if anger were a virus we caught from someone else. It's as if the other person's words were contaminated with the anger virus and as soon as they hit our eardrums we were uncontrollably stricken with the plague of anger. We believe the other person caused our anger, "You did it to me!," and we are faultless, innocent victims.

Fortunately that is not the case. If it were true that someone else *made* us angry, then there would be nothing we could do about our hostile feelings. We wouldn't be able to give up our anger until the cause—the other person—changed. That view makes us into a helpless victim, and then we believe that we are justified in either lashing out at the other person for making us angry or blaming ourselves for being so unworthy that we deserve to be treated like that.

Where does the anger come from? It begins with how we

interpret other people's words; we make up a story: "This person criticized me because he deliberately wants to harm me." "... because she is jealous." "... because I am a bad person and did something wrong." "... because they are prejudiced."

The stories continue to proliferate as we create a drama (or a soap opera) starring ME! "It's all the other person's fault. I hate him! But if it's not his fault, then it must be my fault. I hate myself!" We get ourselves all wound up in a tangled web of our own making.

Is any of this true? We didn't ask the other person what her motivation was. We just assumed that we could read her mind and know her intention. So often these assumptions are incorrect and cause problems in our relationships. Even if the other person did intentionally want to harm us, that doesn't mean we have no other alternative than to be enraged. No matter what the other person's motivation is, we still have a choice about how to interpret their behavior and therefore whether or not to get angry. We have to slow down and see that this choice exists.

We may think, "But any normal person would get angry if someone spoke to them that way." While most people may get angry in a particular situation, it doesn't mean we have to. We are the person who will be harmed most by our anger. The person we are angry with is living their life, drinking tea or talking with their friends. It is us who are stuck in suffering; our anger makes us miserable. If for no other reason than to alleviate our own misery, let's question the story we create that lies behind our anger. Let's investigate if we *have to* get mad.

Usually we believe that if a problem or a bad situation isn't the other person's fault, then it must be our fault. But why do we need to frame the situation in terms of fault and blame to begin with? Instead we could simply say that things arise due to many causes and conditions.

I (Chodron) would like to propose that we go beyond blame. There is no need for there to be a guilty person to blame, be it ourselves or others. No one person is so powerful that he or she can control all the causes and conditions that led up to a particular situation. Situations arise due to many different causes and conditions that themselves stem from a wide variety of other causes and conditions. Rather than point fingers at each other with the thought, "Someone is to blame for this," each of us can accept responsibility for our own part and try to eradicate the ignorance, anger or other disturbing feelings that lay behind it. Even if we believe that we played no part whatsoever in creating the situation, our own emotional responses are our responsibility and only we can change them.

Each of us can play a role in doing this, and since each of us wants to be happy and none of us wants to suffer, it makes sense for us to work together to alleviate the suffering that everyone experiences in a difficult situation.

REFLECTION

Going beyond Blame

Think of a situation where you were in conflict with someone. Remember the thoughts you had, perhaps, "He's such an awful person for doing this," or "It was all my fault. Me and my big mouth!" If you remember blaming someone else, press your mental "stop" button. Instead, remind yourself that the situation is due to causes and conditions that both of you have some responsibility for. There may also be other causes and conditions in play that neither of you are responsible for. Though both of you made mistakes, you want to be happy and not suffer. Examine your share of the causes and conditions, learn from them and try to avoid making similar mistakes in the future. Although you can't control the other person, you can hope that he will do the same. By going beyond blame, you will be able to wish happiness and the cessation of suffering for yourself and others. In short, you will have compassion for everyone involved in the difficult situation.

19 : Establishing
Compassionate Habits

Ψ As with learning any new skill or habit, it takes purposeful effort to establish compassionate habits. We deepen our capacity for compassion by repeatedly reminding ourselves of the desire to help others (and ourselves) move towards happiness and to free them from suffering. Eventually this begins to manifest effortlessly. We can be creative in finding ways to be compassionate: we can establish a routine, using common daily occurrences, such as stopping at a red light or sitting down on the train or bus, to pause and connect with compassion. We can mute the sound during the first commercial of every television program and take a moment to connect with a compassionate thought or exercise. My (Russell's) friend and colleague Paul Gilbert suggested a good one for folk like me who sometimes put our hands in our pockets—carrying a small stone or object to remind us to bring compassion to mind every time we feel it in our pockets. We can get in the habit of bringing a compassionate thought or intention to mind just after waking up in the morning, what we in Compassion Focused Therapy circles call "compassion under the duvet": "Today, I will be kind to one person I don't know," or "Today I will not criticize anyone." For compassionate practices that take a bit longer, we can schedule them into a day-planner, like every other task we value. Be innovative! The idea is to find ways to bring compassion into your everyday life, moment by moment—to weave compassion into the fabric of your life.

When we engage in a particular type of thinking or behavior, there are two effects. The first is the immediate effect of the thought or behavior. In the case of thinking compassionately, the effect may be to shift our perspective on a situation, provoke different emotions in us or inspire us to behave in helpful ways. The second effect gives us the ability to transform our lives in the long term. Every time we think or act in a specific way, we *make it more likely that we will think or behave that way in the future*. Over time, we can deeply embed compassion into our minds, establishing habits and abilities that are strengthened bit by bit through repeated practice. This is the key to transforming ourselves into the people we wish to be.

This sort of change occurs through small steps, repeated over time. Think of a skill you've developed gradually, with repeated practice—playing a musical instrument, cooking, gardening, woodworking, working with electronics or cars, or using computers. In each case, our abilities develop with practice, so that things with which we initially struggled eventually occur automatically and effortlessly. Strengthening and deepening our natural capacity for compassion is like developing these skills, except we can practice compassion in almost any situation, no matter where we are, and we were born with all of the equipment we will ever need—our own minds!

This process also plays out in our brains. Every thought, sensory experience, action, emotion and behavior in which we engage is reflected in a corresponding activation of cells (called "neurons") in the brain. Every time we think in a specific way or perform a certain action, a pattern of cells "lights up" in the brain. When these patterns are activated, changes occur within the cells and in the connections between them, gradually making it easier for that pattern to be activated in the future. When a certain pattern of cells is activated many times, it becomes *very* easy for it to be activated in the future, so that when something triggers it, it can seem to happen automatically.

This process explains why repeatedly familiarizing ourselves with compassion makes it easier for us to be compassionate. It also explains why it can be so hard to break certain habits we'd rather not have. Because these old neural pathways are so well worn, we can find ourselves engaging in those same old behaviors before we're even aware of it happening. So it's important to be patient and kind with ourselves as we gradually work on establishing new neural pathways and stop reinforcing the old ones.

I (Russell) like to use the example of a path in the woods. Imagine I've taken a nice walk through the woods behind my house every day for the past ten years or so, walking the same route every day. Over time, you can imagine that a path would wear in—the repeated walking would create a track, and it would be easier to walk on this track than in other places in the forest, as the shrubs and undergrowth would be worn away there. When it rains, where would the water run? Down the path! Our brains work in somewhat similar ways. Thinking and acting in a certain manner over time "wears in" paths of activation in our brains, so they eventually "light up" almost automatically. This is good if we're studying for an examination; we know if we just review that definition enough times when studying, it will spring forth from our minds effortlessly in the exam. But it can be challenging when that well-worn path corresponds to a habit we want to change, such as a tendency to speak harshly to others or even chewing our fingernails.

However, once we understand how this process works, we can use it to our advantage. Imagine I got tired of the path I'd inadvertently worn into the woods, because it created negative consequences—say, water running down into my backyard when it rains. To change this, I'd need to do two things: stop walking down the original path, and start walking a new route. This is easier said than done, and if I don't make an effort to be aware, I'm likely to continue walking the old way out of habit. But by choosing a new path that is more to my liking, and paying closer attention when beginning my walk, over time I'll form the habit of walking the new path. This is a gradual process; meaningful change seldom happens overnight—not in the woods, and not in our minds. After just a few days the forest doesn't really look much different. But over time, the new path gradually becomes more and more worn in, and the old one grows over. Eventually, we hit the tipping point, and the new path becomes the "path of least resistance," where we automatically walk, and now when it rains, the water runs where I want it to go.

It works the same way when establishing the habits of thinking, feeling and behaving compassionately. It can be slow going and require a good bit of effort in the beginning. We may do the practices, but not really *feel* compassionate. We may inadvertently walk the old path—gossiping, judging or snapping at another person or shaming ourselves, only realizing we're doing it later. The key is to *keep going*, reconnecting over and again with our intention to be compassionate and reorienting ourselves towards this goal. This means learning to catch ourselves while we're judging or shaming, and replacing these judgments with compassionate, understanding thoughts. It can also mean apologizing for our harsh words and renewing our commitment to speaking more kindly in the future, or to *not* speaking when irritated.

This isn't easy, but we can be confident in the process. We know if we keep walking that new path, it will wear in over time. Knowing that it takes time, we can be patient with ourselves. The payoff is worth the effort: it's exciting and satisfying to see compassionate thoughts and behaviors we've practiced finally appearing automatically in our lives. In our Compassion Focused Therapy anger groups in the prison, I've seen men who were serving decades-long sentences for violent offences proudly and excitedly share stories of responding to provocation with kindness and understanding rather than aggression. *This is how we change, and it's worth the effort.*

REFLECTION

Compassionate Practice

Consider a compassionate habit you'd like to cultivate. This may be a way of thinking or approaching a situation, or a considerate behavior you'd like to turn into a habit. It may involve bringing empathy into your interactions, for example by taking a moment during your conversations to pause and consider how the other person might be feeling. Come up with a plan to integrate this habit into your life. For example, you could plan to pause and consider the feelings of the other person during the first conversation you have when you get to work every day. The idea is to find a way to practice this way of thinking, feeling or behaving over and over, so that it gradually becomes a well-entrenched habit.

20 : Imagery and Method Acting: Cultivating Our Compassionate Selves

Ψ AS I'VE (RUSSELL) MENTIONED, our mental state at any given time is a combination of different aspects of experience: attention, motivation, emotion, reasoning and imagery. These mental experiences influence one another—where we place our attention impacts how we feel, which impacts our motivation and reasoning, and so on. There's something really marvelous about the interaction between these various aspects of our mental experience—it means we can use any of them as entry points as we work to develop our minds in different ways. This opens up many new strategies for bringing compassion into our daily lives. For example, one powerful mental tool we'll be using throughout this book is imagery.

Since *purposefully* using imagery in this way may feel a bit foreign (we do it by accident all the time!), it's useful to say a bit about it. Some people may initially feel silly conjuring up mental imagery and doubt it will have much effect. However, imagery is a very powerful tool for impacting our emotional states and developing compassion. Remember our emotions aren't good at telling the difference between things that are happening in the outside world and the thoughts, images and fantasies we produce in our minds. We can keep ourselves angry for hours by playing an irritating scenario over and over in our minds. But we can also use imagery in productive ways to create the motivations and emotions we want to have.

Some people may initially find imagery difficult because they are trying to see things with their "mind's eye" as clearly as if they were looking right at them. Seeing things this vividly isn't necessary. The key is to create *mental experiences* that can help us bring compassion into our minds. For example, imagine your favorite food. Notice the changes in your feelings and mental state when you do this. Bring to mind a wise person who you respect and trust. Your mind changes by imagining them, doesn't it? Perhaps you feel safe or inspired by thinking of them. This mental transformation is what we're trying to do with imagery.

One way we can use imagery to develop compassion is by imagining what it would be like if we succeeded in becoming truly compassionate beings. Bring to mind the characteristics you imagine that you would have as a deeply compassionate being: kindness, patience, wisdom, confidence, courage, distress tolerance, acceptance, creativity and so on. If you struggle to see yourself in this way, think of someone you see as a model of compassion and consider the qualities they possess which you would like to cultivate in yourself.

Self-critical thoughts can get in the way of working to improve ourselves. For example, we may feel we are so far from the goal ("I'm *nothing like* a deeply compassionate being!") that we get demoralized and give up. We can get so caught up in thinking about whether or not we have "what it takes" to develop these characteristics that we never actually try to cultivate them. Paul Gilbert has developed an approach for getting out of this loop that is borrowed from method acting.[9]

To be successful on stage or screen, actors often have to portray characters that are nothing like their real-life personalities. To do this convincingly, they have to "get into the head" of the character—to imagine how this character would feel, think and react to the various situations they are presented with as the plot unfolds. Method actors approach this task *by imagining that they are these characters*, by considering the characters' psychological motives and imagining they actually have the traits of the characters they are seeking to portray. These exercises are also reminiscent of mind-training practices used by Buddhists for centuries. In such practices, the student visualizes herself as a being who embodies the qualities she wishes to cultivate in herself and imagines acting with those qualities throughout the day.

We can apply this approach as we work to develop the qualities of the compassionate self. In doing this, *we imagine what it would be like if we did have these compassionate characteristics,* picturing ourselves having these qualities. We imagine how we would think, feel and act as we manifest these qualities in our daily lives. Doing this, we create and gradually strengthen patterns of activity in our brains that help us to bring these qualities into our lives and to establish them as mental habits.

Professionals in many different fields use strategies like this. Athletes go through the game in their heads, picturing how to respond in various situations. Guitar players run through scales and progressions in their minds. Similarly, imagining ourselves feeling, thinking and acting with compassion can prepare us to bring these qualities into the reality of our daily lives. It helps to imagine ourselves enacting these qualities in specific life situations—imagining our compassionate selves in action can keep this from being a vague, purely mental experience and helping us to bring these qualities into our lives. We can call this the "Compassionate Self" exercise:

Start by considering one or more compassionate qualities that you'd like to develop in yourself:

- Warmth.
- Kindness.
- Acceptance and nonjudgment.
- Confidence.
- Courage.
- Patience.
- Humility.
- Distress tolerance.
- Humor.
- Generosity.
- Loving-kindness.

Think about the qualities you've chosen, becoming familiar with them. Now imagine you already have these qualities.

- Imagine how it feels to have these qualities. What would it feel like to have patience, deep kindness, confidence or generosity? If your internal self-critic begins to argue with you, remind yourself that you're just *imagining what it would be like*. Gently redirect your mind from the critical thought, bringing it back to the quality you're cultivating.
- Having these compassionate qualities, what would you be motivated to do? As these virtues work themselves through you, what desires and intentions would arise in you?
- Consider your thinking. If you had deep kindness, wisdom and confidence, what thoughts would you think? Being kind and patient, how would you understand your own struggles or those of others?

- How would you spend your time, and what sorts of things would you do? How would this compassionate perspective change the way you engage in your everyday activities?
- Allowing your mouth to take on a gentle smile, picture yourself as a compassionate person who possesses the qualities you've chosen. Consider how you would look as this compassionate being. Consider how your voice would sound.
- Picture yourself going through the world, acting with these positive qualities. Imagine yourself interacting kindly and compassionately with others, applying these qualities to specific situations and interactions in your life.

As we do this, we also practice compassion with ourselves—being patient with ourselves as we learn to imagine ourselves in this way. Some people report that while they can imagine how they might think or act if they had these qualities, they don't *feel* it in the beginning. Our emotions are very sensitive to imagery, so if we continue to picture ourselves thinking and behaving compassionately—helping others who are suffering, directing kindness to others, having confidence and wisdom in the face of difficulty—this imagery will come to impact our emotional state in the same way as other mental images. Just as imagining ourselves in an angry scenario can produce feelings of anger in us, imagining ourselves behaving compassionately can help bring up kind, compassionate emotions. As with all skills, using imagery in this way becomes easier and more effective with practice, so we need to keep it up in order to get the results we want. Have fun with it!

REFLECTION

Using Imagery to Develop Compassionate Qualities

At least once per day, bring to mind a compassionate quality you'd like to develop in yourself. Imagining you already have that quality, picture yourself enacting it in your
life. Imagine how your motivation, emotions, reasoning,
behavior and interactions are shaped by this quality. As you
end the exercise, try to bring this quality with you as you
go about your daily life.

PART THREE

Cultivating Compassion

21 : How to
Cultivate Compassion

As a child, I (Chodron) heard, "Love thy neighbor as thyself." It sounded good, but I didn't see any examples of people who did that. People were certainly kind to each other, but they always put themselves first. When others didn't do what they liked, then the kindness went away and was replaced by scolding or retaliation. "Anyway," I thought, "how is it possible to love all these people when so many of them are idiots?"

At college, I had a two-part mind: one part was intensely critical of everything, while the other was searching for peace and harmony. Each week I dutifully went to a class on Love at the University of Southern California, taught by Leo Buscaglia, bestselling author and professor in the department of special education. It was the one thing that gave me hope during those years of self-doubt and self-exploration they call becoming an adult. That was in the late 1960s. Nowadays young adults like myself might be given a bottle of antidepressants.

Actually, in some ways, I'm glad I went through that painful time; in the end, suffering made me more aware of the value of self-knowledge and more compassionate towards others. It also led me to seek a spiritual path that could show me how to train my mind in positive attitudes and emotions.

When I encountered the Buddha's teachings in 1975, I discovered a tried-and-true method to transform my mind. My

Buddhist teachers didn't just tell me to love others, they *showed me how*, according to a step-by-step method that originated with the Buddha and was passed down through centuries of practitioners who applied and developed it. As I learned, meditated on and then practiced these teachings, I discovered that they actually worked. What a relief to find a method to subdue anger and cynicism as well as a path to enhance love, compassion and forgiveness.

Of course, transforming the mind is no quick and easy endeavor. It requires time, energy and a lot of self-acceptance and faith. But it's the most worthwhile thing to do, and knowing that we're making our lives meaningful brings joy in itself, even though it is slow going.

In Tibetan Buddhism there are two methods for developing an altruistic intention: one is called *the seven-point instruction of cause and effect*, the other is called the *equalizing and exchanging self and others*. Compassion is an important step in both of these. I'll briefly share these methods with you. If you want to learn more about them, there are many books and living masters that can help you.

A precursor to both methods is the cultivation of equanimity, which refers to a mind that is free from clinging attachment to loved ones, anger and hostility towards people we don't like—let's call them enemies—and apathetic indifference towards everyone else. When practiced consistently over time, *the meditation on equanimity* brings the feeling of impartial, open-hearted concern for all beings.

REFLECTION

Considering Challenges to Compassion

Consider the challenges and obstacles to your compassion. These may be situations in which you find yourself resistant to shifting into a more compassionate approach, or find thoughts that tend to steer your mind away from compassion—for example, the wish to withhold compassion from another person because you think that she doesn't deserve it. Keep these challenges in mind as you work to develop your compassion through the following entries and reflections, and see if you can find ways to work with them using the methods discussed.

22 : Equanimity

CLOSE YOUR EYES and think of a few people you are attached to and don't want to be separated from. Now ask yourself, "Why am I attached to them?" There's no right or wrong answer; just listen to what your mind says when you ask yourself why you find those particular people so pleasing.

Now, think of some people you *don't* get along with—people you may be afraid or resentful of—and ask yourself, "Why do I feel so much hostility towards these people?" Without censoring your thoughts, observe the reasons that your mind gives.

Finally imagine some strangers—people you pass by who you hardly notice. They are simply part of the obstacle course you navigate each day. Ask yourself, "Why do I feel indifferent towards them?" Again, listen to the reasons that your mind offers.

Your responses may be something like the following:

Regarding the people you are attached to, you may think: "They are kind to me; they respect me; we have similar ideas and interests, they encourage me when I'm down and celebrate my accomplishments. I feel good around them; they bring out the best in me."

Regarding the people you don't like, the thoughts are different, "They interfere with my happiness. They hurt me or the people that I love. They threaten me and make me feel unsafe. They are unethical and their actions go against what I value. They criticize and ridicule me."

Regarding strangers, you may think, "I don't know them. They don't affect me one way or the other. There's no reason for me to care."

What word(s) are present in all these responses? I, Me, My, Mine.

The truth is that while we think we perceive people objectively—as they really are—in fact we see them through the lens of "how do they *affect me*?" and take that as the criteria determining their value. People who help us, like us and basically do what we want we consider good people and friends. We see them as worthy of our affection and become attached to them because they please us. People who do the opposite, acting in ways that displease us or that we find reprehensible, we consider bad or think of as our "enemies." We believe they deserve our anger, dislike and sometimes even hatred and revenge. People who don't affect us one way or the other, we ignore. We often relate to them like objects and may not even think of them as having feelings.

While we are sure that people exist in the way that we perceive them, this is not the case. Thinking only in terms of "I, Me, My and Mine" distorts our perspective because it fails to take into account anyone else and causes us to make up many inaccurate ideas that we believe are true. We believe Susan is objectively an inherently wonderful person, while in fact we may perceive—and even exaggerate—her good qualities and ignore her bad traits. We believe that, objectively, Harry is obnoxious, while it's simply that his behavior is rude in our eyes although he is kind to many other people who like him.

It gets even more complicated. If John agrees with our opinions about Susan and Harry, he becomes our friend, but if he thinks Susan is fussy and Harry is honest, then John is moved into the category of people we don't like. And if Harry changes and acts in ways that please us, then Harry becomes our friend!

Susan, Harry and John all have good qualities and faults, but rather than see any of them as a whole person who has many different, and often contradictory, qualities, we put them into narrow and fixed categories of friend, enemy or stranger and think that is who they will be forever. Here, "enemy" refers to anyone we don't get along with or feel unsafe around.

However, none of these roles is permanent. When we are born, everyone is a stranger to us. Then some of those strangers become friends and others enemies. As we grow up, friends from school become strangers, as do some of our childhood enemies. Meanwhile, people who were once dear friends may go on to become bitter enemies, and when we meet enemies in different situations later in our lives and see new sides of them, they become friends.

And so it becomes clear that "friends," "enemies" and "strangers" are fictitious categories created by our self-centered thoughts that tend to judge everyone in terms of how they act towards Me. Since this is the case, what use is there in being attached to loved ones, feeling hostile towards enemies and apathetic towards everyone else? Since people can change categories quickly and frequently, what purpose is there in holding fixed ideas about other people?

When we open our eyes, look at the big picture and go beyond the superficial appearances of how someone relates to Me, we see that fundamentally all of us are the same. Everyone wants to be happy and no one wants to suffer. That's the bottom line. We may find some people more physically attractive and others less so. Some people may appear more intelligent, successful or humorous and others less so. But all these appearances are superficial and can change very quickly.

Therefore, why allow our mind to be affected by thoughts of attachment, anger and apathy? It makes more sense and is more satisfying to see everyone as having the same ultimate goal of being happy and avoiding pain. In doing so, we will be able to feel connected to everyone and come to have concern for them as well.

Breaking down rigid categories in order to cultivate impartial love and compassion for all beings is something everyone can do. A friend of mine (Chodron's) works for the police as a mediator in hostage situations. He told me that the best way to resolve this fearful situation is to help the hostage takers get in touch with the common humanity they share with the hostages. He counselled, "If you are ever taken hostage, ask the hostage taker about his family and tell him about yours. If he's wearing a T-shirt with the logo of a particular sports team, band or singing group, talk about that. That breaks down the barriers between you. It helps him to see, 'this person is just like me' and makes it more difficult for him to harm you."

One of the qualities we admire so much and that makes us feel safe and at ease is unconditional affection. Similarly, when we have unconditional affection for others, it is a marvellous gift to share with them, one that enables them to relax, trust and be themselves. For this reason, equanimity (a mind that is free from clinging attachment to loved ones, anger and hostility towards people we don't like and apathetic indifference towards everyone else) is important in order to have the kind of love and compassion that extend to all beings equally.

Without equanimity, our positive emotions are limited to only those we like and approve of—those in our "friend" category. In that case, our love and compassion have strings attached, because to get in my "friend" category you have to treat me nicely, agree with my ideas, not comment on my faults ... the list goes on. If you do something I don't like, you'll move to my "enemy" category and my love and compassion for you will disappear. To overcome these judgments and biases, equanimity is essential.

Feeling equanimity doesn't mean that we treat everyone the same way. Clearly how we interact with someone depends on our relationship with them and social roles. We may give our car keys to friends but not to strangers. In our hearts we can equally wish both of them to have happiness and not suffering, but know that it's not wise to give our car keys to just anyone.

Similarly, equanimity also doesn't mean we trust everyone equally. While we may have the same amount of concern for a two-year-old and an adult, we don't trust the toddler with a box of matches. If someone has the habit of not doing their share of work on a common project, we may choose not to work with them, but that doesn't mean our wish for them to be well and happy is less than for another more responsible person.

In short, equanimity gives us the inner freedom to stop making our feelings towards others dependent on the way that they treat us. This is a radical idea that initially may feel uncomfortable: How can I not regard someone who insults me as an enemy and not be angry with them? But when we try to put equanimity into practice, we will see that this is possible. Mother Teresa and the Dalai Lama have done it, why can't we? The beauty of equanimity is that we feel open-hearted care and concern for everyone, which opens the door to cultivating unconditional love and compassion for all.

REFLECTION

Cultivating Equanimity

Consider the ways that bias creeps into your relationships, for example, when you unconsciously exaggerate the positive qualities of friends or overemphasize the negative

SHAMBHALA PUBLICATIONS

If you'd like to receive a copy of our latest catalogue of books and audios, please fill out and return this card. It's easy—the postage is already paid!

Or, if you'd prefer, you can e-mail us at CustomerCare@shambhala.com, sign up online at www.shambhala.com/newsletter, or call toll-free (888) 424-2329.

NAME

ADDRESS

CITY / STATE / ZIP / COUNTRY

E-MAIL

And by also giving us your e-mail address, you'll automatically be signed up to receive news about new releases, author events, and special offers!

BUSINESS REPLY MAIL

FIRST-CLASS MAIL   PERMIT NO. 11494   BOSTON MA

POSTAGE WILL BE PAID BY ADDRESSEE

SHAMBHALA PUBLICATIONS
PO BOX 170358
BOSTON MA 02117-9812

qualities of those people with whom you have conflicts or differences. Consider that, just like you, all of these people want to be happy and to avoid suffering. It may help to recall experiences you've had with people who once were enemies but now are friends—or the reverse—reminding yourself that your relationships to others can change over time, and that all people are worthy of compassion. See if you can feel compassion for all beings equally, regardless of the relationship that you have with them. If you're not ready to do this, then try to have *the wish* to have compassion for all living beings equally.

23 : The Seven-Point Instruction of Cause and Effect

THE SEVEN-POINT INSTRUCTION of cause and effect is a method to cultivate not only love and compassion for others, but also altruism. Given that not all readers of this book are Buddhists, I (Chodron) will explain some of the steps in a way that can be practiced by people of all faiths, as well as those who are not religious.

Step One involves contemplating that we are connected to all living beings. We live in the same universe and so are related to each other.

In Step Two, we reflect on the kindness of whoever took care of us when we were young. It could be our parents, grandparents, babysitter, teachers or a number of people together who made sure that we had food, shelter, clothing, medical care and education. They taught us to speak and to tie our shoes; they protected us from harm when we were in harm's way. They were also faced with the not-very-enjoyable tasks of teaching us manners and disciplining us so that we would act in appropriate ways. They rejoiced in our successes and encouraged us when we lacked confidence. The proof that we were cared for with kindness as children is the fact that we are alive today, have skills, have friends and are able to make a positive contribution to society. Had no one cared for us, we would have died from neglect years ago.

Recollecting the kindness that we received as children makes us feel gratitude to all of those who extended a helping hand. This may have been parents, grandparents, aunts and uncles, siblings, friends, neighbours, teachers, playmates, pets or others. As children we usually took everything our carergivers did for us for granted and complained when we didn't get what we wanted. We seldom thought of what others had to go through to get the money to feed us. As teenagers we may have been rude and rebellious when we thought others were trying to control us and limit our freedom. We may have lied and taken things that weren't ours. When we think about it, we weren't always the easiest children to raise.

In reflecting on the care we received that enabled us to survive, we are filled with a strong feeling of gratitude. As our gratitude increases, we spread it to all other people with whom we share the world. Although they weren't the ones who cared for us when we were young, they could have been if we had been born in different circumstances.

In Step Three, contemplating the kindness that we received when we were growing up arouses the wish to repay that kindness. Through these first three steps our hearts begin to open in ways they hadn't before.

REFLECTION

Gratitude for the Care We've Received

Begin by breathing normally and naturally, observing your breath for a little while to calm your mind. Then bring to mind the many people (and animals, such as pets) who have cared for you in your life. As you think of these people and remember the care you received, allow a strong sense of gratitude to arise within you. Allow your mind to rest in the feeling of gratitude. Extend this gratitude to all other beings. If disturbing emotions or resentments come up in your mind, gently let them go, bringing your attention back to the ways in which you *were* cared for and the feelings of gratitude. After a while, allow the wish to repay their kindness arise in you, and think that you will do that by cultivating compassion and caring for others.

We will learn the next steps in the following entry.

24 : Love and Compassion

 LOVE AND COMPASSION are built on the foundation of equanimity, which makes them stable. Without reducing our attachment to those we consider
"good people" and friends, the love we feel for them will be
dependent on how they treat us. Such "love" is in fact partly
attachment, because it fluctuates according to whether people
are nice to us or not. To have stable love that will endure the
ups and downs of life, we need to reduce our personal sensitivity to what others think of us and how they treat us. This
requires effort and internal strength. It is not about suppressing
our emotional needs; it's about finding diverse ways to fulfil
them. It also involves learning to take delight in caring about
the well-being of others. In other words, the "reward" of loving others isn't that others love us in return, it's that we feel
completely delighted and fulfilled simply to give love.

Steps Four and Five are love and compassion. In the context
of the seven-point instruction of cause and effect method to
cultivate altruism for others, love and compassion have specific
meanings. Love is the wish for someone to have happiness and
its causes; compassion is the wish for them to be free from
suffering and its causes.

We may ask, "What is happiness and what causes it? What is
suffering and what causes it?" From the Buddhist perspective,
there are different types of happiness: temporal and spiritual.

Temporal happiness is happiness that we experience in this life chiefly due to external things, people and situations. For example, happiness is having good food, friends, possessions, success in our career and a happy family life. The causes of this kind of happiness are a kind and generous heart, patience, effort, acting ethically and making wise decisions. Spiritual happiness comes from transforming our heart and mind, liberating them from mental afflictions and developing good qualities such as love, compassion, generosity, ethical conduct, fortitude, enthusiasm and wisdom. The causes for spiritual happiness come from training our mind in these good qualities.

Suffering likewise may be temporal or spiritual. Temporal misery may come from lacking the resources we need to live, not getting what we would like, not feeling good about ourselves and the human condition of being subject to aging, sickness and death. Some sufferings are due to societal inequality. Others are due to how we look at life. When we cannot see the purpose of our lives, we may also experience spiritual suffering. This is due in part to having not yet met wise elders who show us a viable path to inner peace.

By meditating on equanimity, we can free ourselves from attachment, hostility and apathy towards others. In doing so, we can gradually cultivate love and compassion, wishing that others have happiness and freedom from suffering.

Our goal is to feel love and compassion for all beings, including ourselves. It is very important not to leave ourselves out because we are a part of "all living beings." Singling ourselves out for special attention—either denying ourselves love and compassion or being self-indulgent—is a product of unfair bias. Like everyone else, we want to be happy and avoid suffering. There is no reason to treat ourselves differently than others, either better or worse, in that regard.

From a Buddhist viewpoint *all* beings are worthy of compassion and kindness because the fundamental nature of our minds is pure and untainted. This fundamental purity can never be taken away or permanently stained. Furthermore, each of us has the potential to be virtuous, and there is no such thing as an "evil person" who is inherently damaged and corrupt. It is important to differentiate between a person and that person's actions. Although we may engage in misguided or unwholesome actions, it does not mean that we are evil people because our fundamental nature is untainted. That is, wrong conceptions and disturbing emotions have not entered into the nature of the mind itself.

For this reason, every living being is worthy of compassion, even though they may sometimes be overwhelmed by disturbing emotions or act in ways that harm others because of those emotions. We don't have to prove ourselves to others or conform to an external standard to be worthy of compassion. Simply being a living being is good enough. Our negative emotions and mistaken actions are not who we are, they are not our fundamental nature. Therefore we can change and improve; no one is hopeless.

REFLECTION

Cultivating Love

To cultivate love, sit quietly with your eyes lowered or closed. Begin by breathing normally and naturally, observing your breath for a little while to calm your mind. When your mind is calm, imagine a replica of yourself sitting in front of you. Think about how you want happiness and not suffering. Reflect on what this happiness is in your own case. Contemplate its causes: making wise decisions, being generous and so on. Then sincerely wish yourself to have this happiness and its causes. Imagine that you have them and feel safe, satisfied and fulfilled.

Then contemplate spiritual happiness and its causes in detail. Wish yourself to have a sense of meaning and purpose in your life and to be able to fulfil these. Wish yourself to be free from disturbing emotions and to have love and compassion that extend equally to all beings. Feel fulfilled and joyful.

While you are doing this, if any thoughts of "I'm not worthy of being happy," or, "I'm incapable of creating the causes for happiness," arise, realize that these are illogical, self-centered thoughts. We all want and deserve happiness. We all have the ability to create the causes for it. As one of my (Chodron's) teachers said, "If you have the potential to become a fully awakened human being—and we all do—then you also have the potential to create the causes for happiness.

Then visualize a teacher or someone that you respect sitting in front of you, and repeat the above steps of wishing this person happiness and its causes. Send these kind wishes out to that person and imagine that the person is filled with peace and joy as he or she receives them.

Follow that by thinking of a stranger sitting in front of you and repeat the steps.

When you have done this, think of someone you don't get along with. Try to wish him well. Remember that the entire value or meaning of his life doesn't lie in how he treated you for a comparatively short period of time. Extend kind wishes to him. Imagine him being happy and at peace inside of himself. He would be more likeable than the disagreeable person you see him as now. Being happy, relaxed and fulfilled, he would also act differently.

He would be able to express the kindness that is buried beneath the pain in his heart.

Finally, think of all living beings and contemplate the steps, imagining them all having happiness and its causes. Let your love arise and radiate to all of them. Be aware of how you feel when you are able to love everyone—to wish them to have happiness and its causes. Let your mind rest in that feeling.

In this practice and the next, if you get stuck extending positive emotions towards yourself, remember that, like all other beings, you want happiness, don't want suffering and deserve kindness. After all, we are practicing extending love and compassion to *all* beings, not all minus ourselves.

REFLECTION

Cultivating Compassion

As with love, to cultivate compassion, begin with yourself. Imagine in front of you a replica of yourself and reflect on the various sufferings and unhappiness you are subject to due to the human condition. Wish yourself to be free from these sufferings and their causes. Imagine what it would be like to be free from these sources of suffering. Feel your newly found freedom from insecurity, fear, anxiety, anger and emotional neediness.

Reflect in this way towards teachers and those you respect, then strangers, followed by those who you don't like, imagining them all being free of their suffering. If you find it hard to have compassion for people you disapprove of, feel threatened by or for those who have harmed you in the past, remember that whatever traits they have that you find objectionable, and whatever actions they did that harmed you in some way, are based on their internal unhappiness. In other words, people harm others when they themselves are unhappy and miserable. Confused about the causes of happiness and suffering, they mistakenly believe that doing that harmful action will relieve their inner unhappiness, make them happy, and bring them what they want and need. People harm others because of their own inner pain. No one wakes up in the morning and says, "I'm so happy; I think I'll go out and hurt someone!" That never happens.

Imagine what this person would be like if he were free from that pain and misery. He would think and act in a very different way, wouldn't he? Imagine him not being subject to fear, worry, resentment and self-loathing. Imagine him having the recognition, approval, possessions and so on that he needs. Visualize how he would look and behave if he didn't have those needs. In doing so look deeply, not at what he superficially thinks he needs. For example, don't imagine how peaceful an alcoholic would be if he had an unlimited stash of booze. Instead, imagine his mental peace if he were free from the craving that pushes him to get intoxicated. Think of the relief he would feel if he were free from the material and emotional needs that drive him to harm others and thereby himself. Extend compassion to him.

Finally, include all living beings in your meditation, wishing each of them to be free of all the various kinds of suffering and all of their causes. Rest your mind in the inner experience of having a compassionate heart.

Step Six of the seven-point instruction is to develop the great resolve to not only wish others to be free from suffering and its causes and wish them to have happiness and its causes, but also to do something about it. This is similar to the difference between standing on the beach watching someone flailing in the waves and with compassion shouting, "Someone, please go and save him," and jumping in the water ourselves. This sixth step is calling us to be engaged in bringing about the well-being of all living beings. The great resolve arises from repeatedly meditating on love and compassion until we get to the point where we strongly feel we must act to alleviate others' suffering and bring about their happiness.

These first six steps produce the Seventh Step: the altruistic intention. This is a praiseworthy mind that is committed to abandoning all our faults and negativities and cultivating all our good qualities and virtues to their fullest extent in order to give the greatest benefit to all beings. This is truly an admirable and noble motivation, with which we feel full of joy, enthusiasm and purpose in life. It also increases our ability to help others with wisdom, compassion and skillful means.

25 : Equalizing and Exchanging Self and Others

THE SECOND METHOD for cultivating the altruistic intention (the aspiration to abandon all our faults and develop our excellent qualities fully in order to be of the greatest benefit to others) is by "equalizing" and "exchanging" ourselves and others. "Equalizing ourselves and others" involves recognizing that our wish for joy and freedom from misery is just as strong and equally important as others" wish to have joy and be free from misery. "Exchanging ourselves and others" means that we stop focusing on only ourselves and "exchange" that narrow perspective for one that centers on the welfare of others.

As with the seven-point instruction of cause and effect, equalizing and exchanging self and others begins with cultivating equanimity, freeing ourselves from attachment, anger and apathy towards others. Generating unbiased love and compassion will be difficult unless we can overcome or at least lessen our attachment to dear ones, our animosity towards those we don't like and our apathy for strangers. In addition, the love and compassion that we have for our dear ones is not stable, and when they act in a way that displeases us our love and compassion will vanish.

This second method has several steps: equalizing self and others, seeing the defects of self-centeredness and the advantages of cherishing others, exchanging self and others, and taking and giving.

To equalize ourselves and others, we contemplate that we are all the same in terms of wanting happiness and not suffering. This point has been mentioned before and in fact we knew it already, but it's easy to forget. We have to bring it into our hearts. To do this, begin by getting in touch with your own wish to be happy and to avoid misery and pain. Really feel that wish in your own heart. Then bring to mind a variety of people you know, as well as some strangers. Recognize that although each of them may want something different that will bring them happiness, they are alike in wanting happiness. To give a superficial example, one person may like noodles and another rice, but they are the same in wanting to eat.

Similarly, each person may have different unpleasant situations or sufferings he or she wants to be free from, but we are alike in wanting to avoid misery. One person may suffer from bad health, another from losing his job, a third from a break-up and a fourth from feeling unconnected to her spiritual practice, but they are the same in wanting to be free from their difficulties. In addition, we are exactly like each of them in this regard. There is no reason why our happiness is more or less important, or our misery more or less undesirable, than that of anyone else. We are the same.

Regard each of the people you have imagined in front of you one by one and reflect, "This person wants happiness as intensely as I do." Do this repeatedly, looking at each individual and let this universal truth come into your heart. Observe the change that happens in your mind and focus on the feeling that arises. Add more and more people as you gain experience with this meditation.

Since I (Chodron) travel a lot, I do this contemplation in

airports. Sitting in a traffic jam, waiting in line at the grocery store or being in any place with a number of people will work just as well. Look at the people around you and think, "They want to be happy and avoid suffering as much as I do." Let that sink in. That young person who looks like he's on drugs, the elderly woman with a cane, the single mum with a sleeping baby and a screaming toddler, the man in a suit with a mark on his trousers, the young war veteran in a wheelchair, the Pakistani immigrant and his friend a Danish immigrant, the middle-aged man anxiously looking at his watch, the Muslim woman with a head scarf talking to the Jewish woman with a head scarf, the teenager whose thumbs are working overtime texting, the woman wearing political campaign badges—all of them are just like me, wanting to be happy and not suffer. There is no difference among us. What valid reason is there for putting myself first or for caring about the well-being of some people and not others?

REFLECTION

Equalizing Self and Others

Take a few moments in a public place to become aware of the people around you. Shifting your attention away from your own concerns, allow yourself to connect with the understanding that these beings around you have life stories that run every bit as deep as yours does, filled with hopes, dreams and aspirations, and with their own struggles and challenges. Recall that, just like you, they wish to be happy and to avoid suffering. Allow yourself to experience a sincere wish that they have happiness and that they be free from suffering.

26 : The Kindness of Others

IN OUR EVERYDAY LIVES, we are often unaware of how much we depend on others just to stay alive, and as a result we often take their kindness and efforts on our behalf for granted. When we pause and consider that we are all dependent on one another, we realize that everything we have, everything we know and everything we are able to do has come about due to the kindness of others. We are not the independent pick-yourself-up-by-your-own-bootstraps individuals that we sometimes pride ourselves in being.

Think of the food you ate for lunch. Where did it come from? Some people grew it, others harvested it, another person transported it and some others packaged it. Then there are the people who put it on the shelves in the stores, the person at the checkout counter and whoever cooked it. Without the efforts of all these people you wouldn't have even a mouthful of food to eat.

You might say, "But I bought the food with my own money." That's true, but where did the money come from? Someone gave it to you. Even if you worked a job to get it, you still depend on the person who hired you, the customers and clients of the company you work for, the people in the accounts department who issued the check, the people in the bank and more.

"But they don't do this especially for *me*. They work to earn a living," you may protest. But others' motivations for working are not important here. The bottom line is that if they didn't do what they're doing, you would go hungry. You eat due to their hard work and efforts. Surely that makes them kind!

Look around you and pick an item—a chair, a book, a spoon, whatever. Then think about all the people involved in your having it. This includes not only the people directly involved in producing it, but also the people who designed and made the machinery used to produce it. Then consider the miners who got the raw materials and the people in the factories who processed it so that it could be made into the machinery that then produced the item in the room. When we consider all the things we use each day that make our lives possible, the number of people and animals involved in our having them become uncountable.

From time to time one of my (Chodron's) teachers, Zopa Rinpoche, returns to his native area in the Himalayan mountains in Nepal. As is the custom there, the villagers come to visit him and often bring a bag of potatoes—the staple food of the area—to offer. Rinpoche once said that when he contemplated all that the villagers had done so that he had even one potato, he was overwhelmed by their kindness. The only way he could eat it, he told us, was if he generated compassion and vowed to use his life to benefit all beings.

How many of us stop to thank the people installing the fibre optic lines to our home, those fixing the electric or telephone lines, those taking away the garbage or those who work on the roads? Sometimes we are even irritated by them: "Why are you fixing this road now when I need to get somewhere? You should fix it at 2 A.M. when no one is driving on it!" But they work hard in the sun, the rain and, the dark, and we benefit so much from their efforts.

Especially with the global economy, we are indebted to

numberless people in other countries, some working in dangerous or dreadful conditions to produce the goods we use. Do we think about them when we put on our shoes or use our computer? We *can*, and doing so will transform our minds. We should try to use the things in our environment with more care and awareness of what others have gone through to make them. To repay their kindness, we must practice compassion towards as many people and animals as we can.

Not only do all of the objects we use and enjoy come from others, but also everything we know and all the skills we have are due to them. "Wait a minute," self-centeredness objects, "I'm an intelligent person. No one else gave me my brains!" We may have the potential to learn a lot and develop many skills, but that potential is useless without people who encourage us and teach us. Without all the people who taught us how to talk, we wouldn't even have that basic, elementary skill upon which our other abilities are founded. Without people who made the musical instrument and taught us how to play it, we wouldn't be able to play music. The same goes for computer whizzes, builders, athletes, secretaries, artists, engineers and everybody else. We only have the skills we have because others developed the knowledge and then cared enough to teach us.

When we think about it, the web of interdependent relationships connecting us to all living beings is huge, and we are able to live precisely because of their efforts and kindness. When we contemplate this deeply, we will never feel estranged from others. Contemplating this over time will lead us to recognize that we have been the recipient of tremendous kindness from the day we were born until now. Opening ourselves to this fact, our gratitude and feeling of closeness with others will increase and remain constant, instead of jumping from love to hatred whenever we think that they are doing something "wrong." This establishes a firm foundation for generating love and compassion.

REFLECTION

The Kindness of Others

Choose an aspect of your life, perhaps something you use regularly, an activity you frequently engage in or a skill that you have. Consider the many beings whose efforts made this aspect of your life possible. Allow yourself to receive their efforts as kindness and to experience a strong sense of gratitude towards them.

Continue by considering the ways in which so many others have contributed to your well-being. Conclude by feeling that you have been the recipient of tremendous kindness in your life. The wish to repay the kindness that others have given you may arise.

27 : The Disadvantages of Self-Centeredness

THE FACT THAT OTHERS have been tremendously kind to us and that our lives depend on them is not necessarily reflected in the way that we generally think. In our normal daily lives, most of us think of ourselves first and foremost. This self-centered thought believes that we are the most important, that our happiness is more urgent than others' and that our pain hurts more deeply than theirs.

The self-centered thought is deceptive and it has been with us for a long time. Following its advice has brought suffering to us and to those around us. Being self-centered has, in fact, interfered with our happiness. For these reasons we want to counteract it, and remembering its disadvantages is a good way to do this. Thinking of the faults of self-centeredness isn't a matter of scolding ourselves for being selfish—that is not the point. Instead, because we want to be happy and live peacefully, we seek to identify what prevents that and then counteract it.

We naively think that being self-centered—by "looking out for ourselves"—we will protect ourselves from harm and find happiness. However, this is not the case. When we look closely, we are likely to discover that the things we did in the past that we now regret were due to self-centered thoughts: "Criticize this person," and we oblige; "Make love with that person; it doesn't matter that they're married," and we obey. "Forget this stuff about your parents being kind; they spent the family's limited money on your sick brother and ignored you," and we agree. It says, "Eat this food even though you're already full," or "Have a third drink, no one else will know," and we follow suit. Being self-centered makes us very sensitive without our even realizing it. Everything that occurs in the world around us is interpreted in terms of how it relates to me. For example, we see two people talking softly and we're sure that they're talking about us, perhaps even criticizing us behind our back. When someone doesn't say "good morning" in the same friendly voice as usual, we're certain that we did something wrong and that they are mad at us. We become easily offended, jealous and defensive.

Being self-centered makes our relationship with the world very narrow. In the realm of general society, we often look at issues only in terms of how they will affect us in the short term. Not realizing that our own long-term happiness depends on the well-being of others in our neighborhood, city, state, country and the world, we support policies that work for our own immediate welfare or the welfare of our family or group. Thinking in this self-centered way, we may believe that the long-term consequences of these policies do not affect us, that we can just ignore them and others will fix them later on.

Whenever we criticize others or ourselves, we do so under the influence of self-centered thought. Self-centered thought pretends to be on our side and to look out for our welfare, while it actually does the opposite. It make us act inconsiderately and unethically, thus creating the causes for misery. It also ruins any joy that comes our way by making us fearful that it will disappear or envious that others have better. Self-preoccupation gets in the way of any constructive activity we want to do, inflicting self-doubt where it doesn't belong and making us suspicious when there is no reason to be. In short, this self-centered thought—not another person—is the biggest enemy who impedes our happiness.

Thankfully, self-centered thought is *not who we are*. It is simply a thought, albeit a powerful one. We have the potential to overcome our self-centeredness, which causes us much misery, and to cultivate good qualities such as love, compassion and generosity, which lead to our own and others' happiness. It is important to remember that our innermost nature is not inherently selfish. If we forget this, we will feel guilty for being selfish, and that just results in our becoming more self-preoccupied!

Abandoning self-preoccupation doesn't mean we don't take care of ourselves or treat ourselves like dirt. That is just another form of self-centeredness that says, "If I'm not the best, then I must be the worst," or "I'm so important I can make everything go wrong." We must take care of ourselves and look after our health and well-being, and we can do this without self-centeredness. To cultivate love and compassion and to reach out to help others, we must have a healthy body and mind. Otherwise we will become a burden to others and that is counter to our ultimate aim. So we must avoid going to the other extreme and thinking that resting, bathing, eating, studying, going on a meditation retreat and so on are selfish. They are not. We do it to keep ourselves balanced so that in the long term we'll be able to benefit others.

REFLECTION

Rooting Out the Self-Centered Thought

It can be hard to notice when a self-centered thought arises and colors our perceptions, but we can learn to look for clues. When we find ourselves judging and labeling others negatively, the self-centered thought is present.

When we are piqued with irritation or anger, it's usually because things are not going just the way *we* want them to. When we catch ourselves arguing with others, we may be attached to *our* ideas, labeling ours "right" and theirs "wrong." When we greedily crave to have something and act to get it without considering the effects of our actions on others, the self-centered thought is at work for sure.

Noticing these clues, we remind ourselves that self-centeredness creates problems and suffering in our lives and generate the motivation to change it by enlarging our perspective: "I'm determined to win this argument no matter what, but in doing so, I know that I'll damage a relationship that is important to me and hurt someone else. That's not the kind of behavior I want to have. I'm going to calm myself and then approach the situation more openly, without being so judgmental."

28 : "Rules of the Universe"

SELF-CENTEREDNESS IS one of the biggest forces that interferes with the cultivation of compassion. As its name indicates, self-centeredness is self-focused, while compassion focuses on others. They can't both exist in our minds at the same time.

Sometimes we take ourselves too seriously and beat ourselves up for being selfish. This is just another aspect of self-centeredness. Some humor is necessary when stopping self-centered thoughts. I (Chodron) find that one of the best ways to find humor in a situation where my self-preoccupation is flaring is to look at my "Rules of the Universe." Each of us has our own subjective "Rules of the Universe," which consist of the ways that we think other people should act and how we want the world to be. We didn't consciously sit down and write out these rules, and we may not even be aware of them. They are self-centered assumptions that we base our life on. Unfortunately, we live as if these "Rules" were true, but when we expose the ridiculous "logic" of the self-centered thoughts that made these rules, we are able to laugh at ourselves. This in turn helps us to relax and not to follow the autocratic rule of the self-centered mind.

Here are some of my key "Rules of the Universe." Maybe you share some of them. You may have some others to add to the list.

- Everyone must like me. Absolutely no one is allowed not to like me.
- I should get what I want when I want it. The universe owes it to me.
- Everyone should do things my way.
- Everyone should respect me at *all* times.
- I am always right.
- I must win all arguments because I'm right and I'm the best.
- I must always be comfortable.
- I must never experience any hardship whatsoever.
- It's my way or the highway and you should know this and obey.

Some more of my "Rules of the Universe" are:

- Everyone should know when I need help and respectfully offer to help me without me needing to ask.
- I should never get sick or old.
- All the resources at work or home should go towards my project first, because mine is the most important of all. Don't even think of arguing with me about this.
- When people ask me for advice and I give it, they should follow it. If they don't, they're idiots.
- If you don't understand what I'm talking about, it's because you're stupid.
- I'm innocent even when I make a mistake.
- My mistakes are always other people's fault.
- All my mistakes should be forgiven immediately without me having to apologize.
- I should always get the credit for team projects, even when I talked everyone else into doing most of the work.

- I'm always right, and if I'm wrong, it's because you are too stupid to see how right I am.
- My opinions and choices are always correct, even when I change them from one day to the next.
- People must always approve of what I do and never criticize me.
- You must always praise me, even when I'm wrong or did something hurtful.
- You must think my idea is wonderful and listen patiently while I explain to you what is wrong with your idea. Then, you must praise me for being so intelligent.
- You must talk about something interesting. Interesting means something I want to hear about.

And the grand finale is:

- Enough about ME. How about YOU? What do *you* think of ME?

When we look at the way our minds sometimes think, we have to laugh. Here we are, people who sincerely want to develop impartial love and compassion, yet our minds are stuck in the most absurd, self-centered thoughts possible. We need to have some compassion for ourselves and extend kindness and love to ourselves despite our absurd, self-centered ways of thinking.

Being patient and compassionate with ourselves makes it easier to have compassion for others despite their foibles, unrealized potential and bad choices. We see that they are hampered by their self-centeredness just as ours impedes us. But unlike us, they may not have the advantage of knowing that self-preoccupation is the source of their difficulties. We must wish ourselves and them well as each of us goes about freeing ourselves from the causes of suffering and creating the causes of happiness.

REFLECTION

"Rules of the Universe"

Try to identify some of your own "Rules of the Universe": ideas rooted in self-centeredness that interfere with your compassion for others or for yourself. Have fun with it! The idea is to increase our awareness of the ways that we set ourselves up to be judgmental, irritable and self-centered, while introducing some humor into the process. As you consider the examples above and those from your own life, allow yourself to be amused by some of the ridiculous ideas our self-centeredness produces! Compassion works much better when it is expressed with warmth, and humor is a wonderful way of warming things up.

29 : The Benefits of Cherishing Others

CHERISHING OTHERS IS a source of joy and peace. It frees our minds from the problems and pain of self-centeredness and from the regret that self-centered behavior often causes. It brings happiness to those around us, who in turn share their joy with other people. Whether we are "paying it forward" or "paying it back," kindness begets kindness and eases pain. We no longer suffer from feeling excluded because we see the "big picture" and, as a result, seeing others' kindness, we feel close to them. Everyone feels at ease and safe around those who cherish others. All the great religious and humanitarian leaders have this magnificent attitude, and it brings peace without regret in those who have it.

While we contemplate the benefits of cherishing others, we have to keep in mind the faults of self-preoccupation. This involves a process of gradual training. Our self-preoccupation has been with us for a long time, so we cannot expect it to politely bow out immediately. Rather, this process of transforming our mind needs consistent effort over a long period of time. There are no shortcuts, no pill to take or app to download, and we can't pay someone else to do it for us. However, thinking about the benefits of cherishing others and abandoning self-centeredness will encourage us to change. It will inspire us to train our minds to view difficult situations and people from a new, compassionate perspective. These changes, in turn, will increase our enthusiasm for cherishing others. It is a win–win situation!

The Benefits and Joy of Cherishing Others

Bring to mind the many benefits of cherishing others. Think of the times you felt most fulfilled and at peace. You'll likely find that these were the times you felt most connected with others, when your heart was open and caring. At these times we can just be ourselves, peacefully existing together with others. Recall that all of the conditions that make up your life are due to the efforts and kindness of other beings. Let the thought of cherishing others and wishing to repay their kindness rise up in your heart.

Contemplate how cherishing others will benefit both them and you. Experiencing your care, others will feel safe and will be able to be honest and genuine. Perceiving that you want them to be happy, they will release their drive to compete and will be more creative and cooperative. Knowing that you value them, they will consider your opinions and advice and will be able to openly share their own perspectives with you, so that you may better learn from one another. Remember the feeling of being appreciated and valued and think that you can give this gift to others. Feel the joy of being able to give this gift. As you do, consider that cherishing others also weakens the self-centeredness that is the root of so many of your problems. You will feel more connected and less sensitive and self-conscious, freeing you to cultivate your abilities and good qualities for the benefit of all.

30 : Exchanging Self and Others, and Taking and Giving

WHEN WE UNDERSTAND that self-centeredness harms others and ourselves and that cherishing others is a source of joy and happiness, we can "exchange self and others." This means that instead of thinking, "I am the most important person in the world," we think that others are the most important. With this in mind we can learn the "taking and giving" meditation, a meditation technique initially developed by Indian Buddhist sages and later popularized by Tibetan Buddhists. The "taking and giving" meditation is a powerful tool for eradicating self-centeredness and cultivating love and compassion towards all living beings equally.

In our usual self-centered way, we think that if there is happiness to be had, we'll take it, leaving all of the problems and suffering for other people. However, in the "taking and giving" meditation, we shift our attitude, taking others' suffering with compassion and giving them our resources and happiness with love. This is a radically different way to think. Specifically, we reflect on those who are suffering and recognize that our self-centeredness prevents us from helping them. We do this until we find their suffering unbearable and experience strong compassion, wishing them to be free from misery. We then reflect on how wonderful it would be if they had happiness and its causes. With love, we mentally offer them our resources and happiness, imagining they experience the joy they desire.

The rationale behind the "taking and giving" meditation is the opposite of our usual self-centeredness in which we seek benefit and happiness for ourselves and relegate others' suffering and happiness to second place—or ignore them completely. Since self-centeredness causes much of our suffering, it is appropriate and desirable to eradicate it, and since all our happiness is due to the kindness of others, it is suitable and beneficial to cultivate the attitude that cherishes others as much as we care about ourselves.

Each time we do this meditation, we can choose a different type of suffering or a different person (or group of people) to focus on. In this way, our compassion will expand to include a wide variety of living beings and their diverse types of misery. You may be concerned that if you visualize taking on others' sufferings, you may actually experience it. However, since this practice is done in the realm of the imagination and is motivated by compassion and love, this will not happen. If anything, it will create a sense of spaciousness and joy in our hearts, and a feeling of relief knowing that mentally we can give others support and love while simultaneously ridding ourselves of our self-centeredness.

Imagine you are walking home after enjoying a nice pizza, carrying your leftover slices to have for lunch tomorrow. You come across a child in the street, dirty and crying. Asking her what is wrong, she says through the tears, "I'm hungry. Mom is working and we don't have any place to live." What do you feel? You may find that her suffering moves you, and compassion arises spontaneously within you. Perhaps you think, "If I could take her hunger and loneliness away and experience it myself, I would do that." Touched by her suffering, you give her the pizza without a second thought. Her joy in receiving the pizza is all the thanks you need.

The description below is brief but it is sufficient for you to

begin this practice. If you would like a more detailed explanation, please read Chapter 11 of *Transforming Adversity into Joy
and Courage* by Geshe Jampa Tegchok.[1]

REFLECTION

Taking and Giving

Observe your breath for a few minutes and let your mind
settle. Because our own suffering is most potent for us, we
begin to loosen the grasp of self-centeredness by taking
on our own future suffering. While we are still concerned
here with ourselves, it is ourselves in the future. Thinking
in this way is a beginning step in that instead of our usual
focus on our own happiness in the present, we now think
years in advance of the person we will become. The elderly person we will become is sufficiently "other" than
our present self that taking on his or her suffering and
giving him or her our present resources entails reducing
our present self-centeredness.

- Locate the feeling of self-centeredness at the center
  of your chest (your "heart center'), and give it a form,
  such as a hard lump.
- Imagine your future self when you are very old. Reflect on the types of suffering you are likely to experience then: the general sufferings of aging, sickness,
  fear of death and everything they entail, as well as the
  various disappointments and frustrations when things
  don't go well. Generate compassion for your future self,
  wishing that person to be free of all difficulties. Think,
  "I'm willing to take on her suffering so that she doesn't
  have to experience it. Imagine this suffering comes out
  of your future self in the form of pollution, so that

now your future self is free from it. With compassion, breathe in that misery, in the form of pollution. As you do so, imagine the pollution transforms into a lightning bolt that strikes the solid lump of self-centeredness at your heart. The lump of self-centeredness is totally demolished due to the force of your compassion for your future self.

- Now, experience a feeling of openness at your heart—the absence of painful self-centeredness. Stay in that open space, free of self-preoccupation for as long as you can.

- Within that open space at your heart, imagine a bright light appearing. That light is your love. It radiates to your future self, filling your future self's body and giving you whatever you need to be satisfied and live a meaningful life in the future. This may be material objects or people, and it may also include inner qualities that will be essential for you to face the challenges ahead. You may even imagine freely giving your present body, wealth and virtue to your future self by transforming it into whatever your future self will need. Your future self receives this, and he or she feels fulfilled, secure and at peace. Rest for a moment and experience the satisfaction that comes from alleviating someone's suffering and giving her joy.

- Next, visualize a friend that you are fond of. Think of the unhappiness or misery he may be experiencing and cultivate compassion, wishing him to be released from it. Resolve to take on his suffering yourself so that he will be free of it. Do the same visualization as before, your friend's suffering leaving him in the form of pollution that you inhale. The pollution transforms into a lightning bolt that strikes the lump of self-preoccupation in your heart. Feel the joy that comes from knowing your friend is free from suffering and the relief that you are free from your self-preoccupation. Then imagine sending a bright light of love to your friend and transforming your body, possessions and virtues into whatever he needs and giving these to him. He receives these and experiences true happiness and satisfaction. In turn, you experience joy at his happiness.

- Now do the same visualization for a stranger. It might be the person at the checkout in the grocery store, a wealthy person, a homeless person, a person in a war-torn country, someone suffering from cancer or the health-care professionals that care for him. It could be an animal that is mistreated or exploited. Do the visualization as before, taking on their suffering with compassion, destroying the lump of your self-centeredness at your heart center, transforming your body, wealth and virtue into whatever they need and giving it to them with love. Rest in the deep satisfaction that comes from overcoming self-preoccupation and being of benefit to others.

- Continue, doing the same visualization with people you don't like and, finally, with all living beings. Rejoice in the happiness that you have given them and in the relief that you experience from having loosened the hold of your self-absorption. Be pleased that you have awakened this new state of mind. Aspire to cultivate this compassionate wish to help all beings in every way you possibly can.

This practice is especially good to do when you are unhappy or ill. Instead of feeling sorry for ourselves, which only exacerbates our misery, we focus on those who have similar problems and generate compassion for them, thinking, "I am experiencing sickness or unhappiness and it isn't going to go away immediately. Since this is the case, by my being uncomfortable may all other beings be free from suffering. That is, may I take on the misery of others so that they may be free from it." Thinking like this gives purpose to our suffering in that it reinforces our feeling of connection to others and strengthens our compassion. It reminds us of all the other people who are in the same boat as us and puts our own difficulties into perspective so we don't make a mountain out of a molehill. It lightens our mood because we imagine others being well and happy. In addition, when we later encounter situations in which others need help, compassion will easily arise in our minds and we will not hesitate to help. If we do this practice sincerely wishing others to be free from suffering, it amazingly has the effect of lessening our own suffering.

Sometimes we wish we could do something to help others but we don't know what to do, because they live in another country and we don't know how to reach them. In other instances, we know the person but they are not open to whatever help we want to offer. Doing the "taking and giving" meditation keeps our heart open towards them, and deepens our love and compassion. Similarly, this meditation is excellent to do while watching the news. Instead of becoming despondent or cynical because of what is happening in the world, do this meditation. Awakening your love and compassion in this way is a powerful contribution to world peace, and it also counteracts any tendency to feel despair.

Throughout the process of purposely cultivating compassion and later acting with compassion, humility is crucial. Truly compassionate people who are respected in society do not boast about their compassion or their generosity. With a genuine feeling of sisterhood and brotherhood, they go about their lives and remain modest. Try to follow their excellent example.

31 : Self-Compassion and Compassionate Self-Correction

Ψ WE'VE MENTIONED THAT WHILE compassion is often thought of in relation to others, it can also be
directed towards the self. Since our goal is to direct
love and compassion to all beings, we need to recognize that
we are included in this, and direct these positive emotions
to ourselves as well. While we're no more deserving of compassion than other beings, we're certainly no less deserving
either. A compassionate perspective is based on the fundamental assumption that *all* beings are worthy of compassion
and kindness.

The more we are self-compassionate and willing to address
the sources of our own suffering, the better prepared we'll
be to direct compassion towards others. Self-compassion helps
us work with obstacles in our own minds that can get in the
way of our compassion for others, such as disturbing emotions
and troublesome habits. If we're truly going to be effective in
manifesting compassion for others, we have to have some for
ourselves as well.

Western psychologists have given specific attention to
self-compassion because of how pervasive shame and self-
criticism are in the West, particularly in people entering psychotherapy. People suffering from crippling levels of depression
and anxiety often have very powerful internal self-critics.[1]
They spend a lot of time attacking themselves with their

thoughts: "I'm disgusting." "I'm unworthy of love." "I'm hopeless, and can't do anything right." These folks say cruel things to themselves that they would never say to other people, and can find it extremely difficult to relate to themselves in warm and compassionate ways. While we may not all have this level of self-loathing, many of us can be surprisingly resistant to the idea of letting go of our self-criticism and replacing it with a warm, compassionate internal voice. We may think that without the constant torrent of self-criticism we'll be self-indulgent, failing to hold ourselves accountable for our behavior and not trying to improve ourselves.

While self-criticism isn't very effective in helping us take responsibility for our lives and improve ourselves, compassion is. Self-compassion isn't about talking to ourselves in a sweet voice that endorses whatever it is we feel like doing in the moment. Rather, our compassionate internal voice helps us take responsibility for our behavior and coaches us to improve, but does so in a warm, encouraging manner that recognizes the suffering and challenges we face. In short, self-compassion resembles compassion for others, but it involves the ways we relate to ourselves, and the emotional tone we take in doing so.

Some may fear that developing self-compassion will make them self-centered. We don't need to worry about that. Self-compassion is linked to how we deal with challenges and relate to our own failings and imperfections—with acceptance and warmth rather than harsh self-shaming. In this light, developing compassion for ourselves may help *reduce* our tendency to be self-centered by helping us overcome the shame, obsessive self-criticism and self-hatred that keep us trapped in an endless cycle of self-evaluation.

One research study comparing self-compassion and self-esteem found that self-compassion was more strongly related to happiness than was self-esteem. These researchers also found that if the influence of self-compassion was removed, self-esteem no longer predicted happiness at all.[2] In contrast, when the effects of self-esteem were removed, self-compassion was still connected to happiness. Relating to our struggles with warmth and understanding seems even more powerfully related to our emotional health than does positive self-regard. It's important to have confidence in our own strengths and successes, but this study suggests it may be even more important to refrain from kicking ourselves when we're down.

Psychologist Kristin Neff conceptualizes self-compassion as involving three components:[3]

- *Kindness*: relating to the self with kindness and understanding, rather than with harsh self-criticism or judgment.
- *Common humanity*: viewing our experiences, particularly the challenges and struggles, as part of the common human experience rather than as separating and isolating us.
- *Mindfulness*: holding painful thoughts and difficult emotions in kind, nonjudgmental awareness, rather than identifying with them.

Like Buddhist mind-training practices, Neff's approach to self-compassion emphasizes reducing certain habits and cultivating others. Specifically, we want to decrease tendencies to self-criticize, to feel isolated when we observe ourselves struggling or suffering, and to identify with negative emotions, as mirrored in statements such as "I *am* afraid," which reflect the tendency to accept this emotional state as "who I am" in the moment. Instead, we want to learn to relate to ourselves with acceptance, kindness and understanding, calmly observing our struggles and difficult emotions as a part of the human experience that unites us with all other beings.

Another approach to self-compassion was developed by Professor Paul Gilbert, an evolutionary psychologist who spent a good deal of time early in his career studying shame and its relationship to depression. Professor Gilbert developed Compassion Focused Therapy (CFT),[4] which is based in an evolutionary understanding of human emotions and how they play out within our minds and brains. You've already learned about a few CFT concepts (for example, the three types of emotion outlined in entry 12), because I (Russell) take a CFT approach in my own work, and it has influenced my understanding of compassion. Gilbert's model is based on the idea that we, along with every other human being on the planet, have tricky, evolved brains that can influence us to feel powerful and challenging emotions when they are activated by different experiences. These emotions can then organize our minds in ways that can lead to problems for us by shaping the ways we think, pay attention and are motivated to behave, in the manner we discussed in entry 10. This insight allows us to understand our challenging emotions as simply a part of who we are, not as an indication that there is anything wrong with us.

Self-compassion doesn't mean we fail to hold ourselves responsible for our actions or fail to correct ourselves when we've made mistakes. Our brains may have evolved in such a way that they tend to produce certain emotions in certain situations (for example, fear or anger when we perceive a threat), but from the moment these emotions arise, we have the opportunity to work with them. Over time, through mind training, we can even help ourselves learn to respond differently to such situations, for example, with compassion rather than irritation when someone is hostile to us. Remember the "paths in the forest" example from entry 19—over time, we can gradually train our brains to respond differently—gradually helping them shift from a very threat-driven mode to a more compassionate mode.

One part of self-compassion is learning to respond with compassion rather than irritation or harsh self-attacks when we observe our own mistakes or weaknesses. Compassion Focused Therapy makes the distinction between shameful self-attacking and compassionate self-correction.[5] In shameful self-attacking, our internal voice is like a harsh and critical judge. Focused on disappointments, deficits and mistakes, shameful self-attacking relates to the self with anger, frustration, anxiety and contempt. It keeps us stuck in the past, obsessing over our failings and feeling threatened. In contrast, compassionate self-correction is like a compassionate friend—forward-looking and focused on the desire to improve and be at our best. With compassionate self-correction, we encourage ourselves when we're struggling: "This is hard, but I've done difficult things before. Keep going!" The focus here is on building our strengths and cultivating abilities like compassion that will help us continually improve ourselves so that we can do better in the future.

REFLECTION

Compassionate Self-Correction

Consider your internal voice. When you observe yourself making mistakes or struggling with difficulties, how do you talk to yourself? Do you attack yourself with harsh, shaming criticism, or assuage yourself with understanding, acceptance, warmth and encouragement? Think of activities that you would like to do but are difficult or that you initially resist doing—perhaps exercising regularly, changing your eating or drinking habits, or starting a regular meditation practice. Instead of berating yourself for not doing these activities, be kind to yourself. Wish yourself well and, with self-respect, encourage yourself to go in a healthy direction.

32 : Working with Judgment and Partiality

Ψ IT CAN BE SHOCKING to recognize how biased we can be. We assign labels at lightning speed: "friend," "enemy," "smart," "idiot." Once applied, these labels stick in our minds, shaping our future interactions with other people. When we notice we're doing this, rather than assigning *more* labels by shaming ourselves—"I'm so judgmental and short-sighted!"—we can consider why this happens and what we can do about it.

From an evolutionary perspective, there are good reasons for quickly assigning the labels "friend" or "foe," "safe" or "threat." For millions of years our ancestors lived in a world where their survival often depended upon their ability to quickly identify and respond to threats, and their brains evolved to help them cope with such an environment—to fight when they needed to fight, to flee when they needed to flee, and to band together for protection.

Assigning labels and putting people in categories happens very quickly, frequently occurring without our being consciously aware that we're doing it. Often, we don't thoughtfully consider someone's background and characteristics before deciding how we feel about them. Instead, we just find ourselves reacting emotionally to their presence with attraction, aversion, wariness or trust. Once applied, these labels are very powerful—shaping how we feel about people, how we interpret their behavior and how we treat them.

To complicate this, our initial labeling process often has a lot more to do with our own histories than it does with the person who's being labeled. Because our evolved brains work in this "better safe than sorry" sort of way, they are always storing information about "threats" which will help us to be even more efficient in detecting them in the future. So if we've had nasty experiences with a person who has a certain characteristic—say, political affiliation, religion, age, gender or race—we will tend to associate those characteristics with the nasty experiences. This is tricky, because later, we can find ourselves re-experiencing the negative emotions we felt during those experiences when we encounter others who happen to share that same characteristic. This can be particularly powerful when we've had very few *positive* experiences with people who have those characteristics. The next time we encounter someone like that, our brains automatically bring up the negative emotion we've learned to associate with the characteristic they share, and we experience that we don't like them. In this way, we can end up having negative reactions to others who, without our awareness (or theirs!), innocently trigger previously learned emotional responses in us that have nothing to do with this person we're interacting with *right now*. You may have had an experience like this—meeting someone and immediately liking or not liking her, even though you don't know anything about her. Or perhaps you've found yourself having a great conversation with someone until you discover they are of this political persuasion or that religion, and immediately their stock falls in your mind.

This is why we want to make sure to create many more positive interactions than negative interactions with others—

because the emotional tone of our previous interactions with them will shape how we feel about them in the present. If we've a history of many negative interactions with someone and few positive ones, we can find ourselves experiencing negative emotions that are prompted by their very presence, regardless of their current behavior or intentions. I (Russell) have worked with a number of couples and parents who have had this play out in their relationships with their partners and children, and it can be tricky business.

This is a natural process that plays out in our brains—it's simply how they work in their attempts to help us create an understanding of reality. When faced with a situation, our minds automatically draw upon our previous experience, reflected in previously formed connections between patterns of cells in the brain. It's the brain's attempt to help us efficiently make sense of what is happening, so we don't constantly have to relearn everything. When new information comes in through our senses, it activates brain patterns associated with that previous learning. The librarian of our brains goes about collecting previously stored information that seems relevant to the situation at hand, piecing it together into an experience of "reality." The new information coming in and the old information we've stored in the past are woven together to create an experience of the present. Often, we're not conscious of this process at all. We just find ourselves in the situation, feeling a certain way about it, having certain thoughts, but unaware that these feelings and thoughts are echoes of previous conditioning experiences that may have little to do with what is happening *right now*.

Once we've unconsciously attached an emotional label to another person or someone they resemble, it will tend to bias how we experience them in the future. So if we like someone, we're more likely to see their positive qualities and ignore or not even notice their negative qualities. If we've labeled someone as a threat or an enemy, we'll be biased in the opposite way. Since we are caught in this difficult process, we can have compassion for ourselves when these biased emotions arise in us, even as we work to identify and change them. This can also help us feel compassion for those who are being hostile towards us, knowing their reactions may have little to do with us, and much to do with their previous conditioning.

But compassion isn't about making excuses. Fortunately, we don't have to be controlled by our emotions. Now that we're aware of how they work, we can prepare ourselves and plan for how we *want* to react.

When we experience a lack of compassion towards someone, it is often because we've attached a label to him, with a corresponding emotion in tow. Seeing someone as "that idiot that sabotaged my plans," we feel anger towards him. In such cases, our attention is focused on a very small sample of the other person's characteristics, like the quirky thing they do that irritates us. We may be completely unaware of this person as a complex being like us with many other aspects to his or her life. Reducing other people to a caricature, we make them into simply someone to hate. The danger in doing this is evident: it makes it much easier for us to behave harmfully or harbor grudges towards a person when we fail to recognize her or his essential humanity. We need to find a way to see others as they really are—as complex, multifaceted beings who, just like us, want to be happy and to not suffer.

REFLECTION

Compassionate Understanding of Others

Bring to mind an image of someone for whom you'd like to cultivate compassion. This can be someone to whom you feel close, someone you don't know very well or someone you don't like or toward whom you feel other powerful emotions.

- Picturing this person in your mind, remind yourself that, just like you, she or he just wants to be happy and not suffer.
- Allow yourself to be aware that he or she has a life that extends far beyond your experience of them—a story that runs just as deep as yours, filled with hopes, dreams, fears and struggles.
- Picture them going through their life cycle:

  - As a newborn, born into a confusing world they don't understand.
  - As a toddler, learning to move about the world on their own.
  - As a child, making friends, experiencing rejection, entering school.
  - As an adolescent, struggling to define themselves.
  - As a young adult, striving to make their place in the world.
  - Moving through adulthood, establishing priorities, settling into a rhythm of life, experiencing successes and upheavals, and moving on.
  - As an elder, observing their physical strength beginning to fade even as their wisdom grows.
  - On their deathbed, looking back on their life, and closing their eyes.

At each of these points, imagine what this person might have faced and felt—the excitement of exploration and success, the pain of rejection and falling short. Perhaps loved ones surround them; perhaps they are alone. Imagine his or her life—filled with aspirations and experiences, successes and regrets. Imagine this beautiful person who, just like you, only wants to be happy and not suffer. Allow yourself to be filled with the kind wish that he or she may have a life filled with happiness and peace, that her or his life may be free from suffering and its causes.

33 : Compassion and Empathy

Ψ EMPATHY IS A CORE COMPONENT of compassion—both in being able to feel compassion and in acting skilfully upon our compassionate intentions. Empathy enables us to understand what another person is feeling and to know what actions are most likely to be helpful in specific situations. Without empathy, our efforts to act with compassion will likely be doomed to fail, because without *understanding* the experiences of others, it is almost impossible to give them what they need.

Rebecca, a client of mine (Russell's), discussed having this experience with her mother: "I know she cared for me, but she didn't seem to have a clue about what I needed or wanted. On birthdays, she'd make a big show of taking me to an amusement park or noisy restaurant—things she liked and wished she'd been able to do when growing up. She didn't consider that I hated those things and that I'd have preferred a quiet outing with a few close friends. I can't count the times she handed me money when I needed a hug." Rebecca's mother tried very hard to care for her, but because she wasn't good at empathy, she couldn't understand what Rebecca needed and so she couldn't be there for Rebecca in ways that would have been really helpful to her.

Compassion isn't just about good intentions—if we are to

skilfully act on our kind motivation, we must make the effort to understand the feelings and experiences of others and to accept them as valid. Then, we'll know what they really need and will be better equipped to provide it.

Empathy requires us to be emotionally attuned to another person and to use our reasoning, to consider the nuances of their experience. With empathic understanding, we seek to grasp both *what this person is feeling* and *the validity of their emotional experience*—how it makes sense that they might feel and behave in this way. Our mirror neurons—cells in our brain that lead us to feel a bit of what others we are in contact with are feeling—help with this by giving us a taste of the other person's emotional experience. However, we don't want to get caught up in our own emotional reactions to what they are going through, but to use this taste as a clue as to what the other person may be feeling. With empathy, our focus is on developing an understanding of the other person's emotional experience and then checking out our understanding with them to make sure we're on the right track. Again, the focus is on *their* experience.

Here are some tips for developing empathic understanding:

- Pay attention to the other person's nonverbal behavior. What does their facial expression, tone of voice and how they move or position their bodies tell us about how they might be feeling?
- Consider how you might feel (or have felt) in similar situations.
- Consider that this person is different from you in many ways. How might their experience differ from your own?
- If you're wondering how others are feeling, consider

asking them! Often the simple comment, "I'm wondering how you are feeling about all of this," will lead others to tell us *exactly* how they feel. Spoken kindly, it also communicates compassion—that we *care* about how they feel.

- Check out your understanding to make sure you've got it right. Remember, the other person is the expert of her or his own experience, and it is never our place to tell someone else what he or she is (or should be) feeling. "It seems like you're feeling frustrated about this situation. Is that right?"

As a therapist, I (Russell) almost never say the phrase "I understand" to my clients, and I train my students to avoid using it as well. Why? This phrase sets others up to think, "You don't understand at all. How could you? You're not me, and you haven't been through what I've been through." And they'd be right! Instead, my goal is to make my best *attempt* to understand their experience, and then to *demonstrate* my understanding by checking it out with them and responding helpfully and appropriately in our interactions. When it comes to understanding the emotions of others, it can be better to show them than to tell them.

Knowing that emotions can be very powerful in organizing our mental experience and motivating our behavior, empathic understanding offers us a gateway to compassion. Once we understand the factors that led to them, behaviors we previously might have thought were crazy, nasty or irritating can suddenly make a whole lot of sense, and we can find our judgments melting away, replaced by compassion.

During a group therapy session I (Russell) was facilitating at an in-patient adolescent psychiatric treatment center, the teenagers were discussing how things had been going over the last week. One of the group members spoke about another resident, Gregor (not a member of the group), who was from another country, had a heavy accent and hadn't formed many friendships with other kids since he'd been admitted. The discussion focused on Gregor getting in trouble for digging through garbage bins in the facility's dining hall, removing food and stashing it in his room. As the discussion began, the teenagers were laughing and making fun of him for his "gross" behavior, which seemed bizarre to them. As the gossip continued, another group member, Mark, spoke up, "I think it's gross, too. It bothered me so much that I talked to him: "Man, why you digging food out of the trash? That's nasty!" You know what he said? Where he came from, there wasn't hardly any food. His family would go days without having no food to eat!"

Immediately, the mood in the group shifted. The room quietened as ridicule was replaced with empathy and compassion, as the harsh reality of Gregor's life sank in. "I've had to go hungry sometimes. It was terrible." "I didn't know that. Poor guy." Mark continued, "It's like he's always scared that he won't have food to eat, so he hides it. He even gets mad at himself—says he knows it's not true, but he's still scared. It's like he can't help it."

Feeling pleased and moved by their compassion, I sat back and watched as this group of adolescents—all of who had experienced very difficult lives themselves—decided as a group to stop making fun of Gregor and to reach out to him in friendship. This is the power of empathy to create compassion. Once they learned about and understood Gregor's fears, compassion arose within them, and they immediately acted upon it by stopping their ridicule and by committing to treat him with kindness.

REFLECTION

Empathy

Recall a time when you were judgmental towards another person. Think about what they were saying or doing that disturbed you so much and consider: what might they have been feeling that could have led to them to act or speak in that way? If you know even a little about that person's life, consider what they may have experienced and how that might have affected them. Think about how you would have felt in that situation, and let your heart open in empathy, releasing the rigid judgment and replacing it with compassion.

Make an effort to practice empathy during your daily life. As you go through the day, interacting with other people, pause and consider their emotional experience. "What might this person be feeling?" Using the suggestions described above, try to develop an understanding of what others might be feeling and practice "checking out" your understanding with them.

34 : Compassionate Thinking and Mentalizing

Ψ IF WE'RE COMMITTED to deepening our compassion over time, we'll want to pay attention to our thoughts. As we've discussed before, we all have lots of different thoughts as we go through life: happy thoughts, sad thoughts, kind thoughts, cruel thoughts, jealous thoughts and loving thoughts. It's best to avoid getting upset and shaming ourselves for having these thoughts. At the same time, we know that repeatedly engaging in certain types of thinking creates the habit to think that way in the future, as we're wearing in the mental patterns associated with these types of thinking. To develop compassion, we want to choose and nurture the sort of thoughts we wish to have in the future and redirect ourselves when we find we're thinking in ways we don't want to cultivate. This is similar to tending plants we wish to grow in our garden and plucking out the weeds.

One way to understand compassionate thinking is to contrast it with threat-based thinking—the sort of thinking that focuses our minds on ourselves and how best to keep us comfortable in any given moment. Where self-protective threat-based thinking sees suffering and attempts to limit our exposure to it by labelling or avoiding it—for example, by explaining it away or blaming it on the person who is suffering—compassionate thinking considers the other person and seeks to figure out what's really going on in the situation. Compassionate thinking often takes the form of asking questions: "What is going on here?" "What are the causes and conditions that produce this suffering?" "How does it *make sense* that this person is feeling or acting in this way?" While threat-based thinking *judges and blames*, compassionate wisdom seeks to *understand* suffering—what is happening, why it is happening and what can be done to help.

Whereas threat-based thinking is narrow, biased and tightly focused, compassionate thinking is broad and flexible. We are able to consider and understand the situation from different perspectives. Compassionate thinking can move back and forth between empathizing and problem-solving, between directing warmth and acceptance to those who are suffering and seeking pragmatic solutions to address the causes and conditions that create and maintain that suffering.

Some may classify these types of thinking in stereotyped, gender-based, either-or sorts of ways—"Women empathize. Men problem-solve and give advice." Compassionate thinking goes beyond these narrow stereotypes. Compassionate thinking involves both understanding and action: it balances warm, kind understanding with the need to actively address sources of suffering. Thinking with compassion means being able to discern when swift, assertive action is needed, and when it is best to let a situation work itself out without external interference.

Threat-based thinking, whether it is defensive or competitive in nature, directs hostility towards others and the self. In doing so, it keeps us feeling threatened, fueling negative emotions and causing us to engage in even *more* threat-related thoughts and imagery. On the contrary, compassionate thinking is kind, warm and gently encouraging. It's focused on building connections between people and can recognize and validate different perspectives. Whereas threat-based thinking focuses on proving ourselves right to avoid feeling vulnerable or embarrassed, compassionate thinking seeks to understand the wisdom that lies behind others' perspectives. Compassionate wisdom recognizes that appreciating diversity and differences doesn't threaten our own convictions, and when it seems to, maybe it's because our convictions could use some re-examination. In other words, compassion is like a cool jug of water quenching the fire of negativity.

We see this in the way the Dalai Lama discusses religion. We might expect that as a spiritual leader he would try to promote his religion and elevate it above other religions. However, he avoids doing this, knowing that to do so would alienate many people, and his goal is to contribute to the spiritual well-being of *all beings*. In fact, recognizing and respecting that different people are more or less suited to different spiritual approaches, he discourages Buddhists from proselytizing. Instead, he encourages people to follow the path that works best for them in building happy lives, and balances giving very scholarly Buddhist teachings to appropriate audiences with doing public talks and writing books that speak directly to topics of concern to people of all faiths and none. He similarly speaks of science in an open-minded way, even going so far as to say that if science disproves some aspect of Buddhism, Buddhism must change. This is the perspective of compassionate thinking—moved by suffering and the desire to address it, we seek to understand and help, to grow and improve—even when it may mean being vulnerable and even when it means we may need to change. In embracing compassion, we need to surrender our desire to prove ourselves right.

When working to address the psychological sources of suffering in others or ourselves, compassionate thinking can take the form of *mentalizing*.[1] Mentalizing involves considering the mental causes that are at the heart of our and others' behavior. We inadvertently bring much of our suffering on ourselves by engaging in the very actions that lead to our own suffering. As we've discussed, when we see ourselves or other people doing this, we can easily become critical, blaming or shaming. In contrast, with mentalizing, we consider that our actions have causes that originate in our minds, based in our perceptions, interpretations, motives, desires, needs, beliefs and previous experiences. As with other forms of compassionate thinking, mentalizing often takes the form of asking questions: "What might be going on in this person's mind that influences them to act in this way?" "What need is this person trying to meet?" "What does their behavior tell me about how they may be perceiving or interpreting this situation?" Often, when we are able to slow down, stop the negative labeling and understand what is going on in another person's mind, their behavior makes sense, even if we don't agree with their approach.

Mentalizing can be a gateway to compassion. When we see that hostile racism, sexism or political hatred are based on misperceptions—for example, that people different from oneself will "take away all of the jobs for people like me"—we can understand that this hostility is based on fear and insecurity. We'll know that to overcome it, we need to find a way to help this person feel safe. Rather than labeling this person as a "selfish idiot," we can see that he or she is suffering and recognize that when the suffering is addressed, the hatred will abate. In short, once we understand what is going on in another person's mind that is creating their suffering, we're better equipped to help them.

We can also apply mentalizing to ourselves. Observing that we're doing something that is creating problems in our lives, we can look more closely at it: "How am I interpreting this situation?" "What need or desire is being served by this behavior?" "Is this thinking driven by a perception of threat?" Once we understand the mental causes behind our actions, we can ask ourselves: "How could I work to address this need in a way that is more productive?" "What resources can I access that will help me with this?" "Is this belief of mine really true?"

REFLECTION

Mentalizing

In this exercise, we'll use compassionate thinking to consider the mental causes that may be behind another person's emotions and behavior. Bring to mind a person who you'd like to understand better. Consider a situation in which you've observed them struggling. Ask questions to help you better understand their perspective:

- How are they making sense of this situation?
- What needs are they trying to meet with this behavior?
- Do they perceive a threat? If so, what sort (physical harm, being rejected by others, threats to status, reputation or material comfort)?
- How might their previous conditioning/background be impacting them?

Once you've done this, engage in compassionate thinking about what could be helpful to them:

- What would help them to feel safe?
- How can I best help them to meet their needs and develop their own strengths?

35 : The Four Immeasurables

BASED ON THE BUDDHA'S TEACHINGS, the Four Immeasurables—love, compassion, empathic joy and equanimity—present a way to relate to other living beings that is healthy and brings happiness. These four qualities are called "immeasurable" because ideally we cultivate them towards all the immeasurable number of living beings, and we cultivate them to an immeasurable or unbounded extent. Love wishes living beings to have happiness and its causes; compassion wishes them to be free from suffering and its causes; empathic joy delights at the happiness and good fortune of others; equanimity is a balanced mind, free from bias and personal distress. All four are based on a deep understanding in our hearts that everyone wants happiness, does not want suffering, and is worthy of having happiness and freedom from suffering. As mentioned before, we generate this understanding by reflecting on it repeatedly, in relation to each and every living being we encounter.

Based on that understanding, *love,* or *loving-kindness,* is the attitude we cultivate as our general way of relating to people. Whenever we meet, see or greet someone, we are friendly and wish her well. This doesn't mean we become everyone's best friend, but that our heart is open and has a positive attitude when we encounter others. This is very different from being in a grumpy mood and seeing everyone as a pest who is in our way. When we're grouchy, we can remember the kindness of others and how our lives depend on them, and then release the grouchiness in favor of loving-kindness.

When we encounter people who are suffering, our response is *compassion*, wishing them to be free from whatever physical or mental pain they are experiencing, from a small annoyance to extreme agony. Compassion enables us to look at suffering in all its forms without falling into despair and without being limited by our own personal distress. It also enables us to respond in an effort to alleviate it. An active response is a hands-on approach, where we actively engage in helping or in donating the resources enabling someone else to help. The "taking and giving" meditation is an indirect response, whereby our heart is open and engaged although we are not able to actively do a specific task to help the other person at that time.

When seeing others experience good fortune or engage in virtuous activities, *empathic joy* is our response. Instead of making ourselves miserable by being jealous of another's success, we open our heart and share their happiness with them. By rejoicing in others' good qualities and successes, empathic joy enables us to see goodness in the world. It also makes our mind receptive to generating the good qualities we rejoice in seeing in others.

Equanimity (impartial, open-hearted concern for all beings) is our response in two situations. One is when the other person is doing well and doesn't need our help. Here we refrain from interfering in others' lives by giving advice that is both unasked for and unnecessary because they are already doing well. In other words, giving people credit for their ability to manage their own affairs, we calm our "need to be needed" and let others be.

The second situation in which equanimity is the desired

response is when someone is facing difficulties, we try to help, but they do not accept our aid. In this case, rather than chiding the other person or pushing them to do something that they are clearly resistant to doing, we step aside. For example, if our elderly parents want to remain at home when we think they would be safer at an assisted living facility, we need to realize that they are willing to risk taking a fall in return for the benefit of living in the familiar, comfortable and comforting environment of their home. We have to honor their priorities and decisions.

A similar situation may happen with parents whose children are young adults. As parents your responsibility was to care for your children and teach them life skills, including how to manage different situations, to remain safe and to make good decisions. However, when they are older they do not need so much direct care and often resent their parents' well-meant advice, which they perceive as meddling in their life and restricting their autonomy. At these times, parents need to recognize that they cannot control their children's behavior to make sure they are always safe, but must trust their children to make good decisions based on what they as parents taught them when they were younger. If the young adults make bad decisions, parents need to accept that sometimes their children will learn only by making mistakes, the same way they learned from their own errors. Similarly, when a friend doesn't seem to learn from their mistakes, we also need to maintain equanimity, knowing that people create their own experiences through their actions and decisions and that we cannot control them. Our task at that time is to have a peaceful heart, free from guilt or self-blame, and to be open to help the other person should they request help in the future.

Each of the Four Immeasurables has a "close enemy," which appears to be that quality but is a distortion of it, and a "far enemy," which is its opposite and needs to be counteracted.

The close enemy of love is clinging attachment or possessive love for another person. This emotion appears to be love in that it is attracted to another person, but clinging and self-centeredness corrupt it. We remedy this by reflecting that it is our mind that has exaggerated that person's good qualities or projected good qualities that aren't there and then clung to this person, mistakenly thinking that they are the objective source of our happiness. Ill will and hatred are the far enemies of love and are counteracted by cultivating patience and fortitude and by wishing others to have happiness and its causes.

Personal distress and exaggerated grief are the close enemies of compassion. We may mistakenly believe that unless we are overwhelmed with grief or despair when witnessing another's suffering, we don't really care for or have compassion for them. It is neither necessary nor beneficial to become personally distressed when witnessing others' suffering because such feelings interfere with our ability to reach out and help them. Instead we need to cultivate genuine compassion that is focused on the others' suffering. Cruelty, the wish to inflict suffering on others, is the far enemy of compassion. The antidote to it is compassion itself, and the determination to release our resentment, grudges and desire for revenge.

The close enemy of empathic joy is giddiness and excitement, a mind that is too "high" and full of unrealistic expectations when seeing others' success. We free ourselves from this by calming our minds using the reflection Mindful Checking In (see entry 9). Jealousy and boredom are the distant enemies of empathetic joy. Jealousy destroys our internal well-being by making us unable to bear the happiness of others. It also motivates us to act in ways that destroy others' happiness, which, in turn, we usually feel terrible about doing afterwards. For example, we may be jealous that our friend can afford a new car and hope that it gets dented or breaks down. The antidote to jealousy is rejoicing in others' success and good qualities. After all, we often say, "May all beings have happiness and its causes," and here someone has those and we didn't have to lift a finger to make it happen. So why not rejoice? Boredom is a withdrawn mind that doesn't care enough to rejoice at what is good and worthwhile. We can remedy it by getting some exercise and by thinking about things that interest us.

Indifference, apathy and uncaring are the close enemies of equanimity. We have to be especially careful not to slide into these by misunderstanding the meaning of equanimity and closing our heart. Equanimity is open-hearted care and concern felt equally towards all beings, without being biased towards one person and against another. Attachment, anger and partiality are the far enemies of equanimity. The way to cultivate equanimity was described in entry 22.

By consciously cultivating the Four Immeasurables, we will respond to others more gently and more realistically. Love, compassion, empathic joy and equanimity will enable us to have better relationships with others. You may wish to remind yourself of these four immeasurable qualities by reciting in the morning—and at any other time you wish—the following verse:

May all sentient beings have happiness and its causes. (love)

May all sentient beings be free of suffering and its causes. (compassion)

May all sentient beings not be separated from sorrowless bliss. (empathic joy)

May all sentient beings abide in equanimity, free of bias, attachment, and anger. (equanimity)

REFLECTION

The Four Immeasurables

- Slowly reflect on each of the Four Immeasurables, one by one. At the end of each of these four reflections, let your mind rest in the feelings of love, compassion, empathic joy and equanimity.
- Contemplate specific relationships or situations in your life where having one of these four in your mind would be especially helpful. Imagine having that quality when you relate to that individual or are in that situation.
- Consider the close enemies to each of the four and notice if you have the tendency to slide into any of them. If so, remind yourself of the meaning of each quality.

36 : The Importance of Regular Practice

Ψ A NUMBER OF TIMES, we have mentioned the importance of making time each day for practice—time to reconnect with your true values and to build a sense of meaning in your life. It's important to shift out of the hustle and bustle mode of "getting things done" and create space in our lives to connect with our own experience and priorities. Even if we welcome our work, family and leisure activities and find them rewarding, it can be easy to drift away from our core values and again begin to move through life like we're checking items off our list. This can create stress, exhaustion and a gradual erosion of our sense of purpose and compassion—over time, we can find ourselves grumbling and feeling resentful of all we have to do. When this happens, our experience is telling us that it's time to slow down, create some space to relax and connect with our better qualities, and to re-engage with the things that give our lives a sense of purpose and meaning. We don't have to wait until we're feeling burned out, though. Establishing practice as a regular habit can help us avoid getting overwhelmed in the first place. Whether you think of these practices as spiritual mind training or simply as taking your brain to the gym, the key is to slow down and create space in your daily life to reconnect with yourself, your values and what you ultimately want your life to be about.

It can be tempting to put off such practice because so many things seem to be demanding our attention. But if we don't make working with our minds a priority, it's unlikely we'll create lasting change. My (Russell's) son has noticed the difference in me when I keep up with my practice, and when I *don't*: "Dad, you need to go meditate so you won't be so grumpy!" It's like maintaining a healthy body. We may fend off obesity by occasionally going through phases of exercise and healthy eating, but we won't make much progress in terms of getting in shape. Waiting too long between sessions, we lose the progress we've made and we end up just spending our time making it up again.

The easiest way to establish a consistent practice routine is to allocate a time to do it every day, and to make that a part of our routine. This may be a challenge to start with, but it will become easier as your routine becomes established. For example, I do my mindfulness and compassion meditation in the mornings, for a half-hour right before breakfast (unless I'm really starving when I wake, in which case I'll eat a bit of something first!).

In doing this, it's important to consider obstacles that might get in our way. Ask yourself, "What could get in the way of me doing my regular practice?" For example, my routine requires that I get to bed at a reasonable hour. If I stay up too late, I'll be exhausted at that moment when my alarm goes off, and I'll be tempted to set it ahead thirty minutes and use my meditation time to get a little extra sleep. Going to bed on time sounds easy, but it requires a lot of discipline, as I *like* those few hours in the evening after my child is in bed. That's my free "do whatever I want" time, and I cherish it. But I know that if I make it to bed at a reasonable hour, I'll be much more likely to get up and practice—which makes all aspects of my life better.

Another potential obstacle to practice is time. Sometimes we may think there's just not enough time to practice. One way to tell if this is true is to get a daily planner that breaks the days into hourly units, and spend a week recording what you do each hour. When we actually record our activities in this way, we often find lots of time spent surfing the internet, watching television or texting. In this case, we can reallocate some of that time to create 20–30 minutes for practice.

Sometimes, it is *true* that we don't have any free time—we're just racing from one activity to the next from the moment we get up until we collapse into our beds. If this is indeed the case, we need to address it. We won't be able to sustain this pace over time and also be at our best. If we want to develop qualities like compassion, we have to make it a priority. This may mean making tough choices about what we have to eliminate to make space for our practice. That said, we suspect you've made plenty of tough choices in your life already in order to pursue things that were important to you.

In comparison to the rest of our hectic lives, our relatively quiet practice may feel "unproductive," as if nothing is getting done. This is a mistaken perception, a product of an overly busy mind—we've trained our minds to believe that being productive means being *busy*, but they are not the same thing. This busy-ness can keep us stressed out and block our compassion. Mind-training practices involve *slowing down,* and doing things such as focusing attention on our breath, creating compassionate imagery in our minds or reading materials that inspire us and deepen our understanding. This slowing-down is not laziness; it is a basic building block of compassion and sanity. Becoming friends with ourselves, cultivating compassion and generating wisdom take time and dedication. Establishing a regular practice routine is the surest way to do that.

REFLECTION

Establishing a Regular Practice

Think about how you could establish a regular schedule for your compassion practice. Considering your daily activities and anticipating obstacles that might get in the way, make up a timetable and try to follow it. If it doesn't work, figure out what factors got in the way and alter the schedule so that it better fits your needs. It may take several tries to find a schedule you are able to follow consistently. After a period of regularly engaging in practice, the benefits of doing so become clear and keeping to your schedule becomes much easier.

PART FOUR

Compassion and Connection

37 : Connecting with Compassion

BEING IN THE PRESENCE of compassionate people can have a strong impact on us. In one story about the Buddha, his cousin Devadatta, who was viciously jealous of him, released a mad elephant to trample the Buddha to death. As the elephant charged towards him, the Buddha meditated on love and compassion, radiating these out to all beings. The power of his meditation immediately pacified the elephant. As the story goes, the elephant screeched to a halt and bowed on his knees to pay respect to the Buddha.

We see similar, although less dramatic, events nowadays. Several people who are not Buddhists have told me (Chodron) of their experience attending a public talk by His Holiness the Dalai Lama. As soon as the Dalai Lama entered the auditorium, and before he had even begun his talk, they were overwhelmed with an emotion difficult to describe—perhaps it was hope, joy or love—and tears filled their eyes.

A dear friend helped to arrange for my ninety-year-old father to meet the Dalai Lama as His Holiness was returning to his hotel room after giving a talk. My father is not a Buddhist. In fact, he has a scientific approach to life and is not religious even in the faith that he was raised in. The Dalai Lama saw my father and went over to him. They talked for maybe thirty seconds and then someone snapped a picture of them together, the Dalai Lama's arm around my father. There were tears in my father's eyes.

My friend Lee was taken to the hospital after spending the night on a rock ledge following a rock-climbing accident. As he described it, the accident and subsequent hospitalization were like being in hell. His wife brought a picture of the Dalai Lama to hang in his little curtained-off space in the hospital. As Lee told it, "After seeing the photo of His Holiness the Dalai Lama, I felt immense relief just knowing with absolute certainty that someone was thinking about the suffering of others. Now I know from personal experience how much it means just to know someone is aware of your suffering when you are trapped."

This is the kind of peace that we can extend to others when we cultivate compassion. It is also the peace that we experience when being around those who have cultivated deep compassion.

REFLECTION

Compassionate Inspiration

Reflecting on people or ideas that we find inspiring can fuel our compassion for others. Bring to mind an individual—perhaps a teacher, spiritual figure, historical figure or a pet—that exhibits pure kindness. Your source of inspiration could be a poem, song, phrase, mantra or symbol. You may also be inspired by an idea, such as imagining world peace or envisioning a world free of hunger. Think of ways to build this reminder into your life, to provide inspiration when you most need it. You may want to post a picture of your inspirational figure on your desk at work, or print out the poem or phrase, tape it to a place where you'll see it in the morning when you get up or make it the screen saver on your computer screen. The key is to consider what things will inspire you to connect with your compassionate aspirations and to find ways to bring these inspiring reminders into your daily life.

38 : Reaching Out
with Compassion

WHEN WE ARE MISERABLE, what we often want most is to feel connected to others. Yet our actions frequently have the opposite effect. Sometimes we pick a fight with someone close to us just to feel connected to him in some way. Other times we throw ourselves a pity party, replete with lead balloons and a soundtrack playing "poor me, poooor me, poor meeeee, poooor meeee," set on a loop so that it becomes the background Muzak that permeates all other thoughts, if not the major sound in our heads.

We say to ourselves, "If only someone would notice how miserable and lonely I am and show me a little compassion," and then we complain that we live in such a cold, cruel world with so many insensitive people. Yet when a friend comes up and gently says, "What's wrong, you look unhappy?" we turn away from them with a sniff and say, "Nothing." Having been pushed away, our friend leaves and we mourn to ourselves, "I knew it all along. No one cares about me."

Or maybe our pity party is tinged with anger and we slam a few doors so that the "insensitive" people around us will notice that we're unhappy. Then when they come and kindly ask, "What's wrong? Are you angry?" we get shout: "I'm *not* angry! Why are you always accusing me of being angry? Leave me alone and mind your own business!" Put off by our outburst, they do as we've instructed. Then we return to our pity party saying, "It's always the same. They just don't understand me."

What we most want in these situations is to be connected to others, but in our misery we very often create the conditions that disconnect us from those we care most about. How can we break this vicious cycle? A quote attributed to Mother Teresa says:

> When I am hungry, give me someone needing food.
> When I am thirsty, send me someone needing a drink.
> When I am cold, send me someone to warm.
> When I am grieving, send me someone to console.
> When I am poor, lend me someone in need.
> When I have no time, give me someone I can help a
>   little while.
> When I am humiliated, let me have someone to praise.
> When I am disheartened, send me someone to cheer.
> When I need understanding, give me someone who
>   needs mine.
> When I need to be looked after, give me someone to
>   care for.
> When I think only of myself, draw my thoughts to another.

Of course, doing any of these actions is the last thing we want to do when we're stuck in our pity party. But sometimes what we want to do the least is what will help us the most. Opening our hearts to empathize with and care about others frees us from the pain of self-centeredness. We see that we are not alone in having difficulties and that many others are undergoing problems far more serious than ours. We stop being self-absorbed and feel connected to others through the fact of our common humanity, and the universal wish to be safe, happy and free from fear and suffering.

Extending ourselves to another living being—a pet, a child, a friend, a stranger, even someone we don't care for or someone who has different opinions than we do—opens the door to inner happiness. Leave food out for the squirrels, put up a bird feeder, volunteer at the library, smile at someone, bestow a favor that wasn't asked for, praise someone for work well done, point out someone's good qualities when they need a boost. In other words, do something that pulls you outside of yourself, that helps you see that there are billions of living beings who, like you, want to connect to others with compassion. All of us feel better when we experience kindness, empathy and good wishes for others.

It may be helpful to give yourself a homework assignment: "Everyday I'm going to make at least one small effort to connect with someone with compassion. I'm going to do one tiny action without expecting anything back from anyone, while quietly and by myself taking delight in giving." Then, even if you don't feel like doing it, do it anyway.

REFLECTION

A Compassionate "Homework Assignment"

Get creative! Come up with some ways to bring compassion, kindness and generosity into your daily life. Create a list of compassionate actions you could do. Then each day, pick one and do it. As you do so, bring to mind the wish to become deeply compassionate and see this action as a way to move towards this goal. As you complete your "homework," take note of how it feels to behave in this kind, compassionate way. Notice the emotions that arise in you as you purposefully take actions to benefit others.

39 : Finding the Best
in Other People

PEOPLE ARE LIKE PIANOS: what they give back to us depends on how we interact with them. If we are patient and genuinely take an interest in someone, it's possible to bring out their best qualities and interacting with them can be a like beautiful piano concerto. But if we are crabby and treat them poorly, they treat us the same way and our interaction becomes like a child banging on a piano.

There was a colleague we'll call Anne, who I (Chodron) didn't like very much. She seemed to be constantly complaining about something and was melodramatic about small incidents, especially when she didn't feel well. What's more, she sat behind me in our classes and was always asking me to move so that she could be more comfortable. Either that, or she was constantly readjusting her cushions and bumping into me in the process.

I realized that I was either going to be miserable for a long time or that I had to change. So I started asking Anne, "Are you comfortable? Do you need me to move?" and then voluntarily adjusted my seat so that she had more space. I didn't respond to Anne's melodrama when she said that she wasn't feeling well (because the situation was not serious), and she stopped that behavior with me. At a gathering Anne had for her birthday, I asked her to tell the group about her life. I was surprised to learn that Anne had been born during World War

II and as a small child had to flee Germany with soldiers following her family until they crossed the border to safety.

As I got to know Anne better, I realized that Anne had a kind streak. She loved cooking for others, and she took real delight in making the environment attractive by arranging big bouquets of flowers for others to enjoy—two activities that I didn't like to do. When Anne gave things to others, she was so happy. So I started commenting on that to her, pointing out her generosity and the delight she took in it. Anne appreciated the feedback, and I began to see a happy side of her. I realized that if I commented on what Anne did well, her behavior was more pleasant; whereas when I was critical it was more unpleasant. I thought, "Anne is like a piano. If I interact with her in one way, beautiful melodies flow forth; if I bang on the keys recklessly, disharmony is the result."

Sometimes our fixed ideas about people prevent us from feeling compassion towards them. We believe these assumptions, never doubting them for a moment. But as we've discussed, often they are completely false—ideas concocted by distorted ways of thinking. The only way to realize their falseness is to challenge them. Here are some examples.

One of my friends worked for the National Public Radio for a number of years. He was certain that one of his colleagues disliked him. After all, although they saw each other at work every day, they never said hello or made eye contact. "He probably thinks I'm a lousy journalist," my friend told me, "Either that or he's angry because I did something wrong, although I don't remember making a mistake that concerned him." But my friend was sick of the "bad vibes" between them, and so, inspired to overcome his barriers, one day he decided to say hello to the other man as they were passing in the office. The man returned his greeting and a conversation began. My friend later told me, "He turned out to be a pretty nice guy. What was most surprising was he said that he liked the stories I did for NPR. He had nothing against me after all. Boy, did I waste a lot of time being suspicious and miserable over nothing!" This is the benefit of encouraging ourselves to go beyond our preconceptions and to relate to others with kindness.

One of my spiritual mentors, Lama Thubten Yeshe, had a three-month course of teachings in India that he wanted his students to attend. You might think that because monastics wear the same clothes and we all shave our head, that we all think alike. That is far from the truth. In a monastic setting you are around people that you wouldn't necessarily associate with in nonmonastic life. What's more, you live with them 24/7, with no respite. For people with a lot of preconceptions about others—which is most of us—it is quite challenging! "It's the perfect opportunity to transform your minds," Lama Thubten Yeshe would say.

I set myself the challenge of having a conversation with each of the one hundred plus people there during the three months—not just a superficial, perfunctory conversation; I told myself that I had to find something that we had in common to talk about. With some people it was clearly going to be easier than with others. But I kept encouraging myself and creatively brought up different topics in order to have an enjoyable conversation with each person. Sometimes I had to really force myself to overcome my opinions to begin a conversation, "That man is prejudiced against women. He's so arrogant and is always making disparaging remarks but masking it as if he were teasing us," or "That one is such a chatterbox. If I start a conversation with her, I'll be there listening to her go on and on about nothing for hours."

But I tried, and I kept going until I had a good conversation with everyone. Doing so entailed revising many of my negative opinions of others. However, I discovered that if I made an effort, there was a way to connect with compassion with everyone.

REFLECTION

Noticing the Positives

As you interact with others throughout the day, make an effort to notice their positive qualities. Almost everyone that we encounter has strengths that are worthy of our admiration, even if we have a difficult relationship with that person. See if you can discover their positive qualities, and when you find one that you particularly admire, let them know: "I was really impressed with the way you handled that situation. You did not get angry or back down when your neighbour raised his voice, but kept trying to communicate with him." "The project you were working on was completed on time, was laid out in a logical manner and covered all the necessary topics." Be sincere—false flattery is neither kind nor compassionate. Observe how this practice of searching for the good in others impacts how you see them, how you feel about yourself and your relationship with them.

40 : Helping Each
Other Feel Safe

Ψ EARLIER, WE DISCUSSED three types of emotion, each of which exists for a specific purpose. We discussed the threat response, which mobilizes emotions like anger and fear to protect us when we perceive danger, and the drive response, which excites us and motivates us towards pursuing our goals. The third type of emotional response, which we call safeness, involves feeling content, peaceful and most importantly *safe*.

Experiencing safeness is important if we're to feel and act with compassion. Helping ourselves and other people to be at our best begins with helping all of us feel *safe*. When we feel safe, we're able to think more clearly and flexibly, we're less likely to act impulsively or hurtfully, and we're more likely to help others. In contrast, when we feel threatened, our mental resources are focused on what is bothering us. This keeps us locked into feelings of threat, which makes it harder to focus on helping others.

Remember a moment when you've been at your best. Were you spending a lot of time evaluating what you were doing and how well you were doing it, or were you just *doing* it? If you were just *doing* it, this is probably because you felt safe. When we feel safe and comfortable, it's easier to let go of the tendency to self-evaluate and simply focus on the task at hand. Completely present with what we're doing, we see what needs to be done and can focus on doing it. How do we get to this place and how do we help others get there?

Our ability to feel safe, comfortable and at peace is intimately linked with feeling connected to others. We're responsive to what we think others feel about us and how they behave towards us. If we think they are looking down on us or judging us, we'll often feel threatened. On the other hand, if we perceive that others accept us, support us in our struggles and will assist us if we really need it, this helps us to gain the confidence to address the sources of stress in our lives. There is a large body of psychological research showing that supportive, nurturing relationships help us to feel safe and better manage difficult emotions and situations. Such interactions help us manage feelings of threat and can be observed in the workings of our brains: compassionate interactions lead to the release of chemicals in the brain, such as oxytocin, which are involved with feeling safe and connected with others—chemicals which help reduce threat-based feelings like fear by acting on the parts of the brain that produce these emotions.[1] Supportive relationships even help grow the parts of our brains involved in managing difficult emotions and social situations![2]

Cultivating compassion in ourselves helps us create feelings of safeness and peace in other people as well. Feeling safe and supported, we are less likely to focus totally on ourselves and on trying to spot potential threats, and we're more likely to care for (and about) others. When we stop comparing ourselves to others and instead see ourselves as connected to them, we understand that taking care of them and taking care of ourselves is the same thing. Our efforts are supported by the kindness of others: when other people treat us with kindness, they provide us with a model that encourages us to do the same in our own interactions. Similarly, when we help others feel accepted and safe, we help them extend their own kindness to others. In this way, our kindness is multiplied.

This also benefits us in some very direct ways—a growing body of research shows that taking care of others and engaging in altruistic behavior is good for our physical and mental health.[3] One study showed that providing social support to others was linked with a lower risk of mortality in older adults.[4]

We all struggle sometimes. When others experience difficulties, we can offer them support and encouragement. We can treat them with respect and dignity. We come to understand ourselves, in part, through the ways in which others treat us. So when we treat other people with kindness and respect, we are sending the message that they are *worthy* of kindness and respect. When they are at their lowest, we can show them they are valuable human beings.

It doesn't take much. A brief visit, conversation, phone call or text can make a world of difference. "You are in my thoughts." "I can see how hard this is for you." "I am here if you need me." These brief messages remind us we are cared for, liked and valued. Even a kind smile or brief pat on the shoulder can speak volumes.

REFLECTION

Receiving Compassionate Connection

Think of a time when someone gave you the gift of compassion—offering support when you were in pain, encouragement when you were struggling or loving acceptance when you were caught up in feelings of self-criticism. Picture this in your mind, imagining yourself receiving their kind wishes, love and respect. Notice the feelings that emerge in you as you imagine receiving these feelings from them.

Now think of someone you know who is going through a hard time. Think of how you could offer this person support, encouragement or acceptance, and imagine doing this. Picture how she would feel and how you would feel in giving this to her.

41 : Compassionate Communication

COMPASSION CAN BE INTRODUCED into every aspect of our lives, and since we are in frequent contact with others on a daily basis, communication is perhaps the foremost area in need of compassion. Without compassion, our communication with others can deteriorate into a litany of complaints and instructions on how others should change so that we'll be happy. But truly bringing compassion into our communication means that we learn to listen with empathy and respond with true compassion and love—wishing the other person to be free from suffering and its causes and to have happiness and its causes.

Compassionate communication begins with the premise that all living beings want to be happy and not suffer. It involves increasing our awareness of the thoughts and feelings that motivate our speech, and slowing down, listening well, and giving empathy and compassion to ourselves and to others. To do this we have to care about others; if we don't, we won't have the patience to pause and consider what we want to say. In the next few entries, we'll discuss some approaches for helping ourselves communicate compassionately. A number of these are adapted from Marshall Rosenberg's work in nonviolent communication.[1]

REFLECTION

Bringing Compassion to Our Communication

Based on what you've learned so far, consider some ways you could bring compassion into your communications and interactions with others. Bring to mind a recent, tense interaction with another person. Using your imagination, picture yourself interacting with this person in a kind, empathic and compassionate manner. Imagine how this might change the way the situation unfolds. We can use our imaginations in this way before an interaction actually happens as well, practising what we might feel and say to prepare ourselves for conversations that may be difficult.

42 : Describing
Situations Accurately

MANY DIFFERENT MENTAL EXPERIENCES shape how we experience situations. Some of these involve sensory information coming in through our eyes, ears, nose, tongue and body. Other processes involve thoughts, images, assumptions or inferences based on what we perceive through our senses. While some of our thoughts are accurate, in many cases they aren't. Since the way we filter information is influenced by our previous experiences as well as by the emotions we're feeling at the moment, we can easily be mistaken about others' actions and motivations, believing our ideas and opinions are accurate descriptions of reality.

Describing a situation accurately is harder than it may seem. What we believe to be an objective description often turns out to be a series of interpretations and projections, many of which bear little resemblance to what's actually going on. It may be helpful to use Joan's example of a situation she experienced with a friend at a small social gathering: "When I came in, my friend was happily chatting with a good-looking man. She saw me come in and knew I was nervous because I didn't know many people there, yet she ignored me. Instead of greeting me, she was incredibly rude and inconsiderate and kept talking to this man as if I weren't there."

There are a lot of loaded words in Joan's description that go beyond simply describing the situation, embellishing it with her interpretation of what happened and the assumptions that she made about her friend's motivation. Joan became so worked up about what she thought had happened that it was hard for her to hear or consider any other interpretation. However, she knew she was miserable and so decided to try the nonviolent communication approach, which begins by describing just the bare facts of the situation to oneself. After much whittling away of projections and assumptions, her story boiled down to, "I walked in the room. My friend was talking to someone and continued the conversation." Joan was shocked to discover that in fact that's all that had happened, that all the rest was her "story writing." This realization immediately deflated her anger.

The value of trying to describe just the facts is that it stops us from creating threatening fantasies, dwelling on what happened and making assumptions about what we think the other person's motivation was or how his or her mind works. By focusing on the facts, we often come to see that nothing happened that was worth getting worked up about.

REFLECTION

Describing Situations

Recall a recent situation in which you were upset. Write down a description of what happened, leaving out any words that describe the possible motivations of the other person (such as "purposely irritated me"), any emotive words (such as "gave me a dirty look") or any words that describe what was happening (such as "shout" or "gloated"). Just write down who did what and the exact words someone said, if you can remember them.

In what way does the situation appear differently to you now? Do you feel the same about it?

43 : Identifying Our Feelings

EMOTIONS PLAY A HUGE ROLE in our lives, but it can be hard to know exactly what we're feeling at any given time. Some of us may find it difficult to label and describe our emotions. There can be different reasons for this. It may be that we didn't learn how to name our feelings when we were young. Children learn how to identify and label their emotions through their interactions with their parents or early caregivers. But some of us grew up in homes and environments where our parents and caregivers weren't able to teach us these skills, perhaps because they themselves had never learned how to identify and label their own feelings.

Identifying our feelings can be tricky because our emotions may change from one moment to the next. We also can experience a variety of different, sometimes conflicting, emotions seemingly at one time. When faced with a threat or disappointment, for example, we may feel a combination of anger, anxiety and even sadness that seem to happen all at once, making it difficult to distinguish between them. Sometimes these different emotions motivate us in opposing ways, which can be confusing. For example, anger may motivate us to attack at the same time that fear motivates us to withdraw, and we find ourselves caught in the middle. In some situations, such as when we start a new job or relationship, we can feel excited and interested as well as a bit scared. If we experienced only one emotion at a time, identifying them would be a lot easier. But often that's not how it works.

Some of us have a hard time identifying our feelings because we think there are certain emotions we should or shouldn't experience. This may be related to our gender. Some men learn as children that it is acceptable to feel and express anger, but not emotions such as sadness or fear. Some women may have been taught that it is acceptable to express anxiety or sadness, but may have been punished for expressing anger. Of course, these gender stereotypes are just stereotypes and can be reversed: some men are terrified of experiencing anger while some women are comfortable with anger and are unwilling to express anxiety or sadness.

Often, we think we're expressing our feelings when we're actually saying what we think. For example, we'll say, "I feel like you don't care about me." In fact "you don't care about me" isn't a feeling; it's what we think the other person's attitude is. We *think* "you don't care about me" and then, largely as a result of this thought, we may *feel* hurt, scared or lonely.

It's useful to observe your speech and see if you notice any examples of this: "I feel like you're pushing me away." "I feel that you're trying to control me." When you hear yourself begin a sentence with "I feel that ..." or "I feel like ...," pause and reflect: "Are those actual feelings or are those thoughts or assumptions about what someone else is doing?" Anything that can be made into a statement of what we *believe* the other person is doing is an interpretation. What we need to discover is what we are *feeling*.

Chances are when we *think* someone is pushing us away, we *feel* confused, scared or lonely. When we *think* someone is trying to control us, we *feel* vulnerable, apprehensive or insecure. When we *think* someone doesn't trust us, we *feel* hurt, offended or indignant. When we *think* that someone is abandoning us, we *feel* fearful, alone or uncertain. We can see how easily our thoughts and interpretations about others' feelings or behavior can provoke threat-based emotions in ourselves, particularly when we take those thoughts to be true. We can get all worked up over situations we've created in our minds that have almost nothing to do with what is really happening!

In communicating with others, there is a big difference between sharing our evaluation, analysis or interpretation of a situation and saying what we are feeling. In addition, when we tell other people what their feelings, motivations and thoughts are, it usually doesn't go very well. People generally don't like it when we *tell them* what they are feeling or thinking, particularly if we do so in a way that blames them for our distress: "You're trying to make me miserable!" "You're so selfish it's driving me nuts!" "Your anxiety is ruining my day!" It's better to express what we are feeling in non-blaming "I" statements that take responsibility for our own emotions: "I'm feeling really frustrated right now," or, "I'm excited about our collaboration." If we've formed hypotheses or are wondering about what might be going on in the other person's mind, it's best to clarify our understanding by asking *them*: "I'm wondering what you meant by that comment."

Sometimes it is difficult for us to identify our emotions because we're too busy judging ourselves for having them. We may think "I'm pathetic" when we feel anxious or sad, or "I'm a terrible parent" when we shout at our children. Automatically criticizing ourselves can obscure our real feelings and prevent us from understanding what has caused them. In these situations, it's good to pause, try to notice what we are *feeling* (not thinking) and anchor those feelings to real events: "I'm feeling angry that my child forgot his homework, and anxious about how harshly I reacted to him." If our emotions seem to be more than the situation warrants, we can consider if we are thinking in ways that magnify or distort the situation in our minds, producing feelings that are out of proportion to what is happening: "Why would I be so angry about this? Ahh ... I'm thinking the teacher will blame me for him not getting his homework done, and I'll look like a terrible parent. Looks like I'm doing a bit of mind-reading here!"

Sometimes it takes a while before we are able to find words to identify our feelings. It can help to sit quietly and observe our emotional experiences. Mindful awareness, which we discussed in entry 9, can help us slow down and note that our emotions, thoughts and motivations are separate mental events. With practice, we will be able to notice these emotions, thoughts and motivations more easily and see how they influence one another—how a particular thought gives rise to an emotion, which instigates a motivation, which then influences our behavior. We'll be able to identify these as separate but related mental events we can choose to work with and *change*.

Buddhist teachings speak about "introspective awareness," which can help us identify our emotions. Introspective awareness involves observing our thoughts and feelings and evaluating their benefit, harm, accuracy or inaccuracy. For example, we may notice we are angry after a meeting with a colleague. Looking more closely, we may observe that our mind is interpreting an interaction with this person in a negative way: "In the meeting, my colleague made a snide remark about the defects of my report. I know that he is out to humiliate me so that the boss will give the upcoming promotion to him instead of me." Introspective awareness allows us to see that these thoughts contain many interpretations, assumptions and judgments that may not be valid. As such, we can remind ourselves not to let these incorrect thoughts fuel our anger and we can calm ourselves down. Focusing on our breath for a few moments at this time is also helpful.

Once we're able to identify our feelings, we'll be better able to take responsibility for our own emotions when we're in situations of conflict. We will not judge or blame the other person or project our own ideas on them, expecting them to make us happy.

REFLECTION

Identifying Feelings

Think of a conflict you had with another person. Try to identify what you were feeling. Avoid using words that describe what you think someone did. It can help to use single words, not phrases that project a motivation onto another person.

Acknowledge and accept the feeling you experienced. Do you feel different now?

44 : Considering Perceived Threats and Needs

 CORRECTLY ASSESSING OUR PERCEPTIONS is important, because we can misinterpret situations in ways that lead us to perceive threats where there are none. Our threat emotions are very responsive to our perceptions and thoughts—*whether or not* there is an actual threat present. For example, we may believe from the expression on someone's face that he is looking down on us, when in fact he is thinking about something else entirely. Sometimes we perceive others as threats, even if all they are doing is pursuing their own goals, which happen to conflict with our own. It's common to feel threatened when we are having trouble achieving our goals, or when we aren't performing up to our expectations at a task that's important to us, particularly if we compare ourselves to others who seem to be doing better than we are. It's important to be able to identify which threats actually exist in a situation and which ones our minds are fabricating. Are we in actual danger or are these fears unfounded? Doing this allows us to respond appropriately to situations, as well as to take responsibility for emotions that arise due to our own incorrect projections or misunderstandings.

Disturbing emotions can arise from unmet needs. For example, when we need companionship but lack it, we may feel depressed, lonely or angry. Identifying our needs may be even more difficult than identifying our feelings. We can often be mistaken about what we need. For example, a person with a drug problem may think they "need" more money for illegal drugs or more prescriptions for legal ones. In addition, we often confuse needs with things we want others to do. "I need you to tell me you love me more often." "I need you to be a member of this team and get your work done on time." These are not needs, they are demands, and there is a big difference between the two.

Here, we'll use the term "needs" in reference to necessary conditions for us to survive, live healthily and consistently move towards our potential. Psychologist Abraham Maslow defined a hierarchy of five levels of needs:[1]

- Firstly, the basic needs: the most basic needs necessary for our physical survival—food, water, rest, shelter and protection from the elements.
- Secondly, the safety needs: the need to feel safe from harm, to have a stable environment in which to live, to know our basic physical needs will continue to be met.
- Thirdly, the needs relating to connections with others: love, affection, friends, family and harmony with other beings. We need to give and receive affection, to learn and to share.
- Fourthly, the needs establishing a sense of self-efficacy: to contribute, to be efficacious in our work, to receive recognition.
- Finally, the "self-actualization" needs: the needs which, when met, enable us to achieve our highest potential. These needs include creativity, acceptance of reality, spontaneity, problem solving, beauty and lack of prejudice.

These five levels of needs are arranged in a hierarchy because the more basic needs must be satisfied before we are able to work on meeting those on the next levels. For example, we need food and shelter in order to survive; without these needs being met, it is nearly impossible to work towards establishing a sense of achievement in our lives. In such cases, the more basic needs overwhelm the higher-order ones.

Clearly we all have needs, though they may vary among people or communities. All human beings share some needs, such as food, while other needs differ depending on how we were brought up, our psychological makeup and the conditions in which we live.

There's no reason to criticize ourselves for having needs. However, if we fixate or cling to them, giving them undue importance—"I *must* have a romantic relationship or I cannot be happy." "I have to score well on this exam and get the promotion or I'll be a complete failure."—we will inevitably be disappointed.

Attachment also enters the picture when we link the fulfilment of a need to a particular person, object or situation. While we all need to receive affection, that doesn't mean we must receive it from a particular person, in a certain way, at a specific time. While creativity is an important need, insisting that our ideas are the best and must be accepted when we're working with a team of people is unrealistic. All of us need to feel appreciated; however, if we fall apart when someone fails to appreciate us, we will be miserable a lot of the time.

While we may be able to identify our disturbing feelings, many of us initially have a hard time pinpointing the unmet needs that may lie behind those feelings. For example, we may feel agitated about a task we've been asked to do, but unaware that this agitation stems from needing clear instructions on how to proceed. In the case of pleasant feelings, we may not be able to identify what need has been met. We may feel satisfied but unaware of its source—that our need for companionship has been fulfilled. As with our difficulty in identifying feelings, this can happen because as children we were not taught how to identify our needs.

When we practice describing situations more accurately and identifying our feelings and needs in them, we discover that what different people feel and need in a particular situation can vary dramatically. Imagine your boss just gave you some ideas on how to improve your work. You may feel happy and pleased because you appreciated the personal attention. Another person may feel defensive and angry, thinking it indicates a lack of trust. Two people may react in totally opposite ways to the same situation, depending on how they describe the situation to themselves.

What if we felt happy and pleased? What needs were fulfilled? They may not be apparent immediately. We may have to pause a minute to think. We may identify the fulfilled need as "inclusion" while for another person it is "encouragement."

If we're the ones who felt defensive and angry, we can consider: what needs were not met? These needs may not be instantly evident to us because we're not used to asking ourselves that question. After a few minutes, one person may say, "acknowledgment" while another responds "trust and autonomy." These needs differ, just as we all differ as individuals.

Hypersensitivity to perceived threats or a lack of self-knowledge about our needs lies behind much of our frustration in life. We may feel deeply threatened but have little idea that we've created this sense of threat in our own minds. We run around trying to fulfill needs we haven't identified but which affect us strongly. It's similar to trying to fill a gas tank in a car when we can't find the gas cap.

This process of identifying feelings and linking them to

perceived threats and needs is very useful, especially in situations where we are in conflict with other people. It brings us back to exploring, understanding, accepting and taking responsibility for our own experiences, instead of letting our minds fabricate stories about what others did and how unfair it was. It helps us be responsible for our own feelings and needs without insisting the world change and give us what we want when we want it, even when we don't know what it is that we want.

Disentangling our needs from the situations we face gives us the ability to think creatively about how to meet those needs. For example, Susan and Sam suffer from "empty nest syndrome" after their youngest child left home to attend college. Feeling lonely, restless and bored, they think, "Why did we let him go away? He would have been happy attending the local university. We need him, or one of our other children, to come home and be with us as we grow older." This way of thinking makes their purpose in life dependent on the actions of their children; in this case, where their children choose to live. Moreover, if they blame their children for moving away and try to make them feel guilty for doing that, it will likely damage their relationship and the children may visit home less frequently.

Recognizing that their children are not responsible for fulfilling their needs for interests and activity, Susan and Sam decide to attend a pottery-making class together and to go on nature walks on the weekends, activities they love but didn't have time to do while their children lived at home. In this way, they accept responsibility for fulfilling their own needs, do not rely on their children and have a lot of fun in the process.

Sometimes just being able to figure out what our feelings and needs are makes our minds calmer. For example, when we realize we feel lonely because we need to contribute to others' welfare, suddenly the loneliness is not as strong. It's as if understanding and validating our need helps to address it. That does not mean we should ignore the need once we have recognized what it is; but rather, we can now actively try to fill it, for instance, by volunteering. We may want to volunteer at a place where our talents and skills are needed or where we will learn a lot, perhaps by venturing outside our comfort zones.

REFLECTION

Considering Perceived Threats and Needs

Continue with the situation from the previous exercise, focusing on a conflict you had with another person.

Did you think you were being threatened in this situation? If so, try to identify the source of the threat. Consider whether this situation was actually dangerous to you, or whether the sense of threat was rooted in how you perceived, interpreted and assigned meaning to the situation.

What did you need in that situation? Remember to be responsible for your own needs and do not blame other people for not coming to your rescue.

How has your mind changed by exploring your sense of threat and identifying your needs? Does this give you insight into your behavior? Does it help you see the situation more clearly?

45 : The Importance of
Empathic Listening

 CONSIDERING OTHER PEOPLE'S FEELINGS and needs also helps us deal with conflicts and difficult situations. Their feelings and needs are just as important as ours. After all, we all want to be happy and not suffer. Because people who value compassion want to resolve issues in a practical and beneficial way, we have to take others into consideration. A big step in doing this is to listen with empathy.

Others may have as difficult a time as we do identifying their feelings and needs. An empathic attitude on our part enables us to speak and act in ways that can help them. This may mean putting our own feelings and needs on the back burner for a while. Just as sometimes we so desperately need to be heard before we are able to allow new information into our minds, others often need to express their own feelings, thoughts, and needs, and to know we have heard and accepted them, before they can listen to ours. Empathic listening is the key.

We would think that listening would be easy: we just sit there and take in information through our ears. But that's not listening. Empathic listening involves caring about others, and being able to accept their perspectives and viewpoints even when they differ from ours. It means refraining from thinking about the next thing we are going to say and focusing our attention on what the other person is communicating. It also entails refraining from criticizing or blaming them for having these feelings and thoughts. That means when someone is angry or inarticulate, we don't interrupt and tell him he's got it all wrong, he's projecting his frustration on to us or he is inept and stupid. It means we sit there no matter how much they blame or insult us and listen to what they are really saying, which is, "I'm miserable and I want to be happy."

In other words, instead of listening to what the other person thinks about us, we hear his suffering. Instead of labeling him "an obnoxious idiot who is dumping his anger on me and blaming me for something I didn't do to compensate for his own failings," we focus on the fact that this is another person who is just like us and is in pain at this moment. Needless to say, if we have acted badly, it is important to acknowledge that our careless words or behavior have caused others pain and to take responsibility for helping to mend the situation.

In one situation, I (Russell) learned the importance of listening to someone's suffering the hard way. Lucy, a graduate student whom I was both fond of and very impressed by, lambasted me during a meeting, accusing me of neglecting her, not supporting her research project and playing favorites among students. Initially feeling hurt and angry, I started to withdraw, which of course did not help our communication—my experience was that I was very invested and interested in her project, and I was hurt by the idea that I "played favorites." I had to mentally step back and slow things down for a few minutes to realize what Lucy was really saying with her criticism: "I'm confused and anxious about this process, and I need more guidance. This relationship is important to me but I don't know how to express that now. I need support and compassion." However, in the beginning, I felt personally attacked and, as a result, was unable to hear what she was really trying to say. So we paused a moment. I said, "I'm a bit shocked right now. I need a minute to think about this before we continue this conversation, so I can be sure to say what I mean." We slowed things down a bit and were then able to have a conversation in which we each expressed our perspectives. Lucy thought that she was receiving less support from me than she had as an undergraduate, and less than she saw me offering other members of my research team. I was able to validate her concerns—what Lucy was saying was absolutely *true*—but I then shared my perspective, which was that I saw her as an advanced student who was producing excellent work and I was unaware that she needed more support. Where she experienced neglect, I saw myself helping her to develop independence and autonomy. Once we were able to understand one another's perspectives, the conflict melted away and we continued to work together harmoniously.

When we can listen to someone else express pain and know that they want to be happy, we are able to connect with them. This is the time to offer them not only empathy that understands and accepts them, but also compassion that wants them to be happy and free from suffering, even if we can't make that happen ourselves.

Self-centeredness sometimes interferes with our empathy. Imagine we are biased against people who are in positions of authority because we had unpleasant experiences with parents, teachers or the police when we were young. Carrying these experiences with us, we incorrectly project hostility and potential problems on to anyone we consider to be in a position of authority in relation to us. Since our minds are dwelling in the past—which probably is no longer relevant—we now find it difficult to empathize with someone we see as an authority figure. To overcome this, we have to counteract our self-centeredness and see suffering as a common human experience. It's not just our friends, the poor and the oppressed who are suffering; each living being has his or her own inner conflicts as well as difficulties with other people. All of us deal with the loss of things that we like or love, frustration at not getting what we want and disappointment when things don't turn out as expected. All of us deal with the great equalizers—aging, sickness and death. The authority figure also experiences these same things. She is no different from anyone else in this regard.

Another group of people to whom we may find it challenging to extend empathy and compassion are friends and family. Due to our attachment to them, we may have a lot of emotional investment in wanting them to act or think in certain ways. We may want them to approve of us, make a particular choice, or do what we believe is best for them. We are so close to these people that it may be challenging to remember that we are different individuals; that we do not "own" our loved ones and they have their own way of thinking. In this case, as in the case with authority figures, it is helpful to return to the meditation on equanimity (see entry 22) to let go of our excessive attachment or emotional dependency on these people.

It takes some time to learn to listen well. We may have ingrained habits of speech that turn conversations into arguments by attributing blame or telling someone that what they're feeling is wrong. Empathic listening can feel very new to us; it requires listening closely and pausing to consider what is going inside the other person as well as ourselves. At first it may seem unnatural to ask questions like, "It sounds like you're feeling frustrated. Is that right?" and, "Could you help me understand why?" However, with practice it becomes more natural and we find different ways to say it.

Listening to others' feelings and needs is actually "saying" a lot. Often, as soon as the other person knows that she has been heard and feels understood, she is satisfied and the conversation can move on to other topics.

When someone is in pain or when there is a long history behind their conflict with us, we may have to repeatedly reflect back what the other person has said so he will share all of his feelings and needs with us. This might not be easy. His mind, like our own, does not work in a nice, neat fashion, so he may not say everything in a logical order. He may convey negative emotions, blaming himself or us, and exaggerate details. Remember, others are just like us—ordinary, confused people who are sometimes in pain and want to be happy.

As we cultivate patience, open-mindedness, empathy and compassion, we become better able to listen to and care about other people. When listening, we speak only when necessary, keeping the focus on the other person until they have said all they need to say. We know we'll have a chance to speak later, so whenever the wish to interrupt arises, we remind ourselves, "This is not about me. It's about having an open heart," and bring our attention back to what they are saying.

This leads to another important point: although others may express their pain by blaming us, it does not mean we are responsible for their emotions. Just as someone else can't *make* us mad, we can't *make* her mad. Her anger and distress come from her own interpretation of the situation. That doesn't mean we smugly say, "It's all her problem anyway," and walk away. While we don't take responsibility for what isn't our responsibility, we do take responsibility for what *is*. We may not have deliberately intended to hurt that person, but perhaps we were careless in our speech and flippantly overstated facts in order to make a point. While her hurt feelings are not our responsibility, our careless words are, and we need to rectify our own tendency to speak carelessly.

This ability to listen and give the other person empathy and compassion will only happen if we value the well-being of everyone in a conflict. We realize that since all of us are interdependent, caring for others and doing what we can to bring about their happiness means that we will live with happy people. That increases the quality of our own lives as well as the quality of others'.

REFLECTION

Empathic Listening

As you go through the day, try to pay attention to what others' behavior and speech tell you about their needs. Rather than simply responding to the content of what they say or do, consider what these words or behaviors express about their underlying needs. For example, when someone says, "No one listens to me!" she may actually mean, "I feel frustrated and need understanding." When we understand the person's actual feelings and needs, we are better equipped to help them.

46 : Offering Empathy to Ourselves and Others

EMPATHY IS CRUCIAL in cultivating compassion and in forming and maintaining compassionate connections with other people. In addition, offering ourselves empathy is very effective in calming and reassuring ourselves when we feel afraid or apprehensive. In this case, "offering ourselves empathy" means to give ourselves understanding and comfort. Let's say we are planning a project together with a colleague, but we have different ways to go about accomplishing it. Our colleague listens to what we say but doesn't respond to our suggestions. Instead she strongly urges us to follow her ideas. We give ourselves empathy by reflecting, "I feel frustrated because I desire fairness. It's a highly held value in my life, so naturally it's important to me. Fairness in this situation may or may not occur—I can't control the outcome—but I will do my best to express myself clearly and in a way my colleague can understand. I can let her know that while I'm not glued to my ideas, I would like the opportunity to express them and discuss the project with her so that it becomes a mutual undertaking."

In addition to empathy, we can extend compassion to ourselves. "I don't want myself to suffer, so I accept my frustration and need for fairness without judging myself for having them. I also don't want my colleague to suffer, so I acknowledge that she has feelings and needs as well, even though I don't know exactly what they are at this moment." We remind ourselves that everyone equally wants happiness, not suffering, and that we shouldn't see planning this project with our colleague in a narrow way such that if her ideas prevail, she wins and I lose. Instead of seeing the two parties on opposite sides of the table quarrelling, we use a different image: both of us are on the same side of the table looking at the problem together. We suggest this new image to our colleague. While initially she may not see the situation that way, we can continue to emphasize the points we hold in common and respectfully restrain ourselves from acting in ways that may cause her to feel vulnerable. Offering her empathy and compassion will help her to consider this new image of us working together to solve the problem.

To understand the difference between giving empathy and compassion on the one hand and blame on the other, consider these four different ways of responding to an unpleasant situation: blame the other person, blame ourselves, offer empathy and compassion to the other person, or offer empathy and compassion to ourselves. For example, Carl asked his friend John to help him do a home maintenance project on Saturday. John agreed, but an hour before the appointed time on Saturday, he called Carl and apologized, explaining he had another commitment that day that he had forgotten about but he could come the following Saturday to help. Carl was now stuck; he had already removed the old shower stall from the bathroom, and without John's help he could not install the new one. Since this was the only shower in his home, it put him in a difficult situation.

In the first option, Carl blames John, "What do you mean you have another appointment? You told me you would come. You should remember your appointments and not make commitments you can't keep. Now, because of you, I won't be able to take a shower for a week!" Imagine what that kind of response would do to their friendship and to both Carl and John's sense of well-being.

In the second option, Carl blames himself, "I don't know what's wrong with me. All my friends desert me when I need them. It's my fault for trusting John in the first place. Why am I so gullible?" This response adversely affects Carl's self-esteem, as well as his friendship with John.

With the third option, Carl gives John empathy and compassion, "You're my friend and I know you're a person with integrity. I imagine you feel disappointed because you would like to keep your commitments, and in this case you aren't able to." Here Carl is focusing on John's feelings and needs. Carl sees that he isn't the only one adversely affected by John's forgetfulness.

With the fourth option, Carl gives himself empathy and compassion, "Yes, this is inconvenient, but it's not a disaster. I feel disappointed because I need reliability, but I'll be creative and figure out what to do. I know his inability to come today is a simple oversight and he'll be here next week." Here Carl avoids projecting false motivations and meaning onto John's inability to come and accepts the situation, maintaining the friendship and approaching the problem with a sense of creativity.

REFLECTION

Empathy and Compassion in Conflicts with Others

Think of a conflict you've had with someone recently. Go through the four options of how you could respond, imagining each of them in turn.

How would you feel after adopting each one?

What are the advantages of adopting an empathic and compassionate approach for both the other person and for yourself (approaches three and four)?

47 : Humor

SOMETIMES WE AREN'T ABLE to separate our feelings and needs from a situation itself. Desperately wanting something, we are filled with attachment and craving and grumble until we get what we want. In this case, we feel dissatisfied, and our self-centeredness is making a relatively small thing seem very serious. Instead of berating ourselves for how ridiculous our thoughts and emotions are, we can introduce some lightness and humor into our way of looking at a situation. This is a great way to show compassion for ourselves and to gain perspective on the situation's actual gravity. For example, Bill recognized that his self-centered mind craved the acknowledgment and appreciation that he believed he deserved but was not getting from those around him. Rather than criticizing himself for being self-centered, he imagined the following exaggerated scene: his boss, parents, colleagues and friends surrounded him clapping, cheering, throwing confetti and exclaiming praises of his abilities. They took out a golden crown and bending on their knees anointed him their king. He imagined basking in the glory, his gloating self-centered mind being totally satisfied. Then, he naturally started to laugh at the absurdity of the image and his desire for acknowledgment.

Humor can be really useful when applied to ourselves, but it's best to avoid using it to make light of others' feelings unless they've enlisted our help in viewing the situation from a humorous perspective. When others feel vulnerable, it's easy for our well-meaning attempts at humor to be perceived as ridicule.

REFLECTION

Bringing Humor into a Situation

Recall a situation in which you really wanted someone to feel and behave a certain way towards you but they were feeling and acting the opposite way.

Ham it up and exaggerate the situation! Turn it into a humorous skit in which the person feels and does everything you want and even more.

Imagine the entire world reorganizing itself to serve your wishes, with you as the queen or king.

Allow yourself to laugh at the absurdity of how you previously felt and acted.

48 : The Mindful-Emotion Traffic Light

Ψ SO FAR, WE'VE DISCUSSED ways of approaching compassionate communication that involve helping ourselves work with emotions like anger and fear that can interfere with our ability to communicate effectively and kindly with others. The idea is that we manage our own emotions first, and once we're feeling more in control of our threat emotions, we can confidently interact with others without harming our relationship with them. This can be challenging, because emotions like anger and fear carry with them a feeling of *urgency*—a strong motivation to act immediately to resolve the situation. But if we dive into things when we're caught in the grip of these emotions, it's difficult to interact compassionately with others. It's also easy to behave in ways we'll regret; ways that make the situation worse and damage our relationships.

How do we know when we're ready to take on handling conflicts with others? In my (Russell's) anger groups, we came up with a metaphor: the Mindful-Emotion Traffic Light.

Before diving into a difficult situation, we pause to notice and identify our emotions and their intensity. If we find we're in the "red," caught up in the midst of a powerful threat emotion like anger, it's time to *stop*, refrain from diving into the situation and shift the focus to balancing our own emotions. A good way to start is by slowing down the breath and then using some of the approaches described in this book, such as compassionately asking ourselves, "What would help me feel safe and balanced as I approach this situation?"

If we're in the "yellow," our minds still colored by irritation or anxiety, we proceed with caution, pausing to calm ourselves and reframe the situation in our minds using some of the techniques described. Slowing things down, we can try to understand how everyone involved is feeling and interpreting the situation, and approach things with the compassionate intent to benefit everyone and harm no one.

Finally, if we check in with ourselves and find we're in the "green," feeling calm, safe and undisturbed by our emotions, we briefly remind ourselves of the compassionate intention to empathically reflect on our experience and that of the other person, and confidently proceed.

REFLECTION

Using the Mindful-Emotion Traffic Light

As you move throughout your day, take a moment to check in with your emotional traffic light, particularly if you find yourself feeling stressed or frustrated. Notice what emotions have arisen within you, and what thoughts, motivations and behaviors they inspire. If you catch yourself in the red, driven by threat emotions such as anger or fear, take a minute and slow down your breathing. Once you've slowed things down a bit, see if you can adopt a compassionate perspective when examining the situation. Is this situation really that terrible or urgent, or does it just feel that way because you're operating in the red? How might you counsel a friend or loved one who is going through the same thing—what validation, advice or encouragement would you offer him or her? Is there another way of looking at the situation that doesn't keep you locked into threat emotions such as anger? We're learning to notice when we're in the red, and to shift ourselves to the green—bringing up feelings of safeness and calm—before dealing with the situation itself. In this way, we can be at our best as we face the challenges life has to offer.

49 : Making Requests

As HUMAN BEINGS, we often make requests of others to help us to fulfill our needs. Our requests are most effective when we are in a positive mental state and express our request in an appropriate manner and at an appropriate time. When our minds are clear about our feelings and needs and when the other party is receptive, we may consider making a request of them. If we sense they are not yet receptive because we haven't heard their feelings and needs yet, it's wise to hold off on the request, listen to them, and give them empathy and compassion.

When making a request, it is essential that it be a true *request,* not a *demand* masked as a request. A request expresses a specific positive action that a person can do in the present. It is said politely so that the other person can decline without being anxious that we will be angry or retaliate. For example, rather than saying, "Stop stamping your feet when you walk down the hallway, it's driving me nuts!" we would say, "Would you be willing to walk more softly down the hallway? It would help me to have a sound sleep at night."

For example, Carol's roommate often leaves dirty dishes in the sink. Carol feels irritated because she needs consideration and cleanliness. Once she becomes aware of her feelings and needs and accepts them, she may go to her roommate and say, "I really like a clean kitchen and feel irritated when the sink is filled with dirty dishes. I'd appreciate your help in keeping it clean. Would you be willing to wash the dishes within an hour after you finish eating, and I'll agree to do the same?"

When saying this, Carol has to really mean it; that is, "would you be willing to" is not a polite way of saying, "I want this kitchen to be immaculate as soon as anything gets dirty!" "Would you be willing to" is a request and while Carol hopes her roommate will agree, she is okay if her roommate doesn't, and says instead, "Sometimes I'm late for work and can't clean the kitchen immediately."

The key here is to clearly let the other person know what we feel, need and would like them to do without triggering fears that we are threatening or attacking them, and without expecting them to instantly agree. In other words, before making a request, we have to be okay if the other person says, "No, I can't do that." If we aren't, then we're actually making a demand and setting ourselves up for frustration if they don't comply. So, first it's helpful to consider their feelings and use empathy to understand how their emotions and behavior make sense. Our aim is not to express our frustration; it is to maintain a good relationship and act with compassion while inviting the other person's help in meeting our need.

Communicating with care gives us yet another opportunity to deepen our compassion by understanding the other person. We're more likely to communicate effectively when we approach the other person with empathy and compassion. People are naturally more likely to assist us when we treat them with respect and kindness. When we have an ongoing relationship with someone, it's often worth discussing together the best way to express disagreements and to make requests so that we don't inadvertently push each other's buttons.

When we make a request and the other person turns it down, it's best to avoid taking it personally. There's no sense making up stories, "He is trying to make it hard on me," or "She's on a power trip and wants to control me." Rather, extend some empathy. Tell him that you hear what his feelings and needs are. In this case, Carol could say, "Are you feeling pressured because you need to be at work on time?" Her roommate will likely feel validated and appreciate the understanding. Because her roommate knows that Carol understands her situation, she may go on to say, "But when I'm not running late, I'll clean the kitchen right away. And if I am, I'll do it as soon as I can."

Carol made a request that her roommate couldn't agree to, but since Carol was open to negotiating the point, they could find a plan that worked for both of them. If they couldn't do that, maybe Carol would decide to clean the kitchen herself to help her roommate. Or perhaps she would accept that neatness is not her roommate's strong point. In any case, in order to be happy, Carol knows she has to change her outlook and let go of blaming or criticizing her roommate. Acknowledging her feelings and needs takes her in that direction, as does offering herself empathy.

You may consider that if the goal is to get the roommate to wash her dishes, there are other ways to accomplish that. Indeed, in the short term it may work to threaten, cajole or attack another person to get our way: "If you don't do your part, I'm not going to do mine, either!" "If you can't keep the kitchen clean, maybe I'll have to find another roommate who can!" The problem with these approaches is that they create many nasty consequences: they damage the relationship, create tension that will likely lead to other problems in the future, and reinforce unhelpful thoughts and emotions in our own minds that can lead to future problems. *They aren't worth it.* The key is to find ways to address such situations that don't lead the other person to feel vulnerable or unsafe. We would only say, "If this continues, I am going to move out" as a last resort after we've exhausted all other options. In addition, such a statement must be a realistic description of our position and not just a threat. In the end, some behaviors may be "deal-breakers," and it's okay to convey that. But because thinking or saying, "If things don't change, our relationship will have to," increases the pressure on ourselves and other people, it's better to try less extreme measures first.

REFLECTION

Making Requests

Think of a problematic situation in which you would like to make a request of another person. Sit quietly and identify your feelings and needs without thinking of the other person as the source of your feelings or as responsible for satisfying your needs.

Think about the other person's perspective. What might he feel about this situation? How might his behavior make sense?

Is there a request you could politely make to the other person to ask for his cooperation in changing a particular behavior? Invite his help to meet your need. Make sure that this is a genuine request and not a demand. Get your mind to the point where you are okay if the other person declines your request.

Make the request.

50 : Apologizing and Forgiving

SOMETIMES WE SAY OR DO things that harm others, whether intentionally or unintentionally. Noticing this can be painful, because these actions are different from how we like to see ourselves and how we wish to treat others. Since feeling compassion means being sensitive to suffering and working to alleviate it, we need to apply compassion to mend the harm that we have created.

Apologizing simply means acknowledging what we've done in a way that takes responsibility for it, expresses regret and communicates a genuine intention to do our best not to repeat this behavior. "Yesterday when I spoke harshly to you my mind was overwhelmed with anger, and instead of communicating effectively I let my frustration out. I imagine hearing me speak in this way was painful for you. I'll do my best to express what I want in more appropriate ways in the future." Importantly, apologizing does *not* involve adding excuses that let us off the hook or blame the other person: "I'm sorry that I spoke unkindly, but you really ticked me off." "I'm sorry that you took what I said so personally."

Likewise, there will be times when others hurt us. We live in a world in which other people can be ignorant, angry and greedy, just as we can. We will all experience harm from the actions of others, and sometimes this harm can be extreme.

However, when such harm has occurred, compassion can help us heal. One aspect of this is forgiveness. While this may seem counterintuitive and even crazy in our society that espouses "an eye for an eye," forgiveness has the power to relieve our own pain. Forgiving doesn't mean that we approve of someone's harmful behavior. It simply means that we have resolved to stop being angry about it. Learning to put down the anger helps to heal our pain, as anger keeps us feeling miserable long after the action that harmed us has passed. Forgiveness allows us to shift our focus away from the past and into the present.

This form of compassion involves being willing to let go of the hurt we feel over things that occurred in the past. When we have been hurt deeply, this may be difficult to do and may take some time. Nevertheless, it is worthwhile to have the aspiration to do this because the benefit we will experience is great. Imagine for a moment how wonderful it would feel to be free from the hurt and anger you've been carrying with you for years, maybe even decades. You would feel so relaxed and peaceful because the bitterness and resentment that currently weigh you down would be gone. Letting go of our anger in this way paves the way for compassion.

For example, we can have compassion for parents or caregivers who weren't able to give their children everything that they needed; they did the best they could given their own life situations and capacities. It's important for us to appreciate that and be grateful to them for what they were able to give us, instead of only dwelling on what they weren't. A story one prisoner related is very touching. He sobbed when informed by the prison authorities that his mother had died. His friend asked, "Why are you so upset? I thought she was a drug addict and often neglected you kids, leaving you without food." The prisoner responded, "Yes, she did. But she also loved us and did what she was capable of to protect us even though sometimes it wasn't very much. I appreciate her for that." While our minds have the tendency to put people in fixed categories and think of them as all good or all bad, every human being—including ourselves—has both positive and negative qualities. It is more accurate to see others as the complex people that they are.

Letting go of our anger is a way of being compassionate towards ourselves. When we experience pain due to others' actions, we magnify and multiply the hurt by holding grudges and nurturing hatred and animosity towards them. Our hatred continues to harm us by provoking more disturbing emotions. Anger keeps us stuck in the past, obsessing over what has already happened. Seeing how much anger inhibits our growth and brings us suffering can inspire us to put aside our resentment and forgive others. Forgiveness does not ignore the harm or justify a person's misdeeds, but it releases our pain and anger connected to it. When the harm has been great, we may need the assistance of a therapist or spiritual teacher to help us take these steps. Although it may seem very difficult, it is possible to get rid of the hurt and anger. Those emotions are not one with us; they are not part of the pure nature of our minds.

REFLECTION

Apologizing and Forgiving

Bring to mind a situation in which you have caused harm to someone else. Generating a compassionate motivation, imagine yourself sincerely apologizing to them.

Then, consider a time when someone has harmed you. Start with a small harm. Later you can apply this to more severe harm. Imagine what it would be like to forgive him, to let go of the ill will you carry with you as a result of that harm.

Once you've done this, you might consider whether you'd like to express either your apology or forgiveness to them in person. In doing this, reflect how doing so might impact your relationship with the person.

51 : Giving Positive Feedback and Praise

FAR TOO OFTEN WE PAY so much attention to unpleasant situations that we forget to notice and comment on happy ones! Talking about what is going
well and what we appreciate about others is very important,
and it's a good skill to train ourselves in. Sometimes we have
to remind ourselves to do this. For that reason I (Chodron)
often assign the people who attend my classes on Buddhism
"homework": every day they should praise at least one person
to their face and praise at least one other person behind their
back. This is a particularly good assignment to practice in a
workplace environment, as it can help alleviate any negative
energy there. It can also prevent others from ganging up on
and scapegoating another person. The more we express our
happiness and satisfaction about others' behavior to them, the
better both of us feel.

Giving positive feedback is not just saying "thank you" or
"you're very good." In fact, those expressions don't really give
the other person much useful feedback. So often when we
praise children, we say, "You're a good boy/girl." That only
tells the child that we are pleased, but they don't necessarily
understand why or how they have made us happy. But if we
say, "Thank you for picking up your toys. Now I can walk
across the room without fearing I'm going to trip," that allows
the child to know exactly what behavior we appreciate. Then,

because everyone likes to receive positive feedback, the child will do that again.

Communicating appreciation to adults is similar and we do so by telling the person the specific action they did and its positive effect on us. For example, a department manager may say, "Thank you for turning in the report on time. It gives me the opportunity to think about and plan the next step." We can also give praise by sharing our good feelings and met needs, for example, saying, "I'm grateful for your filling in for me at the meeting. I appreciate the support and camaraderie," or "Thank you for calling to say you were going to be late. I appreciate that you gave me notice because it allowed me to catch up on some other work while I waited." Sometimes we don't even need to speak to communicate appreciation— nonverbal communication can be very powerful. A kind smile and nod, or silently mouthing the words "thank you" when someone does something we appreciate can communicate volumes.

Training ourselves to let others know about the beneficial effects their words and actions have had on us increases our joy in life: we feel better when we have kind thoughts about others. It also reinforces our awareness of others' kindness, increases our sense of closeness to others, and strengthens our awareness of good in the world. These, in turn, make our love and compassion more heartfelt and enrich our lives.

REFLECTION

Giving Positive Feedback and Praise

Think of someone whose words or behavior influences you a lot: it may be your boss, a colleague, your spouse or child, or a neighbor. Train yourself to be on the lookout for things they do that are helpful to you, whether or not they do these actions with the intention to help you specifically. When you notice a helpful action, comment on it to them, stating what they did, how you felt and the benefit you received from their action. Notice the positive effect that your words have on them. Notice your feeling of pleasure when you bring happiness to others.

52 : Survival of the Most Cooperative

SOME PEOPLE SEE evolution in terms of "survival of the fittest" and use it as a reason to be competitive. His Holiness the Dalai Lama, however, speaks of "survival of the most cooperative," and points to ants and bees as examples of this. One ant cannot survive on its own; it needs its fellow ants and must work together with them to provide food and shelter for the ant colony so that all of them will survive. It's the same with the bees—they need to cooperate to construct a hive, make honey, care for the queen and protect the eggs. If the bees in one hive formed factions, blamed each other and fought to determine who was most powerful, then all of them would die. But because they care for each other, communicate and work for the common good, they all survive and the hive thrives.

It is the same with humans; cooperation enables all of us to thrive. If the ants and the bees can cooperate for the common good, surely we human beings with our sophisticated human intelligence can find a way to do this. Compassion is vital, and compassionate communication is one tool to bring it about.

What role does competition play? There are two types of competition, one in which we compete with others, the other in which we compete with ourselves. When we compete with others, our focus is on winning. As a result we may not enjoy the activity very much, and in our attempt to win or dominate, we may be rude. For example, in conversation we may not really listen to what the other person is saying, but just wait for a pause so we can express our opinion. At work or school, we may hold back information that might be useful to others or refrain from helping them even when the opportunity presents itself. While in some cases this type of competition makes everyone work harder, it may also result in damaged relationships, hurt feelings, arrogance, and self-recrimination.

We "compete" with ourselves by trying to better ourselves and develop our skills, not because we want more wealth or a better reputation, but because we genuinely care about others and want to contribute to their well-being. The key here is our motivation. Instead of allowing our self-centeredness free rein, we consciously generate a compassionate motivation. We work hard to develop our particular talents so that they can be used to improve the quality of life for everyone. Each of us has unique talents and abilities and the quality of everyone's life is increased when we cultivate them and use them with a compassionate motivation.

REFLECTION

From Competition to Compassion

Consider a time when you adopted a competitive mindset. Would it have been just as effective—or even more so—to be cooperative? As you identify such situations, consider how you might behave if you were to try cooperating with the other person with compassion instead of competing with her. How could focusing on cooperation change your motivation and behavior? How could it change the way that you experience the other person and her behavior? Would cooperation or competition bring you the most satisfaction in the long term?

53 : Compassion and Attachment Relationships

Ψ THE WORD "ATTACHMENT" has different meanings the depending on the context in which it is used. In Buddhism, the term refers to the unhealthy tendency to project good qualities onto people or things, to exaggerate their good qualities and cling to them with the expectation that they will make us truly happy. This often leads us to have unrealistic expectations, to grasp on to our preferred version of reality and become upset when things don't turn out the way we'd like. In psychology, the term "attachment" is used very differently. In this case, it refers to the nature of our interactions with others—particularly our early caregivers—interactions that can profoundly impact our lives. This is the way we will be talking about attachment in this entry.

Starting with John Bowlby,[1] modern researchers in psychology and related fields have looked closely at the nurturing interactions between caregivers and their children. These interactions are vitally important in helping us learn to manage our emotions and to form and maintain healthy relationships. Our early attachment relationships even affect the growth of our developing brains, shaping brain growth in areas involved with regulating emotions and empathy.[2]

These early relationships with our caregivers (and how we remember and make sense of them) also shape how we'll experience and relate to other people, and our understanding of ourselves in relation to them. The patterns of relating we learn in these early, important relationships are called "attachment styles," and they play out across our lives. If we've had many positive interactions with those who care about us, we're much better able to extend that warmth to our own children as well as to others,[3] and we'll be more motivated to do so.

While infant communication isn't very sophisticated, infants are good at communicating distress by crying and fussing. When caregivers respond consistently with warmth and reassurance to an infant's distress, they create what is called a "securely attached relationship" with the infant. When this happens, children learn that when they need help, others will provide it. They learn to be soothed by others and to form soothing mental images of being cared for by others. They also learn to experience themselves as being worthy of love and care, and are given a valuable model of how to behave when faced with others' distress, one that involves empathy and responsiveness. Since compassion involves sensitivity to suffering and the desire to alleviate it, it's easy to see how having secure attachment relationships when we're growing up can give us a head start on experiencing compassion for others as we grow older.

Secure attachment relationships bring many other benefits. They teach children to accept and label their emotions and encourage them to explore their worlds, knowing that they have a place of safety (a "secure base") to which they can return. In short, secure attachment relationships are at the heart of our safeness systems. Those of us who were well-cared for usually have a much easier time feeling safe, comfortable and at peace in ourselves and in the world.

Unfortunately, not everyone grows up in warm, securely attached relationships. In some cases, our caregivers may have been unable to provide us with a consistently caring and responsive environment, which can lead us to develop "insecure" attachment styles. This plays out in different ways, affecting our ability to feel safe in relation to others and how able we are to engage with them.

Some of us had early caregivers who were detached and unable or unwilling to nurture us, so that we learned over time that no one would be there to help us even in times of distress. In response, we may have developed an "avoidant" attachment style, so that when distressed, we pull back and distance ourselves emotionally from others. We've learned our attempts to connect often won't be fruitful, and that we won't be comforted when we're distressed, so we stop bothering with trying to solicit help from others. We also may be less likely to extend compassion to others, because we haven't seen that behavior modeled for us.

Some of us have grown up with caregivers who were unpredictable and dramatic, particularly in the face of our distress. Sometimes they were warm and responsive, but at other times they responded with rejection, harshness or extreme emotional displays. In such cases, we may develop an "anxious-ambivalent" attachment style, finding ourselves very emotional and hypersensitive to any hint of rejection or perceived criticism. We may have a hard time feeling safe in relationships for fear they may end at any moment. We may become preoccupied with ourselves and our perceptions of what others think or feel about us, obsessed with whether they like us, may be rejecting us and so on.

Finally, those of us who have been abused by our early caregivers may have learned to be *afraid* of close relationships with others, having discovered that if we get close to others they will harm us.

Knowing about different attachment styles helps us understand why some people seem to be more interested and capable of feeling and expressing compassion towards themselves and other people, while some of us may struggle to do so. A number of scientific studies show that our ability to feel and act compassionately is related to our experiences of secure attachment.[4] People who have a history of secure attachments with their caregivers—and hence, have a secure attachment style—are more likely to experience compassion for others and to behave altruistically to help them. They have learned to value relationships, and have good models for learning empathy and how to help others.

Our attachment styles also affect our ability to feel and express compassion by shaping how we respond in the face of perceived threats. This plays out both in terms of how threatened we feel and in our ability to soothe and calm ourselves. If we've had a history of securely attached relationships, we're able to draw upon soothing mental images of being loved and cared for. This can help to ease feelings of threat that might prevent us from feeling compassion. We're better able to tolerate and work with our own feelings of discomfort, allowing us to then shift our focus to the suffering of others and how to help them.

Those of us with insecure attachment styles may find ourselves responding to suffering in very different ways. If we've developed an avoidant style, we'll tend to revert to that style when we feel threatened or uncomfortable, pulling back into ourselves and withdrawing from others. Focused on protecting ourselves and managing our own discomfort, we feel less connected to others and may be less likely to help them. Those of us who have anxious–ambivalent attachment styles may be deeply invested in helping others, but become distracted by our own emotions and insecurities. We may be so worried about others liking us that our attention constantly shifts to ourselves, interfering with feeling compassion for others. Caught up in our own distress, we may have difficulty connecting with how others feel. When we do act to help others, our efforts may be skewed by self-interest, more based in the desire to improve our own image and likeability than in genuine concern for others.

As I've said, awareness of the interaction between attachment style and compassion helps us understand why compassion will seem to come more easily and naturally to some of us and require more effort for others. It also helps us recognize that we're not to blame for these differences. We didn't get to choose our caregivers, or their capacity to give us the consistent, responsive, caring environments we needed in order to learn to feel safe in relation to other people. Seeing this, we can have compassion for those of us whose early life situations didn't foster secure attachments. When we see ourselves or other people distancing ourselves from suffering, we can understand that we are attempting to manage our own emotions. When we see ourselves or other people responding in dramatic ways, we will recognize this as a method we've learned to try and manage our own distress. With this awareness, we can respond with compassion rather than annoyance.

While our ability to provide secure attachments for our children is impacted by our own attachment style and how we were treated as children, this conditioning is not cast in stone. It certainly doesn't mean we aren't capable of being compassionate people. However, we may find we need to put a bit more effort into managing our own emotions and make efforts to help ourselves learn to feel safe in relationships. This can involve doing things such as seeking out and joining social groups with people who have similar interests, and working to develop positive relationships with other group members. If we've had difficult attachment histories, any sort of close relationship may initially feel uncomfortable, but over time we can learn to trust others and value our relationships with them.

There are a variety of ways to do this, including psychotherapy and joining supportive communities.

Those with secure attachment styles may sometimes forget that not everyone relates to others with the same confidence that we do. When we are empathic, we can understand that certain people have the emotional patterns they do due to their early upbringing. Realizing this can help reduce our annoyance or impatience with their emotional habits. Those of us with anxious-ambivalent attachment styles can practice differentiating between our own and others' emotions, learning to be responsible for our own emotions and not accepting responsibility for others' emotional patterns. Increasing self-confidence through learning to accept and work with our emotions without completely identifying with them helps calm the anxiety we feel when challenging emotions come up. Those of us with avoidant attachment styles can try to recognize when we're pulling back from others and see if it might be better to try and connect—both with the emotions we're feeling and with others who might be able to help us.

REFLECTION

Considering Attachment Style

Reflect on how you usually relate to others. Can you recognize one of the attachment styles as applying to you? Do you also see tendencies towards other attachment styles arise in certain situations? How does understanding the different attachment styles help you understand your caregivers and other people in your life?

Consider your current relationships. Do you have relationships that are comforting and safe, in which you receive and offer compassion and support? If not, try to imagine how you might create such a relationship in your life.

54 : Inspiring Compassion in Ourselves and Others

Ψ COMPASSION SPREADS. As we've discussed, when we feel cared for and supported *by* others, we're more able to offer care and support *to* others. Here again, the three types of emotion figure in. When we feel threatened, we will focus on the perceived danger and protecting ourselves from it. When our "drive emotions" are running the show, it's more difficult to attend to others because we're fixated on achieving whatever goal has captured our attention. Alternatively, when we feel safe and connected to others, our defences relax, and we're better able to see things from a more compassionate perspective. Compassion is truly the "gift that keeps on giving," because when we behave compassionately towards others, we become the "secure base" from which they can act upon their own compassionate intentions.

You can probably think of people you've encountered who naturally seem to spread goodness, inspiring others to be at their best. If we look closely, we notice that these people have characteristics that we can cultivate in ourselves. People who act with compassion help others connect with it through the power of "modeling." In modeling, we use our own actions to demonstrate the behavior we'd like to see from others. We all learn from observing one another, and every interaction is an opportunity to teach and inspire others through our behavior. One thing I (Russell) try to slip into nearly every psychology class that I teach is, "If you want to be a good parent, become the person you want your child to be." Our children learn by interacting with us and observing our behavior, so the best way to teach them qualities such as compassion is to cultivate these qualities in ourselves, so we will consistently model this behavior for them.

When I (Russell) was an intern finishing up my PhD in clinical psychology, I had a supervisor named John who directed the Cognitive Behavioral Therapy clinic at the hospital. At this point in my life, I was trying to figure out the sort of professional I wanted to be and John was a good model. He was competent, successful and well liked. I learned a lot and thrived under his supervision, even when doing tasks I didn't really like (watching and critiquing videotapes of yourself doing psychotherapy can be *brutal*). I noticed that everyone else who worked under John was also happy, hardworking and engaged, and that the patients in the clinic benefited a lot from our services.

When you find a model like this, it's worth it to pay attention. John was exactly the sort of professional I wanted to be, so I started observing how he did things. What I saw was kindness, consistency, encouragement and compassion—not in a showy way, but in a steadfast one. John was very friendly, and always had a kind smile for everyone. John's job was to supervise and train his students and staff, and he offered constructive criticism, but always kindly and genuinely; he never caused anyone to feel stupid or lose face in front of others. It was clear he liked his staff and *believed in us*, and his correction was designed to help us improve and reach our potential. John never gossiped or spoke harshly about another person behind their back. And finally, if someone needed help with something he could reasonably do, he helped. In modeling these qualities for us, John set the stage for an entire mental health unit of people who worked hard and happily to help others. Those working under him went above and beyond what was expected of us, not because we had to, but because we wanted to. John showed us that helping others mattered, and that it was worth doing well—not by what he said, but by what he did.

Similarly, cultivating compassion in ourselves and in our interactions with others can inspire the people around us to behave more compassionately. Research by psychologists Mario Mikulincer, Phillip Shaver and their colleagues has shown that when our sense of attachment security is activated, we are more likely to feel, think and behave compassionately.[1] Participants in these studies who were exposed to memories, pictures and other reminders of helping interactions and securely attached relationships were more likely to experience empathy and compassion, engage in altruistic behavior and to endorse values such as benevolence (concern for the welfare of others to whom one is close) and universalism (genuine concern for everyone in the world). These studies repeatedly found that helping people bring secure attachment experiences to mind enabled them to connect with their own compassionate qualities.

This means we can directly inspire a compassionate motivation in ourselves by thinking of people who make us feel safe, accepted and cared for, or by looking at a picture, imagining one person helping another or recalling a time when we were helped or when we helped others. Knowing that I (Russell) am a big fan of the Dalai Lama, a colleague gave me a picture of His Holiness looking kindly into the eyes of a somewhat haggard-looking man who was beaming back at him. That picture is on my office desk, and it has inspired me a number of times to be helpful to a student who appeared in my office unexpectedly, interrupting my work with a question or request. We can incorporate prompts into our lives that will help to stimulate our compassionate motivation—pictures on the wall, photos or quotes in our wallets or on our computer screens. This is reflected in the way many of us engage in our daily spiritual practice, using symbols and pictures of deeply compassionate beings that inspire us to imagine, think about and aspire to the qualities these beings represent. The more we find ways to connect with the desire to be compassionate, the more we'll establish these habits in our minds and brains, so that over time, compassion will simply arise in us of its own accord.

As we've discussed, we can also become a secure base for others. It's not magic, and we don't have to be perfect, but we can help others feel safe, accepted and inspired to act on their own compassion. Here are a few ways to do this:

- Smile, letting others know we like them and are glad to see them.
- Speak kindly and refrain from gossip and harsh speech.
- Offer encouragement rather than judgment when we see others struggling.
- Slow ourselves down, pause to listen when others speak, rather than think of the next thing we'll say, and ask questions to clarify our understanding.
- Help others when we're able. This doesn't mean grandiose gestures designed to focus attention on ourselves. Consistent, small, helpful actions let others know we will be there when and if they need us. Often people don't need our help—but they're comforted by knowing it is available if they do.
- Acknowledge others who are suffering, even if we aren't able to help them. Recognize their humanity and offer a kind gesture or nod.

- When offering critical feedback, do so kindly rather than harshly, balancing genuineness with politeness, compassion and encouragement.
- If we're more ambitious, we can make the commitment to become a secure attachment figure in someone else's life by becoming a tutor, mentor, "big brother/ sister" or volunteering at a facility that supports and assists those needing help.

REFLECTION

Spreading Compassion

Think of two things you could do this week: one to help inspire your own wish to be compassionate, and one to help others feel safe, accepted or acknowledged—then do them. Perhaps think of someone in your life, perhaps a co-worker or family member, who seems like they've been struggling lately. Make a point to have a kind connection with them today. Refrain from giving advice—just let them know that you are there, and that you care.

55 : The Importance of Consistency

Ψ WHILE WE WANT TO EXTEND compassion to others and help them, we aren't psychic, so it can be hard to know when another person is mentally ready to receive compassion. Like us, sometimes they will be open to others, and other times they will be so preoccupied with other things in their lives that little we say or do is likely to get through. This means we need to be patient and not force our "help" on someone. It also shows the importance of developing compassion as a consistent way of being, rather than as a "technique" we pull out when we think it's appropriate.

As a professor at Eastern Washington University, this lesson has been made clear to me (Russell) again and again. I love my job—it's inspiring to see students working towards their goals, optimistic and ready to go out into the world and really make a difference. I do my best to help them along the way, through teaching, advising, supervising and so on. Graduation is always bittersweet, because it means celebrating their success, but also saying goodbye.

Every once in a while, a former student will come back for a visit and will say something like, "I just wanted you to know that you said something to me once that had a huge impact on my life ..." Of course, this is really gratifying to hear, and I feel good about it. Sometimes I even say things with the express purpose of trying to affect their lives and futures—bits of encouragement or advice that have been really helpful to me, for example.

But here's the thing. When I later try to guess what I might have said that affected this student so powerfully, I'm always wrong. As the student tells me, I smile back at them, all the while thinking, "Well, that *sort of* sounds like something I might have said."

Why? Because it isn't about *me*; it's about them. We can never be sure of another person's mental space at any point in time. Maybe they are listening and are really able to receive the support we're offering, or maybe they're completely pre-occupied by something going on in their lives that we're un-aware of. It can be almost impossible to know. So if we expect every compassionate word we speak to miraculously change the lives of everyone we interact with, we're going to be dis-appointed a lot of the time.

What we *can* do, however, is try to be consistent. Consistency is much more important than occasional, grandiose gestures of compassion, because if we're consistently compassionate our compassion will be there when they need it the most. This is why it's important to cultivate compassion as a habit (and hopefully, a lifestyle) rather than simply to learn compassion "techniques." While we can never be sure what others will receive at any given moment, if we consistently interact with kindness, understanding, empathy, honesty and a sincere moti-vation to be helpful, eventually our efforts will have an effect. Growing up in Oklahoma, one of my (Russell's) chores was to give the horses water. If you have horses, you don't just carry the water bucket out to the pasture a few random times each day and expect the horses to drink it down on the spot. Just like compassion, you have to make sure there is a trough filled with clean water available all of the time, because you want to make sure it's there when the horses are thirsty.

REFLECTION

Compassionate Consistency

Consider an aspect of compassion you want to bring into your life and establish as a habit. Perhaps it's to sincerely ask at least one colleague each day how they are doing or making the commitment to stop gossiping. Write this commitment on a small piece of paper, and place it somewhere you'll come across it regularly—by your place at the breakfast table, in your wallet or purse, or on your computer desktop—and use it as a reminder to return to compassionate thoughts and actions.

PART FIVE

Bumps on the Road

56 : Compassion and Personal Distress

CULTIVATING COMPASSION BEGINS with being moved by suffering. First we become aware of our own suffering. Feeling that it is unbearable, we aspire to be free from it. Then we shift our focus to others and become aware of their suffering. Realizing that their suffering is no different from our own—suffering is suffering no matter whose it is—we feel that it too is unbearable. Then we consider others' kindness to us and the fact that our lives depend on them. Feeling empathy and gratitude, we experience compassion and want them to be free from suffering.

Some people hesitate to cultivate compassion, thinking that it will only bring them more suffering and that they already have more than enough. However, when we *choose* to look at others' suffering and cultivate compassion, our experience is very different from what we normally feel when encountering others' misery. Cultivating compassion is done voluntarily and for a specific purpose. Using reasoned consideration to understand others' situations, we come to experience an emotion that we see as beneficial and want to have. This is a very different experience from having a sudden emotional outburst that can't bear another's misery. In the latter case, we feel overwhelmed by a sense of distress that we do not want. However, with compassion we are overcome with an emotion that we do want. It is often said that holy beings are "bound by compassion" to those who are suffering. However, their "bondage" is one they choose and honor. In fact, rather than being burdened by compassion, they find freedom: they are no longer imprisoned by selfish concern.

When our compassion is still weak, it may easily slip into personal distress—the close enemy of compassion that we met in entry 35—an emotion that may seem to be compassion but is not. Genuine compassion focuses on the person who is suffering and wishes them to be free from suffering and its causes. Personal distress, on the other hand, focuses on our pain at witnessing another's suffering. With personal distress, we can't bear to see their suffering because *we* hurt when seeing it. Personal distress clouds our minds and may lead us to feeling so much sadness that we become unable to act to help others.

The evolution of personal distress begins with seeing another person's suffering as so bad that nothing can be done to change it. Then, feeling their suffering as hopelessly unbearable, our attention turns to our pain at witnessing their misery. We lose the ability to discern what is our responsibility and what is theirs. We feel guilty seeing another person suffer and think we should be able to do something about it. Not knowing what to do to relieve their suffering, we become distressed. We may become angry at the situation or the person, policy, institution or event that contributed to others' suffering. At a complete loss for any practical remedy, we may stew in depression. Instead of our helping others, they now have to help us!

How do we counteract this unhelpful personal distress? Remembering that we cannot control everything that happens in the world helps us to accept the reality of situations that we don't like. Although we aren't able to undo the complex network of conditions that brought about others' misery, we can think creatively about what we can do to lessen their suffering, make it more tolerable or to reverse its course. Recalling that misery is impermanent by nature—in other words, it cannot and will not remain the same—helps us to put suffering in a realistic perspective. Doing the "taking and giving" meditation (see entry 30) is also beneficial, as is remembering the meaning of actual compassion. We may have learned a number of other effective strategies that help us tolerate distress in our lives; the key is to remember to use them.

With compassion we can see situations more clearly and respond in a helpful manner. Not falling into personal distress, we can assess the situation accurately, seeing what needs to be done, what we are capable of doing, what the other person is capable of accepting and when someone else may be better suited to offer help. An example is parents who refer their teenagers to other wise adults when the teenagers have problems. Parents have tremendous compassion for their children, but they may not be the right people to help their own children at that time—the teenagers may be more open to the counsel of other adults. Being able to step back and let this happen is an act of kindness on the parents' part. For this reason, it's helpful if parents enable their children to form close connections with wise adults when they are very young. Then, when they become teenagers, there are other adults they can go to for advice if they feel uncomfortable asking their parents or if the problematic situation involves their parents.

It takes a lot of courage and fortitude to be compassionate. We have to be able to bear seeing others' suffering. We have to be able to maintain a strong wish that they not suffer even in situations that we can do little to change. It is necessary to have a strong and stable mind that can remember that our foremost aim is to benefit others.

REFLECTION

Compassion and Personal Distress

There is great suffering in our world, and sometimes witnessing it leads us to feeling helpless and hopeless, which impacts our ability to be compassionate. Are there situations in which you feel immobilized by personal distress? If so, give yourself some empathy and compassion: how might you help yourself feel safe so that you can then extend your compassion to others? How might you view this situation in a way that allows you to be compassionate and not be overcome by your distress? You might start by acknowledging that while you cannot control the situation, you can do something to help. Or you may try shifting your attention away from the troubling situation, balancing your own emotions, and then coming back to help.

57 : Empathic Distress

MOTIVATED BY COMPASSION, some people become so busy with caring for others' needs that they experience what is called "empathic distress." Worn out physically and mentally, they are exhausted from their work to help others. They need—and deserve—rest and compassion themselves.

Empathic distress is the result of allowing our lives to get out of balance. To remain sensible and confident, it is important to assess what we are *able* to do, what we *have time* to do and *what is most important* at this particular moment. Doing this requires pausing to reflect on our feelings and the external situation. Sometimes we may have to say, "I'm sorry I can't do that," when we lack either the time or the ability. There is no reason to feel guilty when we do this, because our goal is to keep ourselves balanced so that we will be able to continue to help others for a long time to come.

After a while, people in the helping professions—such as nurses, therapists, social workers, teachers, doctors, clergy, activists and parents—may feel that their energy is depleted. They hear about people's difficulties every day and do their best to help them, and they may understandably become exhausted. At that time, a break and some rest are definitely needed. Yet sometimes people find it difficult to extricate themselves from situations in which others need them, and they protest that taking a break is impossible. Some of us seem to believe that the world—or at least our homes or workplaces—will collapse if we are not there for our patients, clients, students or children.

But we are going to collapse if we don't take a break and rest sometimes. Although we genuinely care for others, we also have the tendency to feel self-important, thinking, "I am irreplaceable and these people can't function without me." This mindset fails to recognize that by not taking care of ourselves, we compromise our ability to help others.

I (Chodron) am the founder and abbess of Sravasti Abbey, a new monastery in the northwest of the United States, and I know all about the tendency to feel that the world will collapse without me. However, I've learned to see this for what it is: a feeling of self-importance. Since early on in the abbey's existence I've had to travel, and the other nuns have gotten used to running the abbey for weeks or even a couple of months at a time while I'm in another part of the world. The abbey doesn't collapse, nor have they; in fact they grow enormously while I'm away on my travels as my absence prevents them from becoming too dependent on me. I'm quite content to know that I am dispensable! I know that when it comes time for me to die that those around me will continue on very well without me.

When we need to rest, we must rest. When we are ready, we extend ourselves again. Taking a break does not mean we have lost our compassion or have become self-centered. Instead we are being practical and kind to those around us, and those that depend on us may actually grow and become more responsible.

As we've mentioned, maintaining a daily spiritual practice is very helpful to nurture physical and mental health. It gives us the much-needed time to reflect on our motivations and actions and to practice the methods to deepen compassion.

Just as we nourish our body every day by eating food, we must nourish our hearts by having some "quiet time" for meditation, self-reflection or spiritual reading every day. Doing this will strengthen our mind and can bring about a remarkable transformation in our ability to be peaceful and to think clearly. One of my (Chodron's) students—a working mother with a child and a grandchild at home—recounted the change regular spiritual practice made in her life:

As I do my daily meditation practice, I find my heart more open to helping other people. My "spare" time is happily spent helping my elderly neighbour, feeding him, trimming his nails and so on, as well as helping an elderly couple living down the street. I have been in hospitals and doctors' offices with them, gone shopping for them and then when I arrive home, I actually hear my inner voice say, "Now I have the opportunity to be of service to my family!"

What is extraordinary is that the fatigue I once felt is no longer there. I feel energized. Of course, I am aware that this can change, but I can't help but think that by meditating daily and living ethically, a small change is happening inside of me. Yes, I still feel the need to take a walk alone, and I do my spiritual practice when the household sleeps, but the *need* to get away or even to lament the fact that I don't have much time to study or read at home is not an issue like it once was.

I'm not sure what I expected years ago when I began my Buddhist practice. It wasn't this, I can assure you. It's not about bliss, about feeling at one with the universe, or even about feeling "clear" or "awake." For me, spiritual practice is about giving without thinking twice, giving of myself joyfully. One moment at a time.

REFLECTION

Recharging Our Batteries

In order to help others, we need to take care of ourselves. Consider how you might create space in your life to recharge your batteries and then try to do so. We recommend beginning a regular meditation practice, but feel free to be creative in finding activities that soothe you and bring you a feeling of peace, safeness and openness. Sitting quietly and listening to music, taking a relaxed walk, chanting a mantra or reading an inspiring book can do wonders to recharge us in the face of a hectic lifestyle.

In addition, try to release the idea that you should be able to do everything or fix everything. No one can do that. Give yourself some empathy so that you feel comfortable about doing what you are capable of doing and are able to rejoice in that.

58 : Removing Partiality

 HAVING IMPARTIAL COMPASSION is challenging, and we may find ourselves experiencing strong compassion for certain people but not for others. For example, when we read about people starving in war-torn Darfur our compassion is aroused, but when we hear about hunger in the inner city we respond with a curt, "Well, why don't they just get a job?" Concerned when civil war, rebels and drought prevent food from reaching the citizens of the Nuba Mountains of Sudan, we don't care that much when a history of family poverty, racism, poor schools and drugs prevents people closer to home from having nourishing food. In this case, having compassion for those further away—whom we don't know much about—is easier than having compassion for those nearby. At other times we have compassion for our friends and family but are apathetic to the suffering of strangers.

Or, we may strongly feel the misery of people suffering from cancer, but ignore Aunt Ethel who suffers from kidney disease and is sometimes irritable. Here it is easier to have compassion for a group of people we do not personally know, than for a specific individual we know that we sometimes find annoying.

Sometimes we may feel strong compassion for the poor in our own country, who we can empathize with, but not for a celebrity dying from substance abuse, whose fame and wealth we are jealous of. Many people find it difficult to have compassion for those whose political opinions differ from their own.

In all these instances bias is at work. In other words, because we understand some people better or are closer to them, our compassion for them is strong, while it is harder to care about those we don't know, like or approve of. While it's definitely good to have compassion for whatever individuals or groups we find it easiest to empathize with, we must continue to work at breaking down our mental barriers regarding comparatively superficial differences and extend compassion to more and more people, seeing that at the end of the day, they are all the same in wanting happiness and not suffering. None of them chose the situations they were born into, but in whatever circumstances they live there is misery of one sort or another. You may want to review entry 24, Love and Compassion, to renew your understanding of this.

In short, it's wise to practice dropping our judgments and abandoning attachment to preferences and to train ourselves to have compassion for whoever is in front of us at this moment. This could be the group of people living on another continent that we see on the news, and a moment later it could be the plumber at our door or our neighbor's child crying after a bicycle accident outdoors. We are always surrounded by living beings; there is nowhere to go where we're totally alone. Animals and insects surround even meditators in remote mountain caves. Therefore, we must try to greet them all with a compassionate heart.

REFLECTION

Working with Partiality

Now it's time to look really closely at ourselves. If you've read this far, you're likely very committed to cultivating compassion. See if you can spot areas where you still have some work to do. Are there individuals or groups of people that you find it difficult to feel compassionate towards? Maybe you find it hard to empathize with people of a different political leaning or religion? Perhaps your compassion stalls when others express certain views or engage in behaviors that run contrary to your values? Challenge yourself. Using the techniques we've discussed throughout the book—for example, empathy, contemplating others' kindness or noticing their strengths—see if it is possible to extend compassion to the person or group that you usually ignore. If you can't, then try to imagine what it would feel like *if you could* have compassion, empathy and kindness for them.

59 : Compassion Gone Awry

IT MAY HAPPEN that our compassion becomes overly confident. That is, we find ourselves determined to help someone whether they want it or not. We think we know what is best for someone and have resolved to save them from what we perceive to be their own foolishness and even from the natural course of events such as aging and death.

For example, imagine an elderly person who is weak, bed-ridden and dying of cancer. He knows he is dying and has a week left at most, and he wants his final days to be tranquil. But he happens to catch the flu, which now threatens to kill him before the cancer does. His spouse, child and doctor are all determined to save him from death by influenza and do one test after another in the desperate attempt to cure the flu. In their own eyes, they are acting with compassion for him, but from his perspective all the poking and prodding are causing him more discomfort.

Or take the young person who enjoys art, is good at it and wants to be an artist. But her parents want her to be an engineer. They only want her to be happy, and feel certain that she will have more job security and earn a better living as an engineer. They badger her relentlessly about going back to school to get an engineering degree and she refuses, knowing that although she is smart enough to be an engineer, she would be miserable being one. Perhaps she will eventually succumb and follow her parents' preferences or perhaps she will refuse. But either way, the parents' pushing has introduced a barrier in their relationship and she distances herself from them. The parents feel hurt and can't figure out what happened since they were only trying to help her.

Compassion gone awry may lead us to try to control others—"for their own benefit," of course. We may become persistently dogmatic in our attempts to "help" someone or we may feel indignant, thinking, "I'm trying to help you, why won't you cooperate?"

My (Chodron's) Buddhist teacher used the term "Mickey Mouse compassion" to describe situations in which we act in ways that superficially appear to be compassionate but lack the wisdom that correctly assesses a situation. Robert, one of the prisoners that I work with (I have done prison work for many years) fell into this when he was a youth. His mother had a huge debt from gambling at the local casino, so with compassion for his mother's predicament, he decided to do a drug deal to get the money to help her. In the process of doing the drug deal, Robert and the other person quarreled. Afraid that the other person would hurt him, Robert shot and killed him instead. Now he is serving life without the chance of parole for a crime committed when he was sixteen.

Mickey Mouse compassion also manifests when people take more animals into their homes than they can possibly care for, creating a hygienic disaster in the name of compassion. Wanting to save all animals, they are unable to care for any of them well and many die. Yet the "animal hoarder" doesn't see any of this and considers what he is doing to be an act of compassion.

In some situations, we put a lot of energy into helping others but are not aware of what is really motivating us. We may think that we are being kind and helpful, but our actions may actually be attempts to feel better about ourselves.

Some people tend to be very sensitive to the feelings of those around them and easily empathize with them. With "compassion" they diligently work two jobs and care for aging parents. But inside they have strong feelings of self-loathing and think that they have no right to live, let alone be happy. The help they give others is an attempt to feel worthwhile or to earn the love that they seek. They often run themselves ragged and then criticize themselves for not doing more. Here we see that being aware of our own feelings and needs is essential for compassionate action.

Although the people in these examples mean well and may even be praised for their kindness, their motivation is not completely pure compassion because they are trying to fulfill a need within themselves. While fulfilling our needs is not a bad thing, when done without awareness it can lead to difficulties. We need to understand our own needs and know our actual motives. Then we can step back and assess if our behavior will bring the results we want and if our actions are actually meeting others' needs. As a way to fulfill our needs, learning to extend kindness and compassion to ourselves will work better than seeking other people's approval or trying to control them. With compassion for ourselves, we can in turn benefit others with genuine compassion for them.

REFLECTION

Considering Our Compassion

Are there times when you've attempted to control someone else's life or behavior "for her own good"? Alternatively, are there times when your behavior looked "compassionate," but underneath you were feeling resentment or condescension? If you discover experiences like this, step back and consider your motivation as we did in the very first entry of the book. Before engaging in any behavior, try to let go of any resentment or desire to control the other person or the situation. Instead, bring forth a kind motivation that cares about others' well-being. If that's difficult to do, try to imagine what it would be like if you already had such a motivation. *If you did* have a purely kind, compassionate motivation, how would that motivation affect your thoughts and behaviors towards the other person?

Are there times in your life when you acted with "Mickey Mouse compassion," thinking that you were helping someone while you were actually unaware of the complexity of the situation? What were the results of the "help" that you gave? How can you slow down so that before acting you will be more aware of the various factors at work in a situation?

60 : Friends Who
Give Bad Advice

Ψ ONE DAY IN MY (Russell's) anger management group, we were discussing how to work with obstacles—things that can come up when we're working to replace our anger, blaming and self-condemnation with compassion. One obstacle that the group identified was reluctance to "let go of the "angry self." One of the group members noted that it would be hard for him to stop being angry, not because he liked feeling that way, but because this anger had been his constant companion for many years. It felt predictable and comfortable, like a friend we've known our entire lives.

The other men nodded as he spoke, and as the discussion continued, they began to identify other such "friends"— aspects of themselves that often weren't helpful, but were hard to let go because they offered some comfort in their familiarity. "I don't know how else to be." "I don't like my anger, but it's always been there for me." "My internal self-critic is continually running me down, but if it wasn't there, I'm afraid I'd completely let myself go." "That judgmental part of me creates problems in my relationships, but it also helps me feel special, like I'm the expert who is in control and knows better than others." "My depression is comforting because I know what tomorrow will be like."

These men had hit on something really powerful: we can have a hard time changing long-standing habits because we may prefer their predictability to the unknown of trying something different, even when these habits cause problems for us. They can feel like old friends who have accompanied us through some very difficult times. But as the men figured out, these habits are like old friends who consistently give us very bad advice.

You may have had some friends like these. They can be fun to be around, and their familiarity is comforting. But they inevitably come up with ideas that end up getting us into trouble. Such friends can be very persuasive—even though we know that our last several adventures with them have ended in catastrophe, it seems to make a lot of sense when they're making the case for the latest exploit. We find ourselves wanting to go along with them, even when we *know better*.

Emotions like anger, fear and sadness can be like this. They truly are our friends—they represent our threat system's efforts to protect us. But unfortunately these friends lack wisdom and don't see the whole picture, offering overly simple answers to complex situations: "He's an idiot! Attack!" "I'm in danger! Let's get out of here!" "That's scary, stay in bed all day." They can't help it. Our anger doesn't know how to be anything but angry. Our fear can't be anything but afraid. Our sadness can only be sad. So if we allow ourselves to continually listen to these friends' advice, we know exactly where we'll end up. Better to simply acknowledge them, thank them for their well-meant advice, and seek out an authority that is better suited to guide us wisely. We need a new friend—one who is kind, wise and competent. One who gives sound advice.

We met this wise friend earlier, in entry 20. It's the "compassionate self,"[1] the kind, wise, confident aspect of ourselves we seek to cultivate. We all have these various emotional aspects of ourselves—personas we find ourselves sometimes inhabiting—the angry self, anxious self, sad self, self-critical self, judgmental self, as well as the kind self, the joyous self, the inspired self. It can be tricky, as we may have had many past experiences in our lives that have strengthened and reinforced the less helpful parts of ourselves, while starving our compassionate and wise aspects. As we've discussed, emotions like anger, anxiety and desire carry with them a strong felt urgency to act, an urgency that can be used by advertisers to persuade us to buy their products or by political parties to mobilize our votes for their candidates. We may have found ourselves surrounded by messages designed to reinforce our competitive, angry or materialistic tendencies, and few that fed our compassion.

If we don't want to get hijacked by these messages, we need to take responsibility for our lives. We can do this by connecting with the compassionate motivation to benefit others and ourselves. If this compassionate aspect of ourselves seems undernourished in comparison to the others—so that it gets drowned out a lot—we can send it to the gym. That is, we purposefully practice these compassionate habits to make them stronger, just as we work out our bodies to make them stronger. We do this by purposefully bringing forth the qualities of the compassionate self in ourselves, again and again:

- Calm the physical arousal—the racing heart, rapid breathing—that fuels the anger and fear by slowing down our breathing.
- Bring to mind the kind wish for all beings, including ourselves, to have happiness and to be free of suffering.
- Shift into an empathic perspective: consider how others may feel and how it makes sense from their perspective that they would feel this way.

- Imagine ourselves acting compassionately, with kindness, wisdom and confidence.
- Meditate and learn to quiet our minds and contemplate things that inspire our compassionate motivation.
- Deepen our wisdom by reading and exposing ourselves to media that broadens our perspectives and allows us to strengthen our compassionate qualities.

As we develop these compassionate qualities, we can prioritize them, establishing our compassionate selves as benevolent, wise authorities in our lives. Just as passengers who spend a long time at sea will inevitably face rough waters, we will all face difficult times. In the face of these rough seas, the various emotional passengers of the ship will do *what they always do* in stressful times. The angry self will get mad and blame. The anxious self will get scared and cower. The sad self will become melancholy and mournful. We can understand all of these reactions in the face of a scary sea-storm, but we wouldn't want to put these passengers in charge of the ship's fate. The compassionate, wise captain, however, has the skills to do the job. He (or *she*) doesn't blame the passengers for getting upset, because he knows that storms are scary and the passengers are reacting perfectly naturally. Instead, he comforts the passengers and takes responsibility for steering the ship to safety. Because the captain is experienced and wise, understanding that stormy seas are just a part of life, he approaches the task with confidence and patience, relying on his experience and drawing upon support—friends, family, spiritual community, therapists—when he needs to.

In this way, we can set up this compassionate self as the "captain" of our emotional lives. When our other old friends—fear, anger and sadness—start shouting, we use these feelings as cues to slow down and shift into the perspective of the compassion-ate self. We slow down our breathing for a minute or two and try to imagine how we would work with the situation if we were at our most kind, wise, confident and compassionate. As we've discussed, from this perspective, we ask questions: "What will help me feel safe so I can best deal with this situation?" "How could I be most helpful to the other people involved?"

This progression is important: we start by calming down the passengers (working with our emotions) first, because it's hard to face the storm (the situation) when the entire ship is in chaos. This starts by listening to the wise captain—the compassionate self. Once we've done this, we can then ap-proach the problem or challenge with kindness, wisdom and confidence.

REFLECTION

Emotional Friends

Consider whether you've had any long-standing emo-tional "friends," perhaps fear, anger, resentment, or jealousy, that have consistently given you bad advice. Think about how you could relate to these emotions from a place of compassion, so you will be better able to face the chal-lenges in your life with kindness, wisdom and confidence.

61 : Fear of Compassion, Steadfastness and Thawing in Our Own Time

Ψ AS WE'VE DISCUSSED, one of the most compassionate gifts we can give another person is the gift of feeling safe. If we look at our own experiences, we will most likely discover that the people who have been the best at helping us feel safe are themselves warm and compassionate. They have a way of accepting and directing warm, unconditional kindness to everyone they meet, creating the sort of interactions that help others feel supported, comforted and at peace.

Although most of us would like to be this kind of friend to others, things don't always work the way we'd hope. As we've explored, some of us have had histories of hurt or abuse and were neglected by those who should have taken care of us. One way or another, we may have learned that trusting others can be dangerous. When this happens, we may feel threatened rather than comforted by close interactions with others, even when we *know* that they have good intentions and sincerely want to help us. Our minds can subconsciously learn to associate feelings of threat with people or situations very quickly and powerfully. Dan Siegel writes about an elderly woman with Alzheimer's disease, who is unable to form new memories. Every day, her doctor comes to her, and every day, it's as if she is meeting him for the first time; she has no memory of their previous interactions. One day, the doctor plays a bit of a nasty trick, hiding a tack in his hand so that when they shake hands, she is poked. The next day, this woman still couldn't remember the doctor, but she refused to shake his hand. Although she didn't remember being poked, the threat centers of her brain and unconscious mind had learned to associate shaking hands with danger. Learning not to trust can occur at a very basic level.[1]

The conditioned fear of closeness with others is sometimes called "fear of compassion,"[2] and it can make relationships very complicated. We can *both* desperately want to have close, supportive or intimate relationships with others *and* find ourselves being anxious and frightened when we're in such relationships. I (Russell) do some work with a residential facility for children and adolescents called the Hutton Settlement, in Spokane, Washington. Many of the children who now live there have had experiences that taught them not to trust others. Some found themselves taken in by well-meaning, loving families who had the best of intentions to provide these children with safe, loving homes. These families had visions of enveloping these young people in love and support, and expected that the children would attach to them in return, feeling safe and thriving. The reality was often very different. In response to these families' efforts at creating closeness, the children often withdrew or even became aggressive. These kids had learned that the people who were supposed to take care of you could hurt you or disappear when you most needed them. So instead of attaching and loving these families back, the children fought them: testing the relationships, distancing themselves, acting out and having extreme emotional reactions—just the way we act in situations of threat.

Feeling upset and threatened that their honest attempts to care for the children were being rejected, these parents would sometimes respond by distancing themselves from the children in turn. This cycle creates a self-fulfilling prophecy that inadvertently confirms these children's greatest fears—that despite the parents' good intentions, their support would not be there when the going got tough and so they couldn't be trusted. This dynamic was played out again and again, and ended with the children being placed outside the home.

Many of us may find ourselves in positions where we want to help others who are afraid of compassion. How do we help those who have learned to distrust the very relationships that could help them feel safe? This is the task faced by countless teachers, therapists, clergy, mentors and volunteers (for example, at homeless shelters and rape crisis centers). It starts by considering how trust works.

A store here in Spokane sells pre-cooked frozen shrimp, which need only to be thawed before serving. Doing so requires a bit of preparation though. The instructions on the bag are very clear: "Thaw by placing in refrigerator overnight. Do not force-thaw under running water." If you thaw the prawns by running water over them, they can absorb too much water and become mushy; they just can't handle all that warm water at once. They can't be forced to thaw.

We're a bit like these frozen shrimp. We have to thaw in our own time. Learning to trust others takes time, particularly when experience has taught us that if we let others get close to us, they will hurt or abandon us. Rushing the process doesn't work. If *we* are the ones who have trouble with trust or closeness, we have to be courageous and allow ourselves to receive warmth and help from others, enduring the discomfort caused by our previous experiences as we slowly learn to trust these relationships.

If we're trying to help others who have learned to fear compassion, we have to go in knowing that things won't always go smoothly. We must let go of the expectation that those we seek to help will automatically respond to our efforts with appreciation, gratitude and affection. Paying attention and responding to the cues they give us—their nonverbal behavior, their level of talkativeness—we should not try to get too close too quickly. We must be willing to patiently weather the storms, sending a constant message of compassion: *I am here for you. You are worth caring about. I will not hurt you. I will wait patiently, and will be here when you are ready.* Although we can be sensitive to their suffering and offer help, warmth and support, compassion is more about steadfastness than action when we're interacting with people whose lives have taught them to fear closeness rather than be comforted by it. We can't change anyone, but we can *help to create the conditions in which change is possible.*

This process can be a long, difficult one, and sometimes it can be too much for one person or one family to handle. This is why places like the Hutton Settlement exist, with its entire staff dedicated to providing a consistent, safe and nurturing environment. It's unrealistic to think that we can "be everything" to another person. In many cases, compassion means helping them to find resources and connect with supportive communities.

REFLECTION

Compassion and Steadfastness

Learning to feel safe can take time when we've been taught to feel threatened by situations or relationships. Consider a situation in your life in which you felt intimidated by closeness. What did you need then? What could others have done to help you learn to trust them?

Now think of a situation in which you were in the other role, wanting to connect with someone who feels frightened or threatened by closeness. Imagine what it would feel like to be steadfast and patiently committed to allowing the other person to thaw gradually, and to accept your support, kindness and affection only as they become ready.

PART SIX

Compassion in Action

62 : Compassion as an Antidote to Low Self-Esteem

IN 1990, I (CHODRON)had the fortune to attend a conference sponsored by the Mind and Life Institute with His Holiness the Dalai Lama and Western scientists in Dharamsala, India. One afternoon Sharon Salzberg, a Buddhist meditation teacher, shared that when Westerners do the meditation on Cultivating Love (see entry 24), they have a great deal of trouble extending love to themselves. The reason was their low self-esteem; they didn't feel that they were loveable. Puzzled, the Dalai Lama asked who had this problem. Most of the people looked around at each other and said, "We all do." "But why?" the Dalai Lama wondered, "all of you are well educated, successful in your careers, have a good income, friends and family. Why don't you like yourselves?"

What followed was a lengthy discussion in which we brainstormed a wide variety of reasons for low self-esteem, ranging from being taught the Christian notion of original sin as children to competition in school to comparing ourselves to celebrities, sports players and models in the media. The concept of low self-esteem baffled the Dalai Lama. Apparently, it is not a problem in the Tibetan community, even though most Tibetans-in-exile don't have factors that Westerners generally associate with high self-esteem, such as university education and high wages.

Several months later, I attended a talk by His Holiness the

Dalai Lama in a major church in San Francisco. At one point he referred to compassion as an antidote to low self-esteem. My ears perked up: clearly he had been reflecting on the discussion in Dharamsala. He recommended that people reach out with compassion and do things for others: volunteer in the community, look after a neighbor's children when she is busy, clean up the coffee counter at work, be kind to a sick relative. But I didn't understand how that counteracted our own low self-esteem. Don't we have to love ourselves before we can love others?

I started to observe my own mind when I felt a lack of self-worth. The inner dialogue was so familiar that I hardly noticed it: "I can't do anything right. Others are better than I am. There's something in me that is inherently defective and unlovable." It went on and on, one statement followed another about "what is wrong with me. Me. ME. *ME*."

Then it clicked. That's why compassion works as an antidote to low self-esteem: it stops us from thinking about ourselves in unhealthy ways. The more we focus on ourselves to the exclusion of everything else, the more self-critical we become. Everything that happens is interpreted through the filter of how it relates to ME. We become sensitive to every small event in the environment, sure that it is indicative of whether others love or hate us. We take innocent statements and read into them comparisons with others in which we come out the losers.

When we practice compassion, we focus on the well-being of others, rather than on *me*. Generating compassion does not involve ignoring our own problems by distracting our attention to others. Instead, being compassionate stops us from being preoccupied with ourselves. The Dalai Lama often says, "We usually believe that compassion benefits others, maybe even at our own expense. That is not correct. When we are compassionate, *we* are the chief beneficiaries. Our minds are happier and more relaxed. Our lives become more meaningful and we feel more connected to others. Others may or may not benefit from our compassionate actions. It depends on their receptivity, and we cannot control that. But, for sure, we benefit from having compassion for them."

Doing the "taking and giving" meditation (see entry 30) demonstrates the efficacy of this approach. When we imagine taking others' suffering with compassion and giving them our body, possessions, and virtue with love, our minds automatically feel calmer and more satisfied.

REFLECTION

From Self-Criticism to Compassion

Try to notice the way that you talk to yourself, particularly when you have made a mistake or are struggling with something. Do you get caught up in self-criticism, berating yourself for your failure? If so, try to shift your focus to compassion. Rather than labeling yourself negatively ("I'm so useless!"), bring to mind your intention to deepen compassion and consider how you might do that. Rather than attacking yourself, what could you do to bring kindness to others? Try replacing that nasty name that you were about to call yourself with a kind smile for the next person you see. Notice how it feels when you do that.

63 : Compassion as the Antidote to the Critical, Judgmental Mind

MANY PEOPLE SUFFER from having a hypercritical attitude towards themselves and others. When aimed at ourselves this attitude results in low self-esteem, as discussed above. When targeted at others, it damages relationships and generally leaves us feeling rotten.

When we look at how the critical, judgmental mind operates, we see that it is trying to make us happy. One of My (Chodron's) teachers, Geshe Ngawang Dhargye, said, "We'll gossip with a friend, criticizing this person and that person, until at the end of the conversation we come to the conclusion that the two of us are the best people in the world." The critical mind thinks that by disparaging others we will make ourselves better than them.

Sometimes we'll sit in a public place and "people watch," commenting on the appearances of strangers: "Why does this person have such a weird haircut? That person is such a slob. This one is too fat; that one is too thin. Oh, there's someone who looks rich and important; he's probably conceited beyond belief. She's pretty but most likely is a spoiled brat. That one can't stand up straight; he's undoubtedly drunk. This one is angry; look at the way she's screaming at those kids." However, doling out criticism does not make us feel good about ourselves; our respect for ourselves diminishes after witnessing the ugly torrent of negative comments about others.

Compassion is a great antidote to a critical, judgmental mind. When we have compassion, we look at others with kindness, understanding their difficulties, knowing that they're doing the best they can, given the external situation and their internal abilities to deal with it. Being compassionate entails understanding that people are usually unaware of how they have been influenced by their misconceptions and disturbing emotions and so remain trapped by them. Yet their fundamental wish is just like ours: they want to be happy and not suffer.

REFLECTION

Replacing the Judgmental Attitude with Compassion

Here's an experiment to try when you're people-watching. Train your mind to say, "There's someone who looks rushed; may she relax, be calm and get to where she's going safely. That person looks unhappy; may he be well and happy. She looks flustered; I hope she regains her confidence. Those kids are giving their parents a hard time. May that family be harmonious and help one another." In other words, look at them with tolerance, understanding and compassion.

Training your mind in such thoughts may seem artificial at first, but after a while your compassionate thoughts will flow like a gentle river, connecting you with others and with your own kind heart.

64 : Slow Things Down and Give Them Some Space

Ψ WHEN POWERFUL EMOTIONS come up in us, we experience the urge to act in ways that can over-shadow our compassionate intentions. If we think we've been criticized, for example, we can feel an almost overwhelming urge to snap back at the other person. One way to counter this automatic reaction is by slowing things down, taking a moment to make sure we've perceived the situation correctly and consider how best to respond so we can prevent impulsive emotional reactions we may later regret.

Andrew, a member of my (Russell's) prison anger group, was sitting in his cell one evening, listening to blues music and reading a magazine he enjoyed. His cellmate entered and loudly proclaimed, "Get your ass out of bed and turn that music off!" After a couple of other nasty comments, he yelled, "You're acting like a little *bitch!*" Those of us who aren't in prison will recognize this as a nasty insult. However, in American prisons, there are certain "code-words" that signify a direct challenge—invoking a dominance hierarchy and almost demanding a violent confrontation. In prison, if someone calls you a "punk" or a "bitch," they are calling you out—*daring* you to respond—with the assumption that if you don't, you have been dominated.

Andrew leapt from his bunk, loudly replying, "What did you say to me?" A fight seemed unavoidable, likely landing them both in solitary confinement, tarnishing their records and per-haps even affecting their release dates. But then Andrew did something extraordinary. He *paused*, took a few breaths and slowed things down, just for a moment. And in that moment, he was able to bring to mind the wisdom of compassion: "I recognized that I hadn't done *anything* to provoke this guy; that this had nothing to do with me. I wondered, 'What could be going on with him that he would act like this?'" Though his mind was telling him to "Attack!," Andrew found it within himself to give the situation some space and withdraw a bit. It wasn't easy, and afterwards he even found himself wondering if he'd done the right thing—if withdrawing while others were watching had made him a "mark," signifying vulnerability that others would later exploit.

It turned out that this didn't happen, but something *else* did. A few days later, Andrew was talking with a peer about what had happened and discovered that his cellmate suffered from severe mental illness and was sometimes disconnected from reality. The remnants of Andrew's anger melted away, replaced by compassion: "I feel bad for the guy—struggling with mental illness, doing things that get him into all sorts of problems. He's got a really hard life. I'd have felt terrible if we'd gotten into a fight."

If we can slow things down, rather than falling into hab-its driven by powerful—but not very clever—threat emotions like anger and fear, we can use compassionate reasoning to consider how best to respond.

Andrew's story also demonstrates that things are not always as they seem, which we can sometimes discover once we slow down and gather more information. Often, we don't have the whole story—we've only gotten a quick glimpse of what is going on. It's like seeing an action-packed thirty-second clip taken from the last third of a movie; we know *something* is happening, but don't have the context to really understand it. Without that context, however, it can be impossible to know how best to respond. So when we recognize a situation is getting out of control, we *slow down and give things (and ourselves, and others) some space.* Since the threat emotions that block our compassion are fueled by arousal in our bodies (racing heart, heavy breathing and so on), slowing our bodies down helps calm our minds as well.

We can practice this in many ways. Instead of rushing to speak, we can listen to what the other person is saying, pausing to consider it and only speaking when we're sure we understand what they're trying to communicate. Before sending that emotionally charged e-mail, we can pause and consider what we seek to accomplish and whether or not this response will address our long-term objectives. Before entering our homes after a long, hectic day, we can pause at the door and remember that we're going to be with the people we cherish the most, and rejoice at our fortune for having them in our lives.

I (Russell) would like to introduce what, in my opinion, is one of the single most powerful psychological techniques I've encountered, and also one of the simplest and easiest to remember. In Compassion Focused Therapy circles, we call it *soothing rhythm breathing*, and it involves taking a moment to slow the breath down and focus our attention on that sense of slowing in our bodies. This counters the arousal that fuels our threat response, helping us calm ourselves down so that we can shift into a more compassionate perspective. This isn't magic; slowing down our breathing won't simply make our anger or fears just melt away. But it *softens* them, helping us shift into a mindset that isn't dominated by those emotions. We're using our bodies as entry points for shifting our emotional state, and it works!

Soothing Rhythm Breathing

Taking a comfortable upright posture, focus your aware-ness on your breath—just gently settle your attention on the sensation of breathing in your body. You may find it helpful to close your eyes.

- Slow your breath down, taking four or five seconds on the in-breath, holding for a moment, and then taking four or five seconds on the out-breath. Take nice, slow, deep breaths. Do this again.
- Feel free to experiment with the breath to find a way that is soothing to you. While most people breathe in and out through the nose, you may find it more helpful to breathe in through the nose and out through the mouth (or vice-versa), as this can help keep your atten-tion on the breath.
- Bring your awareness to the feeling of slowing in your body. Focus on that sense of slowing.
- Spend thirty seconds to a few minutes breathing and focusing in this way. Do it longer if you like.
- If your attention wanders, gently bring it back to the breath and the sense of slowing in your body and mind.

Like anything else, we get better at this with practice. We can practice several times throughout the day with ease—during the first commercial of a television program, every time we get on the internet or after the doors close on the train.

65 : Compassion and
Living Ethically

IN THE PROCESS OF BECOMING friends with ourselves, we will discover that living ethically is the foundation of a happy life. All too often, people see ethics and morals as external rules imposed on them without their consent. Unfortunately, nowadays ethics and morality are increasingly politicized, even while many politicians ignore them in their personal lives. By examining our own lives, we'll see that ethical conduct is the means to live peacefully with others, a way to feel good about ourselves, and the basis for making our lives meaningful.

Ethical conduct has two aspects. The first is abandoning physical, verbal and mental activities that are damaging to others and ourselves. The second is engaging in physical, verbal and mental activities that benefit ourselves and others. Living in this way helps us to live together peacefully. For example, whether we follow a religion or not, we know that harming others by killing or injuring them, stealing or destroying their possessions, and using our sexuality in ways that harm others (such as adultery, spreading diseases or forcing people to engage in sexual activities) creates problems for others and for ourselves. These actions damage our relationships and may result in legal repercussions, whereas abandoning these actions prevents those undesired consequences. Doing the opposite— saving lives, respecting others' property, using sexuality wisely and kindly—goes a step further, creating trust and safety among people.

Likewise, lying, creating disharmony, speaking harshly and engaging in malicious gossip create problems in our families and workplaces as well as between groups and nations; whereas speaking truthfully, in ways that create harmony, with kindness and tact, at a suitable time and about suitable topics spreads good will in families and societies.

Certain mental activities are also damaging: coveting the belongings of others, nurturing malicious thoughts and wrong views such as, "I don't have to be responsible for my actions. I can do whatever I want as long as no one finds out about it," all lead to trouble. Avoiding such ways of thinking prevents these problems, and training our minds in thoughts of generosity, compassion and wisdom creates a positive environment inside us that manifests when we engage in actions that create good relationships.

We all want to live in a safe environment and ethical conduct creates this safety. Imagine for a moment that for one day everyone on our planet abandoned just one of the harmful actions discussed above, for example, killing. That would drastically change the headlines of all the newspapers! So many lives would be saved and so many families would not have to grieve the loss of their loved ones! Living ethically is an expression of our compassion for others. We want them to be happy and not suffer, and we are committed to bringing that about through what we do, say and think.

Ethical conduct also enables us to *feel good about ourselves*. Acting with a kind and compassionate motivation—or at least without thoughts of greed, hatred and confusion—helps our hearts find peace. Going to bed at night, we are not worried about others finding out about our inappropriate conduct. We do not feel guilty, because we've acted in accordance with our values. Our hearts are free from the remorse that comes from hurting others, especially those that we care about the most. Having done nothing that others can use against us, and not giving anyone reason to resent us or retaliate against us, our minds are tranquil. The kind of inner peace and contentment that comes from living ethically is more valuable than any amount of money, fame or recognition. In short, living ethically is a way of treating ourselves compassionately because it prevents our own suffering and enables us to feel good about our actions.

Furthermore, living according to our ethical values *makes our lives meaningful.* When we die—as we all will—we will be able to look back and know that we solved more problems than we created. We will be free from regret and remorse and will be confident that our lives were well spent. We won't lie on our deathbeds wanting to apologize to people we harmed or struggling with anger towards people who harmed us. Rather, we'll rejoice in our lives, knowing that we shared love and acted with compassion. We'll feel satisfied that we touched others' lives in ways that benefited them. Whether we believe in rebirth, an afterlife or are not sure what happens after death, we prepare well through living ethically.

REFLECTION

Living Ethically

Consider the role of ethics in your life—not those based in external rules, but the values and principles you hold. Do you engage in any behaviors or ways of thinking that are harmful to yourself or others, such as abusing drugs or alcohol, nurturing resentment or manipulating others? Do you often lie to cover up something that you did, which you don't want others to know about?

Contemplate how those thoughts or actions adversely affect your life and the lives of others, and generate a strong intention to begin to change them.

Consider how much better you will feel about yourself and how much your relationships will improve if you leave those destructive habits and actions behind. Think of specific activities that would help you to do this. You may want to consult a mentor, clergy member, therapist or life coach to help you.

66 : Compassion, Uncertainty and Listening to Uncomfortable Truths

Ψ As HUMAN BEINGS, we tend to get stressed about circumstances we experience as uncontrollable and unpredictable. We like to *feel* that we have a handle on things, even when we're really clueless. We also don't like ambiguity. Many times, I (Russell) have almost wanted the dreaded outcome to *just happen* rather than having to wallow in uncertainty, wondering if it *may* happen. Have you had experiences like this? We may withdraw from the project rather than face the chance of failure or sabotage the relationship we think might be cooling because disappointment sometimes seems less uncomfortable than ambiguity. We don't like uncertainty, and we don't like *not knowing*. Unfortunately, we can deal with this ambiguity in ways that aren't compassionate at all.

In our attempts to avoid the discomfort of uncertainty and figure out *how things work*, we sometimes create simplistic explanations for things that are quite complicated. This is reflected in beliefs like "Good things happen to good people, bad things happen to bad people." This sounds good at the outset; however, this idea is simplistic and can breed misconceptions and problems. Following its logic, it means that if anything tragic happens to you, you must be a bad person—that it's your fault. It sets us up to judge ourselves and other people, particularly those who suffer the most: "If your life is really that hard, you must be a *really* bad person."

However, reality is much more complex than this. Life is filled with uncertainty and many different factors affect our lives. We know there are ways of living that make it more likely that we'll have good lives. On the other hand, there are many factors outside of our control: the conditions of our birth, the psychological state of our parents or caregivers, our genes and whether or not the driver of the car heading towards us has had too many pints to drink tonight. The truth is that sometimes, bad things happen to all of us, despite our best efforts and intentions. If we're really going to cultivate compassion, we're going to have to learn to deal with the uncomfortable truths of uncertainty, ambiguity, lack of control and tragedy.

In our attempts to come up with personal theories that neatly explain everything, we naturally tend to rely on our own experiences. The problem is that taking our experience as reflective of "the way it is" can set us up to be close-minded and to invalidate the experiences of people whose characteristics and backgrounds are entirely different from our own. If we think our version of reality is the only one, or the only "correct" one, we may dismiss the feelings and interpretations of others, even when their reactions are based on experiences that are just as valid as our own.

We can consider racism, for example. I (Russell) grew up in rural Oklahoma in the United States, where the ethnic mix consisted primarily of white people, Native Americans and more white people. I never thought much about racism and certainly didn't consider myself to be racist. Based on my limited experience of the world, racism meant that you hated other people because of the color of their skin. I didn't hate anybody, and I avoided using racist language or telling racist jokes. My family and friends did as well. I knew people who *did* use such language and didn't think very well of them, but most people I knew weren't like that, so I didn't understand what all this fuss about racism was about.

What I didn't understand, and what it took me a long time to grasp, was that I lived within a culture that systematically advantaged people like me (white, heterosexual males) and systematically disadvantaged pretty much everyone else to one degree or another. This implicit racism, sexism and heterosexism surrounded me, but was invisible to me, because it existed completely outside the range of my experience. I couldn't imagine getting pulled over because of the color of my skin. People had never looked away from me on the street or crossed to the other side when they saw me walking towards them. When I started to listen to people of color, to gays and lesbians—even to white women—it was hard for me to believe their stories were true, because they were so different from my own experience.

They weren't just different. More than that, these stories, these truths, were *uncomfortable*. They described the reality of a world that seemed so unfair and cruel to me that at first I couldn't bring myself to believe it. But once I learned to listen, the stories kept coming. As a young male used to going to concerts by myself, it was eye opening to hear my female friends say they couldn't do that without fear of being raped. A black friend told me of being pulled over in his car by the police on a weekly basis until he got his windows tinted, and then never getting pulled over again. I remembered the pinkish-tan "skin"-colored crayons that I'd used all through elementary school and began to imagine how I might have felt if they hadn't resembled the color of my own skin. Another black friend told me what "for normal hair" shampoo did to *her* hair, and about the thoughts and feelings this fact brought up in her—the subtle communication that she *wasn't normal*, that something was wrong with her. Something was wrong alright, but it wasn't with her.

Since they fall outside our limited understanding of *how things work*, we may find ourselves discounting, minimizing or disbelieving such uncomfortable truths, things we really *don't want* to believe. We convince ourselves that these things can't really be true so we don't have to deal with them, ignoring these aspects of reality in order to avoid discomfort. Sometimes we just stop listening entirely. If we love animals but also love eating meat, we may purposefully avoid documentaries about the unsanitary conditions and tremendous suffering produced by the factory farming industry. We don't like the story, so we change the channel.

Compassion means doing the opposite. If we're really committed to understanding and addressing the sources of suffering in the world, we have to accept that there are many uncomfortable truths out there. If we're going to make things better, we must first be willing to listen to these truths and to accept that the reality of the world is often very different from what we'd like it to be. We have to be willing to let go of the delusions we maintain in order to stay comfortable.

Although listening to these stories and believing them will be disturbing to us, they also present us with possibilities. As we begin to understand these sources of suffering, we see that they don't just happen on their own. *They occur within a system of causes and conditions that can be changed.* For example, children are not born racist—they *learn* to be biased towards some people and against others based upon their interactions with their parents or caregivers, exposure to media that portrays certain groups of people as less competent and desirable than others, and a host of other learning experiences occurring within cultures that systematically elevate some people and disadvantage others. By allowing ourselves to be moved by the uncomfortable truth that things like racism *exist* and are consciously and unconsciously taught, the discomfort this truth produces in us can motivate us to help, to work to *change* the way things are. As we commit ourselves to work with compassion to alleviate suffering, we discover that there are many people who are just as uncomfortable with these problems as we are—people who are as committed as we are to doing something about them. As we join together with the diverse community of people who are actively working to make the world a better place, we find an antidote to our discomfort that works far better than avoidance and ignorance—genuine, warm connectedness with other people.

By repeatedly facing uncertainty, we learn it is possible to be comfortable with not knowing, and with not being able to control everything. We learn to calmly accept that life is inherently uncertain, and perhaps even appreciate that our profound lack of knowing creates the possibility of wonder, awe and appreciation for the amazing enormity of life.

Opening ourselves to the stories of those who are different from us is also a powerful gateway to wisdom. While some of those stories are tragic, many others are fantastic, inspiring and filled with knowledge that open us to entirely new perspectives on life. It all starts with learning to listen.

REFLECTION

Learning to Listen

Spend some time listening to someone whose experience is entirely different than your own. When their experience seems to conflict with your understanding of how things work, try to set your judgments aside and remind yourself that each of us has different experiences in life. Allow yourself to see what you can learn from others. Accepting their experience of life as valid, commit yourself to hearing, understanding and learning from their perspective. Practice listening without interrupting, keeping your attention on what the other person is saying.

67 : Small Acts of Compassion Can Have Big Results

SOMETIMES WE THINK that to be a truly compassionate person we must be like His Holiness the Dalai Lama or Mother Teresa. Looking at their great deeds, we think, "What can I do? I'm so selfish."

This way of thinking is not helpful. The Dalai Lama and Mother Teresa don't live in our families or work in our workplaces. If our spouses, bosses, employees, colleagues, neighbors, or family members need understanding or compassion, the Dalai Lama or Mother Teresa can't give it to them. But we can. So we should not belittle ourselves or the importance of showing compassion, even if it's only a little. Consider some examples.

One day a resident of my (Chodron's) monastery came to me and said, "There's another person here who is often in an angry, bad mood. I'm tired of being around her negative energy and so keep a distance from her. However, from studying the Buddha's teachings, I recognize that I don't have a very good attitude. What can I do?"

I recommended that she do small acts of kindness for that person—smile at her, give her a snack, help her when she's doing her chores. In short, just be pleasant. That evening I received the following note:

I would like to share with you something wonderful that happened after I spoke with you today. While walking past the person I told you about I gave her a big smile, and she gave me a big smile back! Later she gave me a note (because we are in silence today) that said, "When I see you smile, I will make an effort to smile also."

This made me realize how self-centered I was. Everything was all about me. Often enough I show others a sad face because I'm not satisfied. At those times I forget and lose the ability to practice compassion.

It's so wonderful that she reminded me! Now I will work to strengthen my love and compassion. Thank you for your advice.

Everyone who comes to Sravasti Abbey eventually hears the "Toilet Paper Teaching." I usually give it at the beginning of a retreat, when explaining that we do a meditation retreat not to shut ourselves off from the world, but to learn to approach the world with compassion. We show compassion to our fellow retreat participants by arriving to sessions on time, not leaving in the middle unless it's an emergency, and being mindful of how we walk and move. Knowing that we can communicate compassion, hostility or apathy to others by seemingly small actions, we practice compassion by bringing mindfulness to them.

Then I tell them to pay attention to small acts of compassion. One way to do this is to change the toilet paper roll when it runs out. Replacing the old roll with a new one is such a small thing, but it's something we're often too lazy to do. We think, "The next person who comes to use the bathroom will notice and put in a new roll. I have more interesting things to do now."

Have you ever been in the bathroom and noticed that there was no more toilet paper only when you were already in a compromised position? Oh, how we would have appreciated it if the person who finished the old roll had put a new one in! In this way, we see how a small kind act that takes less than thirty seconds can be greatly appreciated. So whenever we have the opportunity, we must overcome even a little bit of laziness and do a small act of kindness.

After attending a Buddhist retreat, some people ask, "I'm finding these teachings and the practice very helpful in my life, but my family wonders what I'm doing. How can I get my family interested?" I tell them, "Take out the garbage!" Imagine: Your mother will think, "I've been trying to get my son to take out the garbage for thirty years with no success. But after attending Buddhist teachings, he did it without my even asking. Wow!" Small acts of kindness like this attest to the value of your spiritual practice more than hours of talk.

Compassion can change and save lives. As a teenager, a friend of mine was very depressed and thought of killing herself. One day she was walking down the street, her eyes fixed to the ground. A stranger passed and she looked up for a moment. The person smiled at her. It warmed her heart and she began to think that maybe her life had some value. After all, someone appreciated her existence enough to smile at her. That was the spark that began her path to recovery.

My friend Kalen is a chaplain for the Missouri Department of Corrections as well as the founder of Inside Dharma, a Buddhist group that reaches out to those in prison. Kalen worked with an inmate who was in administrative segregation because he was considered dangerous. Administrative segregation—or "The Hole" in prison slang—is an isolated, maximum-security area where inmates are locked in windowless cells except for three one-hour periods of exercise per week. Realizing that he was in a bad way, Kalen asked Inside Dharma's supporters to send him messages of support. Later she received the following letter from him:

Dear Friends,

Being in prison has been very hard for me, especially in a state where I have no family or friends. My home is in Chicago, where I have lived all my life until I came to Missouri and got myself into trouble I could not get out of. After that, things got worse: I lost my house and my job. My wife died and then my grandmother died. Then my mother died too, and at her funeral my father had a heart attack and it seems that he won't make it either.

I hated my life. I hated prison. I hated the world. I didn't want to live anymore and I gave up. All I wanted to do was die. One day the chaplain came to see me. She had heard that my mother had just passed away, and she tried to talk to me, to comfort me and to ease my pain. We talked for a while and when she left I felt better. Nevertheless I planned to take my life a few days later. I had nothing left but pain, sadness and HATE! Hate is such a powerful emotion. It takes so much energy out of you to hate. It is like draining out the life that's in you until you are just a dried-up prune. That is how I felt.

The day I planned to commit suicide is a day I will never forget. I was going to do it at night, but an officer came to my cell door and told me I had mail. When he passed the mail under my door I saw over twenty letters and cards. I couldn't believe I had received that much mail, at least not at one time. As I sat down and opened the letters and cards, I was shocked to receive so much love from people I didn't know and who didn't know me. I felt their love and it moved me deeply. I cried and I knew that I could not give up. I knew I had to stop hating.

The brothers and sisters at Inside Dharma and the

Dharma center opened my eyes with their love and concern. I am forever indebted to you. As one teacher said, "Life is what we make it. Nothing lasts forever, not even bad times. They too will pass." I look at things differently now and realize that hate can be replaced with love and joy. I can't express in words how much all of you have changed and affected my life. Prayer and meditation are wonderful, and I am more peaceful now. I send you lots of prayers and good wishes. May you have success, health, happiness, peace, insight and receive the blessings of the Three Jewels. I love you all.

We never know the far-reaching effects of a small action undertaken with compassion, but they can be great. Let's not miss the opportunity to share even a little kindness with others, even strangers.

REFLECTION

Small Acts of Kindness

Reflect on the kindness you have received from others during your life and let the wish to repay that kindness arise in your mind. Think of small things you can do in your life to show kindness to those around you, and imagine the happiness you will feel knowing that you made someone's life even a little bit easier or more pleasant. Make a strong intention to do that action, and smile at the thought of doing it.

68 : How Compassion Changes Us

WE ARE THE CHIEF BENEFICIARIES when we cultivate compassion. To illustrate this, I (Chodron) would like to share some stories that people who are in prison have shared with me about how their practice of compassion has benefited them.

A Family of Mice

George was a tough guy, a former member of a white supremacy gang. He found a Buddhist book while in prison and began to learn about compassion. In one of his letters, he shared this story:

Last night the sound of a mouse chewing on something woke me up. I had not seen any mice around this cell since I moved here in April, and I assumed it was in the wall where the plumbing was because mice get in there pretty regularly.

This morning when I woke up I saw some bits of paper in my locker. One side of the locker has a door but the other side is open, and that is where I keep all of my hygiene articles and stationary. Seeing the mouse had been in my locker, I decided to clean out any mess that she may have made. I started pulling stuff out and putting it on the floor. I got all of the hygiene articles out, and as

I grabbed an envelope with legal pads in it, she jumped out and ran straight towards me. I was sitting on the floor in front of the locker and had nowhere to go. Even if I did, there wasn't any time because she was pretty quick on her little feet. I squalled like a child, and I'm glad that I was here alone so that no one saw me. Meanwhile, the mouse rushed past me and ran into the pipe chase where the plumbing is.

After my heart rate settled down a bit, I went back to the task at hand. While doing so, I found the paper that she had been chewing all night long. I also found her babies that she was building her nest for. Six little pink ones. They were so tiny, and I had no idea what to do with them. I kept looking at the door, thinking that she might come back and get them, but she didn't. I thought about just leaving them there but I didn't want to encourage that type of behavior from her.

Finally I picked them up and put them into the pipe chase one at a time through a hole by the sink. I put the nest and everything else in there with them. Then I put some chips in there, hoping she would find them and build another nest in there for them. I didn't know what else to do with them.

I hope that she finds them and takes care of them. A couple of them were making noise so hopefully she heard them crying and came to their aid. A few years ago I would have sent them down the toilet. Today I worried all afternoon hoping they were okay.

The Kitchen and the Cat

Steve murdered someone as a teenager and was tried in court as an adult. He has been in prison for nearly two decades now. He told me this story about his job working in the prison kitchen.

Today, after the kitchen was cleaned up, I took my break-fast tray outside and ate on the service ramp. Considering that the institution has been on lockdown status with no regular movement for nearly two months now, the fact that two other workers and I were outside at all was a treat that few others were able to enjoy.

As an added bonus, we were paid a visit from one of the few stray cats that still roam freely about the institution. Despite the administration's repeated attempts over the years to remove the feline population who wander in and around the prison, others still manage to find their way in and make themselves at home.

Some of these cats end up having kittens which, if found in time, are often adopted by caring staff or, if not, grow up wild along the perimeters of the institution. The latter, while avoiding nearly all human contact, manage to live quite well off the bounty provided in and around the prison dumpsters.

This particular stray, a young tabby, had not grown up wild. She was so familiar and comfortable around people that the first time we made her acquaintance was when she took up position next to our kitchen line early one morning and followed us straight to work as though it were the most natural thing in the world for her to do.

We had only seen her a couple of times since then, and not at all in the last week and a half. There was specula-tion that she'd been scared off by some dog-loving officer who'd chanced across her path. Worse yet, we wondered if she hadn't met an all-too-common fate on the busy street in front of the prison. Happily neither misfortune had befallen her.

I watched as our little friend slid her way through a chink in the security fence at the front of the kitchen and proceeded to casually make her way to just within ten feet of us. She stood there looking at each one of us expectantly, gave out a single "meow" and sat down, waiting for what she seemed confident would soon be coming her way.

Now, this is prison, something one does well never to forget. It's filled to overflowing with men who have committed some of the foulest deeds imaginable. Yet, when I went inside to find something suitable for her highness's palate, the guys' eyes lit up just to hear that she was outside. Smiles broke out from ear to ear as a few workers made their way to the cooler looking for milk, leftover fish or bits of turkey. Several otherwise "hardened criminals" headed straight out the door where their gravely voices could be heard trying as best they could to purr and meow a welcome to our visitor.

I found myself simultaneously amused and touched by the spectacle playing out before me. For several minutes I just stood there, watching as the defences dropped away and men serving decades behind twenty-foot walls secured by armed towers and razor wire forgot all about where they were and did their level best to pamper the closest thing most of them would ever get to having a pet again.

Once more I was reminded that, deep down, even the supposed worst of the worst of us have at least a spark of compassion inside, a spark that no matter how dim it may sometimes appear can never entirely be extinguished by mere outward circumstances.

A Teacher I Didn't Expect

Jerry is a young man imprisoned for a violent crime he foolishly participated in with the encouragement of his girlfriend. He is quick to anger and has been involved in several fights in the prison. An intelligent person who wants to be more compassionate, he told me this story:

> I've been having an interesting time practicing patience with my cellie [his cellmate]. He's a sixty-something-year-old man who has been in prison since he was seventeen. He heard about my reputation from others and, although nothing had happened, one day he suddenly jumped up and announced that he wasn't afraid of me and wanted to fight. I refused and said to him, "Why should I fight you?" Although he insisted, I declined and eventually he settled down. This happened several times.
>
> As time went on, I saw him worry himself silly about people trying to take advantage of him. I watched him complain about everyone and everything and witnessed his wife leave him after seventeen years of marriage. Basically, I saw someone who was coming to the end of his life wracked with hatred and loneliness, trying to figure out what his life had meant. I began to feel for him, so when he wanted to talk, I listened, and when he wanted to fight, I laughed, and eventually he would too.
>
> I came to have compassion for this person who was in such a state. He taught me patience, not with him but with myself because I had to learn to rethink what I thought. I learned that I don't have to have an opinion about everything, that I don't have to trounce someone just because he challenges me, that my previous snap judgments got me in a lot of trouble.
>
> I don't care so much about my opinions now. I want to stop the cycle of beating someone up and being beaten up. There are more important things than defending my ego and its turf. All this I learned from a man that the people around me called psychotic.

REFLECTION

How Compassion Changes Us

By now, you've spent a good deal of time reading about, thinking about and practicing compassion. Consider how this has impacted you. Has actively bringing compassion into your life changed how you view yourself, other people and the world in general? Has it changed your relationships to others? Has compassion affected your sense of meaning in life and what you aspire to? Observe the effects that cultivating compassion has had in your life and allow yourself to enjoy them.

69 : Bringing Compassion into Every Moment

Ψ IN CLOSING, WE'D LIKE TO POINT out the importance of each moment. Every moment presents us
with an opportunity to bring compassion into our
lives, and give it to others. Every time we think a compassionate thought, direct kindness towards another person, relate
warmly to ourselves and others, or bring to mind something
that inspires our compassionate nature, we plant and nurture
the seeds in our minds that will eventually grow into a garden
of kindness and compassion. We, and only we, have the power
to transform our lives. The key is to continually find ways to
bring compassion into every day. Here are a few final suggestions for doing this:

- As often as possible, take a moment to connect with
  your compassionate motivation.
- Seek and create opportunities to cooperate and act
  "in-sync" with others. One research study showed
  that simply tapping our fingers in time with another
  person leads to increased compassion for that person.[1]
  Spiritual communities have long used such methods
  to enhance the feeling of community such as chanting
  and bowing together.
- If you find yourself caught up in self-pity, self-criticism
  or other thinking that keeps you locked in a state of

threat or self-centeredness, gently redirect your attention to helping others.

- Volunteer!
- Do your best to make sure your own needs are met, starting with giving your body what it needs: nutritious food, adequate sleep and regular exercise.
- Find ways to help yourself feel safe, particularly when threat emotions arise. Studies show that giving support to others helps to reduce feelings of threat and corresponding threat activation in the brain.[2] One of my favorite studies looked at the relationship between feeling social threat (for example, fear of being embarrassed) and helpful behavior. When people feel socially threatened, their likelihood of behaving altruistically often disappears—but this effect was erased in participants who held a teddy bear![3] Find ways to soothe yourself and help yourself feel safe—and use them!
- Practice relating to yourself and others with *warmth*.
- If you find yourself thinking unhelpful thoughts, don't try to push them out of your mind. Instead, try to let those thoughts go, gently shifting your attention to more helpful, compassionate ways of thinking.
- Whenever you find yourself beginning to judge, try instead to understand.
- Rather than continuing to beat yourself up for past mistakes and transgressions, focus your attention on finding ways to do better.
- Practice pausing and slowing things down.
- Engage in regular practice that helps you make friends with yourself. Make time daily to reconnect with your values and a sense of meaning in your life.
- Seek and frequently bring to mind things that inspire you to be compassionate—stories, images, poems, songs,

quotes and memories of times that you have acted, been treated with and observed compassion.

- Be creative in applying compassion to new areas of your life. As you go through the day, ask, "How can I bring compassion into this moment?"
- Commit to take responsibility for your own emotions and needs, and refrain from blaming others for your own internal experiences.
- Frequently remind yourself of the many ways your life is positively impacted by the kindness of others—that everything that makes your way of life possible occurs as a result of the efforts of other beings.
- As often as possible, connect with empathy. Try to understand what others are feeling, and how it might make sense that they are feeling this way. Direct empathy towards yourself, too!
- Finally, allow yourself to rejoice in your growing capacity for compassion.

If you give yourself over to compassion, compassion will give you back a life filled with good relationships, peace, confidence and joy. When we learn to let go of the constant need to prop up our egos at every turn, we can engage in life directly and meaningfully, participating fully in our activities and actively engaging in our relationships. From the bottom of our hearts, we want to welcome you to the community of people who, for thousands of years, have used the power of compassion to transform their lives, and the world. You are in good company.

Notes

DEDICATION

1. Santideva, *A Guide to the Bodhisattva Way of Life*, trans. Vesna A. Wallace and B. Alan Wallace (Ithaca, NY: Snow Lion, 1997), 10:55. See also Shantideva, *The Way of the Bodhisattva*, trans. Padmakara Translation Group (Boston: Shambhala, 2006).

INTRODUCTION

1. There are several versions of the Cherokee "Legend of the Two Wolves." The version presented here was adapted from that presented on the following website: www.firstpeople.us/FP-Html-Legends/TwoWolves-Cherokee.html.

CHAPTER 2. WHAT IS COMPASSION AND WHY DO WE NEED IT?

1. The metaphor of the critical versus compassionate teacher is commonly used in Compassion Focused Therapy, developed by British Psychologist Paul Gilbert.

CHAPTER 8. A DIFFERENT KIND OF STRENGTH

1. Shantideva, *The Way of the Bodhisattva*, trans. Padmakara Translation Group (Boston: Shambhala, 2006), 6:14.

CHAPTER 9. MINDFUL AWARENESS

1. There is an evolving body of research showing that mindfulness and other forms of meditative practice can actively develop the brain. The two studies below are a good starting point for those who are interested: B. R. Cahn & J. Polich, "Meditation States and Traits: EEG, ERP, and Neuroimaging Studies,"

Psychological Bulletin, 132:2 (2006), 180–211; Britta K. Hölzel, James Carmody, Mark Vangel, Christina Congleton, Sita M. Yerramsetti, Tim Gard & Sara W. Lazar, "Mindfulness Practice Leads to Increases in Regional Brain Gray Matter Density," *Psychiatry Research: Neuroimaging,* 191 (2011), 36–43.

2. The RAIN acronym as it applies to mindful awareness is explained nicely in Jack Kornfield's *The Wise Heart: A Guide to the Universal Teachings of Buddhist Psychology* (New York: Bantam, 2008).

CHAPTER 12. THREE TYPES OF EMOTION

1. This discussion is based on the three-circles model of emotion as featured in Compassion Focused Therapy (CFT), developed by Professor Paul Gilbert. The following references are good places to start for those interested in learning more about the three-circles model and CFT: Paul Gilbert, *The Compassionate Mind* (London: Constable, 2009); Russell L. Kolts, *The Compassionate Mind Approach to Managing Your Anger Using Compassion Focused Therapy* (London: Robinson, 2012); and, for mental health professionals, Paul Gilbert, *Compassion-Focused Therapy: Distinctive Features* (London: Routledge, 2010).

CHAPTER 13. WORKING WITH UNWANTED THOUGHTS AND EMOTIONS

1. Daniel M. Wegner, David J. Schneider, Samuel R. Carter III & Teri L. White, "Paradoxical Effects of Thought Suppression," *Journal of Personality and Social Psychology,* 53:1 (1987), 5–13.

CHAPTER 20. IMAGERY AND METHOD ACTING

1. This method of cultivating compassion using imagery and method acting is a core component of Compassion Focused Therapy treatment, and was developed by Paul Gilbert. More can be learned about these approaches in Paul's books: Paul Gilbert, *Compassion-Focused Therapy: Distinctive Features* (London: Routledge, 2010); Paul Gilbert, *The Compassionate Mind* (London: Constable, 2009); and in my book applying CFT to anger: Russell Kolts, *The Compassionate Mind Approach to Managing Your Anger* (London: Constable, 2012).

CHAPTER 30. EXCHANGING SELF AND OTHERS, AND TAKING AND GIVING

1. Geshe Jampa Tegchok, *Transforming Adversity into Joy and Courage: An Explanation of the Thirty-Seven Practices of Bodhisattvas* (Ithaca, NY: Snow Lion, 2005).

CHAPTER 31. SELF-COMPASSION AND COMPASSIONATE SELF-CORRECTION

1. Paul Gilbert, *Overcoming Depression: A Self-Help Guide Using Cognitive Behavioral Techniques* (London: Robinson, 2009) and Paul Gilbert, *The Compassionate Mind* (London: Constable, 2009).
2. Kristin D. Neff & Roos Vonk, "Self-Compassion versus Global Self-Esteem: Two Different Ways of Relating to Oneself," *Journal of Personality*, 77:1 (2009), 23–50.
3. Kristin D. Neff, *Self-Compassion: Stop Beating Yourself Up and Leave Insecurity Behind* (New York: William Morrow, 2011), and Kristin D. Neff, "The Development and Validation of a Scale to Measure Self-Compassion," *Self and Identity*, 2 (2003), 223–50.
4. Paul Gilbert, *Compassion-Focused Therapy: Distinctive Features* (London: Routledge, 2010).
5. Paul Gilbert, *The Compassionate Mind* (London: Constable, 2009) and Russell L. Kolts, *The Compassionate Mind Approach to Managing Your Anger Using Compassion Focused Therapy* (London: Robinson, 2012).

CHAPTER 34. COMPASSIONATE THINKING AND MENTALIZING

1. The concept of mentalizing was introduced by British psychologist Peter Fonagy: Peter Fonagy & Patrick Luyten, "A Developmental, Mentalization-Based Approach to the Understanding and Treatment of Borderline Personality Disorder," *Development and Psychopathology*, 21 (2009), 1355–81; and Peter Fonagy, Gyorgy Gergely, Elliot Jurist & Mary Target, *Affect Regulation, Mentalization, and the Development of the Self* (New York: Other Press, 2005).

CHAPTER 40. HELPING EACH OTHER FEEL SAFE

1. C. S. Carter, "Neuroendocrine Perspectives on Social Attachment and Love," *Psychoneuroendocrinology*, 23 (1998), 779–818.

2. One of the most exciting developments in modern psychology is the discovery of the dramatic ways that our experiences impact our developing brains in ways that continue to reverberate throughout our lives. Dr Dan Siegel is a pioneer in this area, and a good place to start is with *The Developing Mind*. We've listed a few other references below as well, which provide a few more texts to read through for those wishing to explore this exciting area of psychological science. Dr. Siegel's audio-CD set *The Neurobiology of "We"* provides a particularly accessible entry point into this area of study. See Louis Cozolino, *The Neuroscience of Human Relationships: Attachment and the Developing Social Brain* (New York: Norton, 2006); Joseph LeDoux, *The Emotional Brain: The Mysterious Underpinnings of Emotional Life* (London: Weidenfeld and Nicolson, 1998); Allan N. Schore, *Affect Regulation and the Origin of the Self: The Neurobiology of Emotional Development* (Hillsdale, NJ: L. Erlbaum Associates, 1994); Daniel J. Siegel, *The Developing Mind* (New York: Guilford Press, 1999); Daniel J. Siegel & Mary Hartzell, *Parenting from the Inside Out* (New York: Tarcher, 2003); Daniel J. Siegel, *The Neurobiology of "We": How Relationships, the Mind, and the Brain Interact to Shape Who We Are* (Audio CD, Boulder, Colorado: Sounds True, 2008).

3. Carolyn Schwartz, Janice Bell Meisenhelder, Yunsheng Ma & George Reed, "Altruistic Social Interest Behaviors Are Associated with Better Mental Health," *Psychosomatic Medicine*, 65 (2003), 778–85; Tara L. Gruenewald, Diana H. Liao & Teresa E. Seeman, "Contributing to Others, Contributing to Oneself: Perceptions of Generativity and Health in Later Life," *The Journals of Gerontology, Series B: Psychological Sciences and Social Sciences*, 68:6 (2012), 660–5; C. E. Schwartz, P. M. Keyl, J. P. Marcum & R. Bode, "Helping Others Shows Differential Benefits on Health and Well-being for Male and Female Teens, *Journal of Happiness Studies*, 10 (2009), 431–48.

4. Stephanie L. Brown, Randolph M. Nesse, Amiram D. Vinokur & Dylan M. Smith. "Providing Social Support May Be More Beneficial Than Receiving It," *Psychological Science*, 14:4 (2003) 320–7.

Chapter 41. Compassionate Communication

1. Marshall B. Rosenberg, *Nonviolent Communication: A Language of Life,* (2nd ed., Encinitas, CA: Puddledancer Press, 2003).

Chapter 44. Considering Perceived Threats and Needs

1. A. H. Maslow, "A Theory of Human Motivation," *Psychological Review,* 50 (1943), 370–96.

Chapter 53. Compassion and Attachment Relationships

1. John Bowlby, *Attachment and Loss: Vol. 1. Attachment* (2nd ed., New York: Basic Books, 1982, first published 1969).
2. Louis Cozolino, *The Neuroscience of Human Relationships: Attachment and the Developing Social Brain* (New York: Norton, 2006); Allan N. Schore, *Affect Regulation and the Origin of the Self* (Hillsdale, NJ: L. Erlbaum Associates, 1994); Daniel J. Siegel, *The Developing Mind* (New York: Guilford Press, 1999).
3. Daniel J. Siegel & Mary Hartzell, *Parenting from the Inside Out* (New York: Tarcher, 2003).
4. Mario Mikulincer & Phillip R. Shaver, "Attachment Security, Compassion, and Altruism," *Current Directions in Psychological Science,* 14:1 (2005), 34–8.

Chapter 54. Inspiring Compassion in Ourselves and Others

1. Mario Mikulencer, Phillip Shaver and a number of their colleagues have done a series of wonderful studies showing how activating a sense of attachment security—of being connected to and supported by others—can help us be more compassionate. Here is a selection of Russell's favorites: M. Mikulincer, O. Gillath, V. Halevy, N. Avihou, S. Avidan & N. Eshkoli, "Attachment Theory and Reactions to Others' Needs: Evidence that Activation of the Sense of Attachment Security Promotes Empathic Responses," *Journal of Personality and Social Psychology,* 81:6 (2001), 1205–24; Mario Mikulincer, Omri Gillath, Yael Sapir-Lavid, Erez Yaakobi, Keren Arias, Liron Tal-Aloni & Gill Bor, "Attachment Theory and Concern for Others' Welfare: Evidence that Activation of the Sense of Secure Base Promotes Endorsement of Self-Transcendence Values," *Basic and Applied*

Social Psychology, 25:4 (2003), 299–312; Mario Mikulincer & Phillip R. Shaver, "Attachment Security, Compassion, and Altruism," *Current Directions in Psychological Science*, 14:1 (2005), 34–8; Mario Mikulincer, Phillip R. Shaver, Omri Gillath & Rachel A. Nitzberg, "Attachment, Caregiving, and Altruism: Boosting Attachment Security Increases Attachment and Helping," *Journal of Personality and Social Psychology*, 89:5 (2005), 817–39. An excellent summary of this research can be found in the following chapter: Omri Gillath, Phillip R. Shaver & Mario Mikulincer, "An Attachment-Theoretical Approach to Compassion and Altruism," in Paul Gilbert (ed.), *Compassion: Conceptualisations, Research and Use in Psychotherapy* (London: Routledge, 2005), 121–47.

CHAPTER 60. FRIENDS WHO GIVE BAD ADVICE

1. Paul Gilbert, *The Compassionate Mind* (London: Constable, 2009); Russell L. Kolts, *The Compassionate Mind Approach to Managing Your Anger Using Compassion-Focused Therapy* (London: Robinson, 2012).

CHAPTER 61. FEAR OF COMPASSION, STEADFASTNESS, AND THAWING IN OUR OWN TIME

1. Daniel J. Siegel, *Mindsight: The New Science of Personal Transformation* (New York: Bantam, 2010).
2. Paul Gilbert, Kirsten McEwan, Marcela Matos & Amanda Rivis, "Fears of Compassion: Development of Three Self-Report Measures," *Psychology and Psychotherapy: Theory, Research, and Practice*, 84:3 (2011), 239–55.

CHAPTER 69. BRINGING COMPASSION INTO EVERY MOMENT

1. Piercarlo Valdesolo & David DeSteno, "Synchrony and the Social Tuning of Compassion," *Emotion,* 11:2 (2011), 262–6.
2. James A. Coan, Hillary S. Schaefer & Richard J. Davidson, "Lending a Hand: Social Regulation of the Neural Response to Threat," *Psychological Science*, 17:12 (2006), 1032–9.
3. Kenneth Tai, Xue Zheng & Jayanth Narayanan, "Touching a Teddy Bear Mitigates Negative Effects of Social Exclusion to Increase Prosocial Behavior," *Social Psychological and Personality Science*, 2:6 (2011), 618–26.

Index